Rational Reinsurance Buying

Rational Reinsurance Buying

Edited by Nick Golden

RISK
BOOKS

Published by Risk Books, a division of the Risk Waters Group.

Haymarket House
28-29 Haymarket
London SW1 Y 4RX
Tel: +44 (0)20 7484 9700
Fax: +44 (0)20 7484 9758
E-mail: books@risk.co.uk
Sites: www.riskbooks.com
www.riskpublications.com

ISBN 1 904 339 00 X

British Library Cataloguing in Publication Data
A catalogue record for this book is available from the British Library

Head of Risk Books: Conrad Gardner
Risk Books Commissioning Editor: Sarah Jenkins
Assistant Editor: Kathryn Roberts

Typeset by Penrose Typography, Maidstone, Kent

Printed and bound in Great Britain by Bookcraft (Bath) Ltd, Somerset.

Contents

List of contributors

Jonathan Barber is the founder and chief executive officer of SERM Rating Agency Ltd, which uses its methodology to rate listed companies for social, environmental and operational risks. Following his early years with *The Times* newspaper and in a City-based public relations firm, he founded Falcon Asset Management in 1986. In 1993, he joined the Committee of the European Federation of Financial Analysts Societies (EFFAS) for the Edinburgh Conference, and began developing the concept of environmental risk rating, leading to the formation of SERM Rating Agency Ltd in 1996. He is a member of the Centre for the Study of Financial Innovation (CSFI) Advisory Council and a Registered Insurance Broker. He read engineering at Brunel University, and has become a leading authority on social and environmental risk assessment.

Philippe Derieux has been chief executive officer of AXA Cessions, the AXA captive reinsurer in charge of the AXA Group insurance risk management and reinsurance protections, since July 1999. Prior to that he was deputy chief financial officer of the AXA Group from 1996 to 1999. Philippe has also been corporate finance officer and chief group controller for UAP and direct European controller for AIG. Philippe's other interests include teaching strategy, finance and insurance techniques at the French National School of Insurance. He is a qualified chartered accountant and has a PhD in law from the Institut d'Etudes Politiques de Paris.

James R. Garven is professor of finance and insurance at Baylor University, where he holds the Frank S. Groner Memorial Chair in Finance. A prolific researcher, Dr Garven's research applies principles of finance and economics to topics such as corporate risk management, economics of insurance and reinsurance markets, and insurance pricing. Dr Garven currently serves as associate editor of the *Journal of Risk and Insurance* and as a member of the American Risk and Insurance Association board of directors. Dr Garven has previously held faculty appointments at Pennsylvania State University, University of Texas and Louisiana State University. He has also had private sector experience, having served as vice president of economic analysis and product research for InsWeb Corporation and as a consultant to industry.

Until June 2002, **Nick Golden** was the director of reinsurance for the Royal and Sun Alliance Group (R&SA) worldwide. His responsibilities included formulating and implementing the reinsurance strategy for the group and integrating the risk management strategy with capital management. He implemented a risk and capital management discipline that was supported by a global dynamic financial analysis (DFA) model for the group as well as each of the regional territories. By consolidating the territory DFA analysis into a global DFA model, R&SA was successful in evaluating the trade-off between regional vs global positions. His success in co-ordinating a global DFA discipline was instrumental in R&SA's ability to replenish capital following September 11, 2001 through the purchase of a quota share reinsurance with Munich Re, the largest single reinsurance contract ever effected. While at R&SA, Nick was a founder member of the TSUNAMI initiative, a UK government initiative to form a bridge between insurance and academia. This work has produced a number of research projects and consequent findings. Nick has spoken extensively on the issues faced by the global insurance industry and the support needed from academia. Nick is a fellow of the Chartered Insurance Institute.

Dougal Goodman is the director of The Foundation for Science and Technology (FST), a UK charity devoted to promoting effective dialogue between the UK parliament, senior civil servants, academics and senior managers in industry on policy issues with a science and technology content. He began his career researching the mechanical properties of ice at the Cambridge University physics department, the Cavendish Laboratory and at a Japanese university. His work included mounting expeditions to the Arctic and Antarctic to study ice in nature. In 1995 he became deputy director of the British Antarctic Survey, which is responsible for the UK's Antarctic research effort. He was awarded a Polar Medal by the Queen for his contribution to research in the Arctic and Antarctic in 1998. He worked for BP for many years and in several different contexts, including research, oil field operations, strategy, analysis of catastrophic events and alternative risk transfer instruments. He secured the funding for and managed the TSUNAMI initiative to bring the UK insurance industry closer to the UK research base and was principal organiser of a Short Programme at the Isaac Newton Institute for Mathematical Sciences on the theme of managing uncertainty.

Kathrine Huelster is president and chief operating officer of inreon. Prior to joining inreon, Kathrine served as chief operating officer at WISe, the industry-owned e-commerce enabler and played a leading role in integrating the organisation's standards-setting activities with those of its US counterpart, ACORD. Mrs Huelster also worked for RINET, the Reinsurance and Insurance Network, that merged with LIMNET, the London Insurance Market Network, and WIN, the World Insurance Network, to create WISe. Mrs Huelster is a graduate of Florida State University where she earned an honours degree in business management. She also holds a master's degree in international business from the University of South Carolina.

Chris Klein is chairman of the Benfield Group Reinsurer Security Committee and is the group's senior credit analyst. On joining Benfield, he instigated and led the development of a credit rating model with an enviable predictive capability. He was recruited from FitchIBCA rating agency in 1998, where he was a founding director of the European insurance rating division. His analytical career started in 1994 with Quest Insurance Research following retirement from the British Army in the rank of Major. His military service included a wide range of postings, including active service in the infantry and financial staff. He has a BA Honours degree in economic and social history from the University of York and is a graduate of the Royal Military Academy, Sandhurst. He has had several articles on industry and historical topics published.

Paul Koronka is currently head of the Non Marine Mutual Division of Charles Taylor Consulting plc. After reading law at Oxford and a short period as legal assistant to the General Council of British Shipping, Paul joined the management of a mutual insurance company in 1977. Since then he has been associated with a wide variety of mutuals both marine and non marine and in particular with start-ups.

Joan Lamm-Tennant is the senior vice president and practice leader for GeneralCologne Re Capital Consultants (GRCC) – a consulting arm of GeneralCologne Re who advise insurance companies on risk and capital management strategies. Prior to establishing GRCC, Joan was the Thomas G. Labrecque chair in business and professor of finance at Villanova University. Her publications appear in such journals as the *Journal of Business, Journal of Banking and Finance* and *Journal of Risk and Insurance.* During these years, she also consulted with numerous insurance companies, actuarial firms, accounting firms and consulting firms on risk and capital management. She currently serves on the board of directors for Selective Insurance Company, Charter Oak State College and Connecticut State Academic Awards. Prior to completing her doctorate, she worked in finance and systems at United States Automobile Association. Joan received a BBA in accounting and a MBA in finance from St Mary's University. She also received a PhD in finance, investments and insurance from the University of Texas at Austin.

Morton Lane is the president of Lane Financial, LLC, a broker-dealer engaged in consulting and transaction activity at the intersection of the reinsurance and capital markets. He has consulting arrangements with a number of major clients in Europe and the US. Previously, Morton has been senior managing director of the Capital Markets Division at Gerling Global Financial Products (GGFP), president of Discount Corp of New York Futures, senior managing director and head of commodities of Bear Stearns & Co, president of Lind-Waldock, investment officer for The World Bank, and lecturer at the London Graduate School of Business Studies. He has also designed and taught courses at the University of Chicago Graduate School of Business and at the University of New

South Wales in Sydney. Morton is a prominent speaker on insurance and securitisation and has written numerous articles on this subject. In 2001, he was awarded the Charles A. Hachemeister Prize for his article on "Pricing Risk Transfer Transactions" (ASTIN Bulletin). He edited *Alternative Risk Strategies* in 2002 and has co-authored two books, *The Treasury Bond Basis* and *Eurodollar Futures*. Morton earned his BSocSc from Birmingham University, and his PhD in mathematics, business administration and computer science from the University of Texas.

Christian M. Milton is vice president reinsurance officer of the American International Group, Inc. (AIG), where he has worked since 1980. Prior to AIG, Mr Milton has held reinsurance positions at various companies (National Union Fire Insurance Company, American International Underwriters, American International Reinsurance Company, for example) in a variety of locations (New York, Bermuda and London). Chris was educated at the City of London Polytechnic. He is and adjunct professor of the College of Insurance, a member of the MGI Creditors Committee and director of Rom Reinsurance Management Inc.

Adam Rose is head of research at Falcon Asset Management. He has previously headed research teams at economic development consultancies and a corporate governance research organisation. During the 1990s he was a private sector consultant advising government upon sustainable and local economic development opportunities. He is a member of the Centre for the Study of Financial Innovation (CSFI), and associate member of the Chartered Institutes of Management and Marketing. He read economic geography at the London School of Economics and holds postgraduate qualifications in management and marketing. Adam has become an authority on researching social and environmental risk and the economic/marketing benefits of addressing these risks. He is currently involved with numerous research panels including the SERM Advisory Panel.

Reto Schneider is member of senior management of Swiss Re, who he joined in 1994. After two years of working as a non-proportional property treaty underwriter for the UK and US markets, he moved to Risk Engineering Services where he is currently heading the casualty team. He holds a diploma in cell biology and a PhD in natural sciences from the Swiss Federal Institute of Technology in Zurich. His work is focused on assessing general liability and product liability risks in various industry segments. In addition he specialises in the fields of risk culture and risk management in hospitals.

Herbert Sedlmair is currently in charge of Natural Catastrophe Management and Counterparty Exposure Accumulation and Reinsurance Security with Allianz AG, where he moved to in 1990. He has had more than 15 years experience in the reinsurance industry, starting his career as a pricing actuary at Swiss Re. His responsibilities in the reinsurance department include active underwriting, actuarial and natural catastrophe management, and reinsurance placement of Allianz AG's industrial corporate business. Herbert gained his degree in mathematics from the University of Regensburg in 1988.

David Simmons is head of risk consultancy, one of seven specialist teams within Benfield ReMetrics, the analytical arm of the Benfield Group, and is a member of the Benfield ReMetrics executive committee. At Greig Fester, and later Benfield Greig, he pioneered the use of PCs and new mathematical methods in the modelling of the utility of insurance/reinsurance risk mitigation. Earlier in his career, he developed the first computerised reserving routines for Sun Alliance. David was instrumental in the creation of the Benfield Greig Hazard Research Centre, Europe's largest multi-disciplinary hazard resource body, and sits on the board of the centre. David is closely involved in the creation of the RISK Group – a new insurance market body to act as a form to discuss all aspects of risk. He is a regular contributor to print and broadcast media. David gained his honours degree in mathematics from the University of Bristol and is a fellow of the Chartered Insurance Institute.

Robert Stevenson is chief reinsurance officer and head of the Group Technical Center for Zurich Financial Services, where he is also chairman of Zurich's group underwriting and reinsurance boards. He is responsible for managing the development and implementation of the Zurich Group's technical underwriting, reinsurance and claim policies and also has executive responsibility for Zurich's specialist TPA and run-off services unit, Zurich Risk Management Services. Prior to joining Zurich in 1995, Robert was the senior reinsurance officer of Home Insurance and a member of the company's executive council. He started his career at AIG, where he spent 17 years with AIG's international operations, initially in London and from 1981 in New York. Robert was born and educated in England.

Dickie Whitaker is the principal of Guy Carpenter plc. Dickie has worked within the London market for over 20 years, initially as a reinsurance broker. He then helped to form EQECAT, one of the leading catastrophe modelling companies. More recently, he has held a number of positions within Guy Carpenter in both London and New York.

To Norman Robinson,
Marine Underwriter

whose early example and guidance
endured throughout my career

Preface

After a long and interesting underwriting career with Royal and Sun Alliance (R&SA), in 1996 I became R&SA's first world-wide director of reinsurance. This is the book I would have liked to have had then.

Reinsurance is the technique insurers use to try manage their risk and protect their shareholders capital. It is to insurance what insurance is to industry, commerce and the private individual.

In 1997, the global reinsurance volume was US$124 billion (Sigma 9/98). Not all of this was in respect of reinsurance premiums flowing from insurers to reinsurers, increasing amounts of reinsurers' income comes direct from the insured. Nonetheless, it is safe to assume that in 2002 insurers will pass to reinsurers more than US$100 billion. They will return eventually a figure of between US$80 billion and US$140 billion, depending on the final outturn of the year. Huge sums of money.

Most insurers will pass between 5% and 25% of their income to reinsurers, representing for most their second biggest area of expenditure after claims.

There is much published on reinsurance theory; what the contracts cover, the law, the risks, the solutions. Yet so far there has been little to guide the market observer or the new practitioner on the issues involved in professionally managing this massive expenditure.

This book draws together the views of expert and highly experienced professionals in the field.

The book is in four parts:

1. Alternative strategies of insurers.
2. Risk assessment.
3. Integration of risk management with capital management.
4. Alternative perspectives.

It is designed to move from a discussion of the realities of life, through the tools available to help solve the problems, then to the academic and capital markets' view and finally a look at future issues and opportunities.

It begins with a series of essays from major global buyers. As editor I was delighted to find how different they each were, ranging from an analysis of historical issues and how the past can determine current strategy, through an expert discussion of the current perils faced by multinational insurers and on to the identification of an ideal structure and framework for the analysis and purchase of reinsurance. We owe a huge debt to the real leaders in this field, Messrs Stevenson (Zurich Financial Services), Derieux (AXA), Sedlmair (Allianz AG) and Milton (AIG), and who gave so much of their time during an especially demanding reinsurance renewal season.

The views of the practitioners are supplemented and balanced by the views of the professionals. In Part II, four experts from the reinsurance broking and reinsurance industry discuss four of the key issues that all reinsurance buyers wrestle with on a day to day basis:

Chris Klein (Benfield Group Ltd) addresses the issue of relative reinsurer security and why the claims-paying ability of the counter party is rarely factored into the price. He offers a solution.

Dickie Whitaker (Guy Carpenter plc) unravels catastrophe modelling and discusses the degree of faith that we are entitled to have in the predictions of the models.

The emergence of a new risk and the associated failure of existing reinsurance programmes to respond to new emerging losses is a constant concern of any reinsurance buyer. Reto Schneider describes the world of emerging risk and explains how Swiss Re is tackling the subject.

Last but not least, David Simmons (Benfield Group Ltd) explains the concepts of dynamic financial modelling and identifies both opportunities and pitfalls.

In Part III, James Garven (Baylor University) and Joan Lamm-Tennant (GeneralCologne Re) contrast the pragmatic approaches of the practitioners in Part I with economic and financial theory as to what drives organisations to hedge risk, be it commercial organisations with insurance, or insurance companies with reinsurance.

They present a fascinating exposition of the conditions in the market place that lead to insurance firms creating economic value through risk/reinsurance management. They also demonstrate how certain types of insurers who are more exposed to these conditions are more likely to reinsure and will reap the greatest benefit from their hedging activities.

We are indebted to Morton Lane (Lane Financial LLC), fresh from editing his own book, *Alternative Risk Strategies*, who found the time to contribute an excellent piece on the evolution of capital in the insurance business and the options available to those who wish to explore different risk transfer options.

Lastly we try to look into the future.

The reinsurance world is changing rapidly, no more so than in the area of execution. Many have argued for years that the frictional costs (the incidental expense of doing business) are far too high, business methods have changed little in the last 25 years, save maybe for the advent of emails and faxes. Lurking around the corner lies the world of electronic business platforms that could transform the market by increasing the speed of transactions and radically reducing cost. We have an eloquent chapter on that from Kathrine Huelster of inreon.

Capital and regulation are key to this business in 2002/3 and we reproduce two very important papers from the International Association of Insurance Supervisors (IAIS). The way in which the international community regard reinsurance security and the adequacy of reinsurance programmes is critical.

The industry is often accused of relying too much on the past to price the future and it is important that we continually look for reliable indicators of future loss experience. Jonathan Barber from SERM Rating Agency Ltd, with Paul Koronka of Charles Taylor Consulting plc and Adam Rose of Falcon Asset Management Ltd contribute an interesting alternative view, arguing that management skill and competence with environmental and health and safety issues are a good proxy for management quality and thus loss experience. It is possible that this could lead to risk quality assessment of insurer's risk portfolios which in turn could lead to greater fluidity in the way that risks are traded, even securitised.

Lastly, from Dougal Goodman of The Foundation of Science and Technology, we have an examination of the benefits the industry could gain from working more actively with the global academic community and identification of the issues it could help us address.

Reinsurance can be an arcane subject and there are many misunderstandings about its role in the financial world. It is hoped that this collection of views will go some way to clearing the fog.

Part I

Alternative strategies of insurers

1

The Evolution of Purchasing Strategy

Nick Golden

Royal and Sun Alliance

INTRODUCTION

This chapter aims to provide the reader with an insight into the reinsurance decisions that were taken by Royal and Sun Alliance in the early years of the new company, beginning with an outline of the heritage to provide a degree of context.

Royal and Sun Alliance (R&SA) is the product of the merger between, unsurprisingly, Royal Insurance PLC and Sun Alliance PLC. The merger took place in 1996 and it was the first of the big UK insurance groups to come together. The rationale behind the merger was cost saving and the need for size when competing in a global environment.[1] It also came at a time when the UK Government in the form the President of the Board of Trade, Michael Heseltine, was keen to see bigger British international insurers.

Cost savings were expected to flow from moving to best of breed practice throughout the new group and from better and more efficient use of capital. Reinsurance expenditure was an early target; using the thinking that twice the capital should lead to, if not half, certainly less reinsurance.

Given that reinsurance purchasing strategy is such a cultural issue for most global insurers, it is first necessary to provide some history to give background to the events that unfolded later.

Royal Insurance, founded in 1845, has its origins as a provincial UK insurer that expanded globally in the footsteps of the British Empire. Its financial metal was tempered in the 1906 San Francisco earthquake where it paid all losses promptly and in full, leading to a culture of security and dependability at all costs.[2] It regarded reinsurers with suspicion preferring to write gross and retain 100% – "if it's not good enough to keep then it's not good enough to write" was the unspoken credo.

Royal recognised the need for reinsurance on peak risks in order to provide capacity and of course for catastrophe accumulations, but even as late as the 1960s it had no truck with treaties, preferring to use facultative reinsurance as and when necessary. The senior management were often heard to say "We don't want to encourage our underwriters to write on the back of other people's capital nor do we want to make ourselves hostages of fortune to reinsurers who might increase terms or withdraw cover." It was all to do with control and a culture of complacent self-sufficiency, soon to be rudely jilted by the emergence of direct writers and the collapse of the UK property market in the early 1990s.

CHANGING CULTURE

To be more specific, four things changed this thinking and culture:

1. **The seductive powers of excess of loss (XoL) reinsurance.** By moving from proportional to non-proportional reinsurances RSA found an instant and painless injection to the premium line that flowed straight through to that year's underwriting result.[3] Excess of loss was regarded as modern efficient reinsurance for an established player with good capital. Proportional reinsurance was only for the new guys who had little experience or little capital or both. Royal Insurance certainly would not have included themselves in the latter category. Never mind that its excess of loss introduced differential pricing; never mind that it began to change the principle that reinsurers follow the fortunes of their insurer clients; it was irresistible. So the surplus treaties were cancelled and replaced by coded XoL facilities.
2. **The storms in the UK in 1987 and 1990.**[4] Until October 1997, the prevailing view in Royal was that their UK catastrophic threat was flood and freeze. Flood because the Thames barrier had yet to be built and London was very flood exposed (as was (is) East Anglia), and freeze because houses were poorly insulated yet carrying ever increasing amounts of domestic consumer goods at risk from water damage following pipes bursting. What Royal

wanted was a stop-loss to cap the accumulated weather claims. Royal did not expect hurricanes to happen in England. Wrong. "Cat 87J", as it became known, brought Royal Insurance losses of £130 million which it carried entirely net. Very slightly against its better judgement the company decided to enter the reinsurance market, wary that it was repaying other people's losses and believing a second 1:100 in the near future was unlikely. Common sense did prevail however, to everyone's huge relief when the second and third events struck just three years later in 1990.

3. **The collapse of the UK property market.** Sadly, as luck (to Royal Insurance) would have it, the 1990 storms were accompanied by an equally catastrophic collapse of the stock market, high inflation, and high unemployment and ultimately the collapse of the UK property market. At that time Royal was a heavy property investor and was suddenly facing a collapse of both its assets and a mushrooming of its liabilities, particularly domestic mortgage indemnity. Reinsurance suddenly became an attractive source of additional capital, although in the end rescue came primarily in the form of release of imbedded value on the overseas business, notably Australia and Holland. Royal Australia was sold to the Sun Alliance and was merged with their Australian operation and two thirds of Royal Nederland was sold to Fondiara of Italy and Aachen and Munich of Germany in an attempt to create a joint venture (EPIC) with European aspirations. The idea failed and EPIC disappeared some three years later.
4. **A culture change from being insurance managers to business people.** In 1987 Royal embarked on one of its many strategic reviews and, among other conclusions, branch managers were to cease being administrators and custodians of underwriting values and become local entrepreneurs with complete control of their business, from risk selection and pricing to staff selection and terms. They were to be judged and remunerated on their profit contribution. Reinsurance became hugely attractive to them, limiting the downside in their local results and thus protecting bonuses and jobs.

REINSURANCE STRATEGY DIFFERENCES

So, from a reinsurance point of view, Royal approached the merger with Sun Alliance in 1995 with an open mind. It had learnt that it was not self sufficient in terms of capital, that it needed close and effective relationships with reinsurers that it could trust, and that it could learn from reinsurers. Royal acknowledged that there could be huge opportunities if only it could resolve the inherent conflicts between group or central risk aspirations, based on the total group capital and risk tolerance and local risk tolerance, which was heavily influenced by local capital and compensation incentives.

Sun Alliance came from a different place. Much older than Royal (founded in 1745) and based in London, it had had much more sophisticated relationships with its reinsurers and a much stronger capital base with a solvency margin (premium to capital ratio) in the high nineties compared to Royal's of about 50%.

It also had a strong relationship with the City and the financial markets.

Sun and Alliance were neighbours on the stock exchange site and their merger (minus Sun Life who were excluded) occurred in the late 1950s when consolidation within the industry was rife. It was relatively gentle; as systems were predominantly manual, their merger was painless with limited computerisation, later cementing the merger through introduction of new processes. The takeover of the London in 1966 and the Phoenix in 1986 provided accelerated growth in common areas of business without the need to generate this from new businesses and it reduced competition. It also provided lessons in assimilation of other businesses.

Sun was originally a fire insurance company, as was the Phoenix, with the Alliance and London originally marine insurance companies, but all had become composite insurers. The combined group achieved significant penetration within the UK property market, both commercial and personal, and an account that was both of good quality and highly profitable.

The UK centric focus resulted in an unbalanced worldwide distribution of exposure combined with a distrust of the management of their overseas businesses. This was in part due to the differing conditions and practices particularly beyond the old Commonwealth countries and part due to an inherent belief that returns would not match those from the UK. So, little was invested in development of viable stand-alone businesses overseas. Expansion through takeover was limited and reliance on overseas agents was allowed to continue with a demoralising effect on the management. With each takeover, control of the business was ceded to the defeated party as a standard operating procedure, but without central trust.

In particular, from early times, the USA had been viewed as a difficult territory with significant potential to destabilise the business. Having met their obligations, San Francisco Alliance and London were happy to leave their marine and property business with Chubb as their managers, and this relationship continued into the 1990s. Peripheral involvement with Jones Manville and asbestosis in the 1950s had reinforced a strongly held tenet not to write North American casualty business. This principle presented a sheet anchor to the companies' growth, proving both a strength and a weakness. Where it was necessary to write business with exposure to USA, heavy reliance was placed on facultative reinsurance.

Underwriting philosophy through the company was focussed on case underwriting with little consideration for account underwriting. There was a belief in the inherent quality of the book. Underwriters were confident in accepting large net exposures and confident in their underwriting skills.

Care had also been taken in plotting the incidence of large losses within the account. This statistical base assisted in both loss reserving and providing a platform from which underwriters could derive their retention strategy.

If purchasing philosophy is divided between case and account, or risk and catastrophe, then between account size and capitalisation of the business, comfort with the relationship between the size, quality and profitability of the UK property account ensured that limited risk cover was purchased. Control of exposure from accumulation of risk was ensured by controlling exposure through effective identification of risk, risk assessment by a large team of surveyors and effective identification of EML, As with the Royal, the major perceived problem was UK flood particularly for the personal account, but here the means to identify exposure was still limited. Adoption of postcodes would assist in providing this later.

Like Royal, Sun Alliance also had no reinsurance for the 1987 storms in the UK, but for different reasons. Theirs was not a peril analysis, but a capital decision. Sun Alliance argued that over time reinsurance had brought them no benefits, results were no more stable, the group result always ended up with a net transfer of profits to reinsurers and they had more than enough capital. So why buy it at all?

Like Royal, Sun Alliance were not persuaded by the likelihood of catastrophic storms in the UK, but unlike Royal, they believed that risk retentions could be much higher. In 1996, Royal's retention on a top quality property risk was £7.5 million; Sun Alliance's retention for an identical risk was £22.5 million. In the early 1990s Sun Alliance was the epitome of a confident well capitalised gross insurance company, with the philosophy "we know our book, we have more than adequate capital, what we write is what we keep". At the time it was a bold and intimidating strategy, if luck had been with them they would have been engaged in a virtuous circle; not buying reinsurance would enable them to retain greater underwriting profit over time, greater profits would lead to greater assets, and greater assets lead to greater retentions and so on until they would potentially dominate the market.

But t'was not to be. 87J forced them reluctantly back into the reinsurance market as they could not take the risk of second loss of this size in the near future. The manner of their departure in 1986 had caused resentment in the market and their terms were not attractive.[5] The storms of 1990 followed soon after and that, together with the collapse of the stock market, brought an end to the experiment. However, if nothing else, it had awakened a real interest in the cost and effect of reinsurance and led to Sun Alliance developing a global reinsurance strategy built around control. The company knew it had to fully understand who bought what and why, so they established an internal facility to which all external treaties purchases had to be offered (as shown in Figure 1). This had the virtue of revealing what was being bought but also provided an opportunity to constrain the financial effect of the purchase by forcing short placements, the balance being retained in the facility. They regarded offshore captives as only offering the advantage of tax deferral and instead carried the new exposures directly on the main balance sheet.

Royal and Sun Alliance (R&SA) merged in 1996. The merger followed a series of deals with each other around the world – for

Figure 1 Sun Alliance's internal facility

Without internal facility

Client	**Insurer**	**Internal facility**	**Reinsurer**
100% of risk passed on	60% of risk retained	—	40% of risk retained

With internal facility

Client	**Insurer**	**Internal facility**	**Reinsurer**
100% of risk passed on	60% of risk retained	10% of risk retained	30% of risk retained

instance Sun Alliance bought Royal's Australian operation, Royal bought Sun Alliance's Canadian operation. These transactions led to the senior managers of both groups building a working partnership and led them to believe that a total merger was feasible and desirable. Shareholders were encouraged to support the merger with an annual expense savings target of £175 million and an increased ability to control price in R&SA's chosen markets as a result of greater size. Savings of £225 million were eventually delivered and the early years of the new company were very profitable; profit before tax in 1996 was £582 million and in 1997 was £683 million, more than twice as much as in the subsequent years.

Cost savings were to flow from a multiplicity of sources working on the principle that the merged company would be able to establish the most efficient process within either of the two organisations and change to that process. This was a logical and well intentioned strategy but questionable with the benefit of hindsight as it led to hours of in-fighting as each side set out to prove their heritage was best. For instance, the processing system for the broker motor was not finally established until 1998, due to internal conflict.

In the first full year after the merger, 1997, Royal and Sun Alliance passed to reinsurers premiums of £1,368 million. This was more than twice the administrative expenses (salary costs) and was an obvious area for investigation, especially as claims recovered from reinsurers were only £790 million.

EFFECTS OF SYNERGY

So far, this chapter has established that each side came to the reinsurance discussions with slightly different cultural backgrounds, but both saw reinsurance as an expense and an unavoidable cost with little real and tangible value that would have to be minimised. Beneath that sweeping statement lay hundreds of individual underwriters at the time who believed that reinsurance would turn their accounts "from dross to gold", but at group level it was regarded with a jaundiced eye as the result over time appeared no more stable after reinsurance than before.

The thinking that underpinned the reinsurance side of the merger considerations was that, by merging, the combined company would have twice the capital of either of the original two, therefore there was a feeling that twice the capital must, if not half, certainly lead to less reinsurance.

So in that first renewal at the end of 1997 the central directive was to reduce reinsurance expenditure. There were neither the data nor the models to calculate the financial effect properly, but an impetus was placed on reducing the top line outflow of premium to reinsurers. The target was a global reduction of £200 million, which, given an average profit transfer to reinsurers of 10%, was expected to yield an improvement in Royal and Sun Alliance's annual underwriting result of some £20 million. Retentions were increased, both risk and catastrophe, quota share treaties were cancelled and where possible facultative reinsurance not renewed. The £200 million was duly achieved but not without some nervousness as territory and portfolio managers saw their businesses suddenly more vulnerable to large losses and thus their bonuses, perhaps even careers more exposed.

This group-driven central objective also sat uneasily on the emerging culture of R&SA, which emphasised full devolution of authority and decision making to territories and getting decisions made close to the customer by those who are best equipped and motivated to make them. In these circumstances, businesses were given full control over product range, pricing, distribution, claims, staff compensation, etc, but it then created tension if the organisation gave the view "Ah, you can do all that, but on reinsurance you do what we say from the centre". This is the very nub of the challenge of reinsurance in a multinational with devolved accountability.

R&SA's solution was the re-working of Royal's old offshore captive and Sun Alliance's onshore internal facility. Why not permit the territories to buy as much external reinsurance as they wanted but insist that it all be offered to the group head office for them to participate in if they so wished and so reduce the amount placed externally by acting as an internal reinsurer? The arguments in favour were that:

- ❑ by obtaining external prices for each treaty the businesses would remain on level terms with their competitors;
- ❑ by keeping a minimum in the market (60%), local reinsurer relationships would not be disrupted; and
- ❑ R&SA now had a truly global book; is this not just what a new reinsurer would be seeking – global spread of uncorrelated risk? Surely R&SA could construct a book with such global balance from its own external reinsurances that would be inherently profitable over time? This must be a more intelligent approach than the blunt instrument of "spend less".

PRICING PROBLEMS

The fly in the ointment in this otherwise elegant solution was the reinsurance market itself. Or to be precise the reinsurance market pricing cycle. Like its larger sister, insurance, the reinsurance market is relatively easy to enter and thus quite open but it is not a perfect market, ie, there is imperfect information about losses that leads to periodic eruptions of disastrous under-pricing which continues until underwriters lose their jobs when losses become unsupportable. Only then do prices rise again until the same cycle repeats itself, usually in about three years. Logically R&SA should have been able to at least elevate itself from the reinsurance cycle by simply not participating in external reinsurances when the price was uneconomic, ie, the business being retained in the captive was likely to generate greater losses than the premium being saved. There were, however, two problems with this strategy:

1. the message to the reinsurance industry that R&SA was an opportunistic buyer and the damage that then did to the reputation and cost/availability of its reinsurance; and

2. without a full team of reinsurance pricing experts and all the accompanying data, how would you know whether the price was adequate or not?

R&SA decided to take the long-term view that reinsurers make a profit over time and as the internal facility will make a profit for the company four years out of five, it is worth riding the fifth when it happens.

Next question, what to put in the internal facility?

The argument for catastrophe (cat) reinsurance is straightforward. With the exception of the Caribbean/United States and United Kingdom/Northern Europe, cat risks are uncorrelated. If the chance of an earthquake in New Zealand at, say, Richter scale 7 is 1:100 and there is a chance of a European wind storm with hurricane intensity, again with a 1:100 return period, the probability of them both happening in the same year is 1:10,000. So, why buy full protection for each event in each territory when all the group should really be worried about is the accumulation of cat losses in any one year? Why not drive retentions to a consistent level in the group businesses around the world and buy a cover to cap out frequency.

The argument for individual risks is less obvious and hinges on consistency of retention. Assume for a moment that the group's capital is just that – the capital that supports each risk written around the world and is perfectly fluid (meaning there is no restriction on moving capital from one part of the world to another). Then, why does risk A have a retention of £x million in territory A and an identical risk has a retention of £x/2 million in territory B? The answer of course is that the group's capital is not perfectly fluid. In fact it is far from perfect as the capital is parcelled into various territories of the world, retained there for good and sensible regulatory reasons (for example the protection of local consumers against insurer failure) and the retentions are driven by the local capital and local risk aspirations. But how tempting it might be to seek some sort of global uniformity by including individual risk losses (both property and casualty) in the facility.

While this work of building a global reinsurance strategy through dialogue and compromise was plodding slowly on, group thinking on capital was progressing. One of the concerns investors had when R&SA was formed in 1996 was that it had too much capital. Perhaps this is hard to believe now, but it is true. The group had a solvency margin in the nineties and its investors felt that the company had too much of their money. So the question was addressed "how much capital do we need if we are to retain the company *within its risk tolerance* but no more?"

The risk tolerance was articulated to be no more than a 1 in 100 chance of the solvency margin (assets/premium) falling below 25% in any one of the next five years, from any cause. This resulted in a target solvency margin of 47% and some £750 million was returned to shareholders to achieve this new leaner capital base. From this a new financial target emerged – 10% net real. To cover the cost of capital R&SA had to achieve an annual return of 10%, net of tax and net of inflation.

Capital was allocated to the lines and territories around the world and the injunction given that the 10% net real had to be achieved at all costs.

Not only was 10% net real to be achieved, it was to be achieved each year, hence the unpredictability of R&SA's results were to cease forthwith. Implementation of this policy began in earnest in 2000, throwing the internal facility (by now offshore in a captive in the Isle of Man and registered as "Globe Isle of Man") into question. The capital was no longer to be retained at the centre; it was fully allocated and therefore there was no longer any such thing as group capital. But the captive, as constructed, following the market cycles, included a balance of both risk and cat that could only increase volatility. By definition it would make good years better and bad years worse. Good years for insurers are when claims are less than expected and therefore reinsurance recoveries are also lower than usual. In those circumstances reinsurance becomes a less efficient purchase and the more that is retained the better. The reverse effect takes place in bad years; claims are higher than expected, reinsurance recoveries should be higher too but, as some reinsurance has been retained in the company, it is forced to pay its own reinsurance losses.

The real issue became really understanding the profile of the book worldwide and being able to work out when it was better to use a reinsurer's capital and when it was better to use R&SA's.

ENTER DYNAMIC FINANCIAL MODELLING

Dynamic financial analysis (DFA) was introduced to the reinsurance business in the late 1980s to exploit the emerging computer capabilities to build statistical models of insurance portfolios. In recent times, the technology, especially computer run times, has improved immensely.

DFA will be discussed in more detail elsewhere in this book but in essence the process is to:

1. capture historic loss and exposure data, with and without reinsurance;
2. add inflation and pricing expectations including the cat model predictions for each territory, and thus produces a model of the business, segmented as you wish;
3. then you can invite the model to randomly sample different outcomes for each one of say, the next three years; and
4. run the simulation enough times to be sure that you have captured a good range of all the possible outcomes. That number is usually between 4,000 and 10,000 times for each year.

This produces a range of outcomes for each year with a range of probabilities, ie, "in an average year with these assumptions the result is going to look like this" or "you have a 20% chance of it looking this or a 1% chance of it looking like this."

This turned out to be a huge step forward. R&SA could clearly and objectively see how the effect of reinsurance as a resultant stabilising tool diminished as risks were accumulated or pooled. The tool is capable of validating the view that reinsurance is hugely effective at an individual risk level, slightly less so at branch, less so again at territory, etc, until the group consolidated result level is reached when the effect of reinsurance on stabilising the result is minimal.

CURRENT STRATEGY

This summary is being written in the autumn of 2002. R&SA is battling with the effects of September 11 with additional losses surfacing in 2002 of £66 million, the collapse of the stock market requiring additional capital of at least £800 million and the emergence of asbestosis losses (£384 million new provisions made in 2001). Not good times and certainly not an ideal time to make bold and radical moves with the risk transfer philosophy. So the hard won experience is currently consolidated into the practicalities of making the best of a difficult situation. This author believes it can be summarised as follows.

1. Set the company's risk standards centrally, ie, specify the models to be used for catastrophe risk assessment and then dictate the level to which each territory should buy protection.
2. Control the risk assessment of counterparties by publishing and constantly revising the names of acceptable reinsurers for internal distribution.
3. Use the global DFA model to assist in individual treaty purchase evaluation, and regional reinsurance strategy.
4. Buy all reinsurance locally with local profit and risk tolerance guidelines but subject to the retentions being consistent with local capital and premium. R&SA's investors seem to be interested in the period that a territory would take to recover a large loss, ie, they find large losses in small territories, such as the storm losses in Taiwan or the volcano in Montserrat difficult to accept.
5. Mechanise the purchase of facultative reinsurance with a global electronic purchasing system. Such a system is capable of reducing frictional costs and accumulating global data on facultative premium and claims.
6. Co-ordinate the purchasing with a formal network of reinsurance buyers to maintain best practice and achieve consistency of style and approach.
7. Use the DFA model to better allocate capital between territories and businesses.

This structure results in the efficient purchase of local reinsurance. The businesses are able to establish one-to-one relationships with their reinsures, supply authoritative answers to their questions and tailor their programmes exactly to the local commercial and regulatory requirements. The absence of central participations increases the degree of control over accumulations and minimises the effect on the volatility of the result.

It does not maximise the group purchasing power, or construct any programmes to protect the group rather than the local result. It does have a tendency to result in the overbuying of reinsurance: a reasonable thing in soft reinsurance market conditions when reinsurance is underpriced, a bad thing in hard market conditions when reinsurers raise price beyond the economic levels and destroy shareholders' wealth in the ceding company.

MOVING ON

In an ideal world reinsurers would...

1. *Address the issues of inadequate catastrophe models.* Shareholders and regulators alike should be concerned that cat modelling is a competitive adventure. The different modelling firms (EQECAT, RMS, AIR for instance), operate as commercial ventures and reinsurers regard cat modelling expertise as an area of competitive advantage. The calculation of the maximum probable loss at a location from a predetermined series of events is critical to both pricing and solvency and should be taken much more seriously by the industry. It is time for reinsurers and insurers to share expertise, establish agreed levels of uncertainty in the outcomes and work with the scientific and academic communities for real and tangible improvement. Without really good and authoritative curves for each territory, far too much of insurance becomes "feel and sentiment" as opposed to fact and rational process.
2. *Think global not local.* As results get worse following unexpected loss size or frequency increase, the natural reaction of reinsurers is to restrict their offerings to more focussed and simpler products. These tend to be product-specific and usually non-proportional. Despite the fact that most modern multi-national insurers are actively working to construct a global business model, many reinsurers and reinsurance brokers like to regard them as a collection of separate businesses operating under a single franchise. It suits their purposes to sell locally; they are likely to have access to better information, they are able to sell smaller more containable deals and the buyers may be less ambitious in their negotiation of terms. On the other hand, it may well suit less the reinsurer who sees things quite differently from a global perspective and who is more interested in global results protection and capital relief and less interested in local account protection.
3. *Consider themselves as stakeholders in the insurers business.* Many reinsurers reading these words will no doubt be bristling, and one can imagine them muttering "We are more than stakeholders

already, we subsidise their business". True, the last few years have been bad for reinsurers – losses have significantly exceeded premiums, late emerging issues such as asbestosis have got worse and new ones have emerged.[6] Yet neither side can exist without the other and especially without the end customer. In hard markets reinsurers tend to think only of their responsibility to their shareholders and to the exclusion of the issues related to the customer and how the problem is going to be solved. Reinsurers will come and go as business models change or capital finds more attractive places, but to flourish, insurers need committed long-term partners who share in the construction of solutions.

4. *Cut cost from the process.* Transacting reinsurance is a hideously expensive business with huge amounts of energy expended in the construction of presentations, negotiations with brokers and reinsurers, dispute over claims etc. That is not to say that the gatherings in Baden Baden and Monte Carlo, the visits around the world, the symposiums and the conferences are not pleasant and stimulating.[7] They are. They are also expensive and time-consuming. One wonders how the capital markets view these arcane methods of doing business. Where are the commonality of language, the common use of wordings, and the standardisation of accounting information?

And in an ideal world insurers would...

1. *Concentrate on the gross.* This is the "before reinsurance" line in their management information, especially that concerned with pricing and remuneration. Reinsurance is clearly valuable when brought to bear on low-frequency, high-severity events such as earthquake or conflagration. It saves capital, and provides capacity for the world's peak risks by employing the rules of risk diversification. But it is harmful at an operational level as information mismatch can deepen the cycle. It works like this: an insurer's account sinks into loss following late emergence of claims or change in frequency but the insurer has reinsurance so their cash position is protected as recoveries against earlier losses continue to flow in. The insurer delays increasing price. Similarly, all their competitors are in a similar position. Eventually the reinsurer realises that they are being damaged

and have been so for some time. Then the decision will be taken to increase price radically. The insurer can not raise price as quickly (they have a renewal cycle to go through) so the increase further worsens their book and price increases become savage as the insurer compensates for bad gross results, higher than expected reinsurance costs and the timing mismatch. The insurer might then over-compensate and eventually start making excessive profits, at which point new capital enters. So the cycle becomes deeper and longer in frequency resulting in greater uncertainty for the end consumer.

2. *Get a grip on the reinsurance brokers.* Despite the commission payment flowing from the reinsures they are, in effect, being paid for by the end customer. The system whereby brokers work for the insurer (but are paid by the reinsurer) to deliver a product which is designed to pay claims and yet have no incentive to ensure performance is bizarre and fundamentally unacceptable in modern times. Brokers must have their interests tied to their customers and move to a new business model as consultants rather than transactional intermediaries.
3. *Make the capital dynamic.* If the Australian office of an UK-based multinational insurer elects to buy a particular treaty then it should do so in the knowledge of what the effect will be on its capital and should be able to contrast the benefits of operating against reduced capital, compared to the additional hit to local earnings of the reinsurance. Included in this calculation should be a provision for counterparty security, the lower the value of the security, the higher the additional capital charge, otherwise the subsidiary is getting a free put on the group's capital every time it uses capital with a rating less than the parent's.

If shareholders and regulators were to measure the quality of the reinsurance programme what would they look for?

1. Absolute excellence in modelling, both cat exposures and the insurers' own book using the latest DFA techniques.
2. Strong correlation between the global DFA model and the operational plan.
3. Dynamic capital, with capital flowing in response to profit and development opportunities and accurate measurement of the opportunity cost of using others' (reinsurers') capital.

4. Clear evidence of partnership, commitment and community of interest between insurer and reinsurers.
5. Evidence that the reinsurer has a professional fee-based relationship with his reinsurance broker supported by a clear list of deliverables, including claims collection, management information and an explicit commitment to the corporate strategy.
6. Sound control of risk within the company, with risk transfer to reinsurers being just one weapon in the armoury that it uses to manage value-at-risk (VAR) and keep the company within its risk tolerance.

Quite a challenge, but, as always, travelling will be more fun than arriving.

CONCLUSION

For those not in the insurance business reinsurance must seem arcane indeed; risks and customers for which insurers strongly compete and then are bundled together and laid off around the world either to protect insurers balance sheets or to gain competitive advantage, or both. For those in the insurance business the reinsurance strategy of R&SA may have appeared complex and inconsistent.

This chapter provides an insight into this particular company to illustrate the drivers behind reinsurance and to explain why R&SA adopted the strategy it did.

The author will leave it to future business school students to evaluate the success or failure of the merger, but as far as reinsurance is concerned, he would suggest that the lessons are:

- reinsurance is not a cost but is an alternative source of capital and should be evaluated as such; and
- the behavioural impact of reinsurance buying on underwriters should not be underestimated. Those who write purely on their own capital with no reinsurance tend to be much more conservative then those who write using extensive reinsurance protection and therefore "other people's" money.

1 In the 1997 report to shareholders the then new CEO Bob Mendelsohn stated:

> Projected annual expense savings from the merger will exceed the £175m previously reported. The target has now been increased to £235m per

> annum by the end of 1998. The one-time costs of achieving these savings will increase from the £201m charged in 1996 to £265m, with the balance of £64m being charged against 1997 earnings.

The merger has put the Group in the top 10 of worldwide general insurers covering risks in over 130 countries. With total assets of £60bn we are increasingly becoming a preferred choice for international brokers and multinational clients.

2 The scale of fire loses following the San Francisco earthquake in 1906 was staggering for the newly emerging insurance industry and there was much concern about the ability to pay. Of the 90 American offices involved, 15 defaulted, of the 15 continental European offices, 4 defaulted. None of the 18 British insurers defaulted. Royal's gross loss was US$6.7 million, a massive amount for the time. It would appear that non-US insurers were not especially welcome at the time but the *Insurance World,* a US magazine said in 1906:

> "Just at a time when there is flurry in the financial circles in this country the Royal Insurance Co. sends over three quarters of million dollars in gold with which to settle losses... Great institution is Royal! Always on deck in an emergency and never quibbling about the payment of losses. Is it a foreigner? Well we guess not.
>
> It has been here so long and has buckled down to so many problems which applied directly to the welfare of this country that it became "one of us" long ago.
>
> There is a need for institutions like the Royal and this is without regard as to where the real home office may be."

3 Reinsurance can be divided in to proportional and non proportional. Proportional reinsurance takes a predetermined share of the ceding insurers business. A 50% quota share treaty would be paid 50% of the premium for each risk and pay 50% of any subsequent claims. Non proportional or excess of loss reinsurance pays claims in excess of a predetermined figure and the premium is calculated by the reinsurer to reflect his liability and does not follow the original premium.

4 Cat 87 J was the name given by Lloyds Claims settling bureaux to the 87th major loss of the year. It referred to the storm on the south east of England on October 1987 that caused levels of damage to trees and buildings. The insurance loss was in excess of £1 billion. Although at the time 87J was believed to have a return period of 100 years, there was a more intense storms in January and February 1990.

5 At that time Lloyds was the main market for catastrophe reinsurance and some syndicates, F R White for instance, declined to participate in their programme purely on the basis of the company's previous behaviour in the market.

6 See *Daily Telegraph* 22/06/2002.

7 Senior executives of insurance, reinsurance and reinsurance broking industries gather each September in Monte Carlo for three to four days to discus the forthcoming (year-end) renewals and the prospects for the following year. Managers from the same groups gather in Baden Baden each October to negotiate terms, transmit corporate messages and bid for corporate capacity.

2

Managing Reinsurance within a Multinational Environment

Robert Stevenson

Zurich Financial Services

While the reinsurance industry has long been truly global in scope, insurance is a more local enterprise. The regulatory environment largely dictates the way in which insurance companies operate in many countries, particularly the United States. For those select few insurance companies who have chosen to expand beyond their national borders, the challenges presented by multiple regulatory environments coincide with the challenges of their own business operating model. The mixture is, at the very least, interesting. To this mixture we can add the fact that multinational expansion has often been achieved through acquisition as opposed to organic growth and with it multiple national and organisational cultures. This proves to be a true challenge for those charged with managing and mitigating risk!

It is a common trait to regard reinsurance purely as a financial instrument or, at its most basic, just another source of capital. This chapter will argue that the successful use of reinsurance involves both the behavioural and financial aspects. It will lead the reader though the need for a clear policy framework, the need to create a feeling of ownership by the internal constituent and the issues involved with successful execution. It will also tackle the thorny subject of internal reinsurance and the pricing thereof, together with a brief look at the technical and regulatory issues that the modern reinsurance team needs to take on.

DRAWING UP THE POLICY FRAMEWORK

The first order of business when given the charge of managing the reinsurance process has to be to define a policy framework that recognises the company's business and financial models and consequently is reflective of the business and financial objectives. Irrespective of the fact that the combination of a business and financial model will result in each company being individual, there is a common need for a reinsurance policy to incorporate an effective framework of governance. Companies may choose to execute their reinsurance strategy using a centralised or a decentralised model, and in some cases a combination of both, but in all instances the strategy will not be consistently executed without a robust framework of governance.

The use of reinsurance, both internally and externally, is a key component of a company's risk mitigation and financial management strategies. An effective group reinsurance policy has to address:

1. Protecting the group's balance sheet and facilitating sustainable earnings power.
2. Delivery of large risk capacity to the company's underwriters.
3. Risk retention and performance management.
4. Reinsurance as a financial management tool.
5. Reinsurance operating platform (the systematic and operating environment of a given company).
6. Reinsurer credit risk and credit risk management.

This framework of governance needs to recognise the dynamics of the entire reinsurance process, not simply the act of purchasing reinsurance. It is the "whats", "whens" and "hows" of the process. Explicit recognition needs to be given to the review and authorisation of reinsurance security, the review and approval of contract language, the provision of management information, the purchase authorisation process and most importantly the policies and processes to be followed when things go wrong. The framework of governance has to be, to large degree, prescriptive while the actual execution can introduce some pragmatism based on the market conditions and the objectives of the company.

Returning to the need for reinsurance policy to be prescriptive, reinsurance is a process that incorporates many elements of risk.

These range from reputational risk, legal risk and credit risk, all the way through to management risk. Reinsurers and insurers simply cannot afford to compromise in these areas – reputations are hard to win and easy to lose, legal risks bring about significant cost but can be avoidable and credit risk is directly and immediately erosive to both the profit and loss statement and the balance sheet.

ENGAGING YOUR INTERNAL CONSTITUENTS

Now the fun starts! You may have just been told that you are the worldwide reinsurance manager for ACME International and that you are responsible for the entire reinsurance process, but you are about to find out that the reinsurance process is pervasive within a large multinational organisation involving underwriting, claims, finance, risk management to name but a few. Everyone is involved and everyone has an opinion, but how do you pull all of these constituents together in order to implement reinsurance policy and strategy? If a company operates a true management matrix[1] the task may be slightly less challenging, but most companies operate with strong vertical "silos"[2] challenging the wits of all those whose task it is to operate on the horizontal plane, such as the reinsurance manager. Issuing mandates from the centre without engaging these multiple constituents, and addressing the fundamental questions "why should I?" and "what's in it for me" is a recipe for failure.

So, what to do?

- ❑ Identify those internal constituents and engage them at the highest level within their respective silo. While it may well be one person in accounting who is the key individual in managing the reinsurance accounting on a day to day basis, without explicitly gaining the support of the head of finance, that person cannot be effectively engaged.
- ❑ Create a network at multiple levels, at the most senior functional level as well as at the level of the day-to-day practitioner.
- ❑ Ensure that there is minimal organisational distance between the promulgation of reinsurance and its execution.
- ❑ Consider a group reinsurance board that includes geographic and functional responsibilities and ensure that this body is empowered to act on behalf of their unit with the minimum of internal communication.

- Make these board members responsible for execution. Principal responsibilities of your group reinsurance board might be:
  - To promulgate and execute an explicit risk retention strategy that recognises the group's tolerance for risk within the design of external reinsurance structures.
  - To develop and maintain reinsurance capacity for key lines of business, and to provide regions/customer segments with ready and economic access to this capacity.
  - To provide competent consultancy to business divisions/customer segments on all reinsurance related matters.
  - To optimise financial performance through the use of reinsurance vehicles.

The concept of a consistent approach to risk retention, based on the highest common denominator, coupled with global capacity for selected lines, are at the core of the reinsurance policy and strategy of a large multinational company. It is the responsibility of group reinsurance board to ensure that business divisions/customer segments are fully aware of available global capacity and that a professional level of service supports their mandated role.

PRAGMATIC EXECUTION OF POLICY

You have to remember that, having established a group reinsurance board you have created a platform not only for the promulgation and implementation of policy but also for the development, refinement and execution of a mutually agreed strategy. The sum of the collective expertise within your board is the key; operating individually that expertise can be valued greater than the whole, but, operating as an effective team, the whole is worth considerably more than the sum of the parts. You have to recognise that your own organisation is as dynamic as the external environment in which you operate. Underwriting is a key constituent and creating a fundamental partnership with underwriting is essential. This partnership needs to be replicated with finance and risk management. The notion of partnership is important because of the mutuality of interest that it creates and the most important element of an effective partnership is recognising each other's needs and being able, to a certain degree, to compromise.

Looking at the relationship between underwriting and reinsurance, it can be seen that neither can operate in a vacuum detached from the other. In order to secure reinsurance capacity underwriters have to clearly articulate their needs and provide the information to support the development of the most appropriate reinsurance solution. Reinsurance on the other hand has a lot of market information and knowledge that is essential for underwriters' understanding of the broader market environment. When creating effective reinsurance solutions the reinsurance department facilitates a process of engagement between the primary and reinsurance underwriter that is both explicit and implicit. It is likely that underwriting will be highly demanding of reinsurance but this should be taken with a degree of pragmatism. However, you cannot be pragmatic about something without effectively communicating the areas of policy where some latitude may be allowed and where there is no compromise; some areas are inviolable, reinsurance security, for example; to compromise your reinsurer security standards is to play with fire.

CORE COMPETENCIES

In order to effectively develop, execute and maintain any viable reinsurance strategy you need to define where the core competencies lie within the organisation. What can and cannot be effectively accomplished with internal resources is a key issue that undermines both the ability to promulgate effective policy and to effectively engage internal constituents in meaningful discussions regarding the whole process. It is highly desirable to identify a centre of reinsurance competence and capability within the company. Core reinsurance services can be provided to internal constituents directly by the centre of reinsurance competence or by third parties with the approval of the centre. Some of the key competencies are:

Data mining

The ability to extract essential data from multiple data sources is a skill that becomes of paramount importance in the multinational environment where the presence of common platforms that facilitate the timely and accurate extraction of data are the exception rather than the rule. Essential data include risk-profile, claims-profile and trend-related information.

Data analysis

The ability to take the data that has been mined and construct meaningful analyses in a cogent form is another skill that becomes an imperative. The ability to build a reinsurance structure based on data no more constructive than that written of the back of an envelope has long since passed. The utilisation of a standard tool-kit is highly desirable.[3]

Risk assessment

The data will tell much about a given business, but it falls well short of giving the whole picture. In particular, the data will allow a backwards look at history, but does it (or can it) really tell us where we are going in the future? Risk assessment, including the multiple disciplines involved in the insurance business process cannot be underestimated in its importance. What needs to happen here is identification of key risks and an assessment of their importance and magnitude. Simply put, risks that are assessed above the line of tolerance must have an action plan and this information has to be incorporated in the overall analysis of any risk mitigation strategy such as the use of reinsurance.

Understanding the underlying business

This sounds obvious but is often not paid the attention that it demands. Understanding the underlying business involved requires the development of a partnership between the reinsurance area and the owners of the underlying business. The practitioners in the reinsurance area may be well versed in a given line of business but they are not responsible for the underwriting of that business; you have to go directly to the "horse's mouth" to get the real picture. Remember the reinsurer is reinsuring the underlying business and therefore the partnership with the managers of that business needs to also become an integral part of the value proposition presented by the ceding company to the reinsurer. The mere existence of a given reinsurance structure does not guarantee the support of a reinsurer for any given piece of business.

COMMUNICATION

The preceding section briefly touched upon the subject of communication , but it shall be expanded upon here in terms of the importance of effective internal and external communication.

As the worldwide reinsurance manager of ACME International you have already identified your key internal and external constituents and must have developed a plan of communication to address each party's needs. It is not a "one size fits all" environment; each department/level requires individualised information:

- Senior management needs the overview of the programme in a manner that allows them to understand the impact of the reinsurance process in a concise manner. This should not consist of sound-bites, but precise identification of key issues both internal and external.
- The finance department needs to understand the importance of the most relevant financial components of the reinsurance process and the measurements applicable to them.
- The underwriting department, as mentioned above, needs interactive communication on multiple levels from identification of key issues to macro economic trends and their potential implication, even for a local or regional portfolio.
- Risk management needs to know that risk policy is being complied with.

To the internal constituents we must add key external constituents such as the reinsurer and broker. The reinsurance department has the responsibility of representing ACME International to reinsurers and brokers. While reinsurers will judge an individual transaction on its merits, the underlying relationship between the ACME International and the reinsurer cannot be underestimated. ACME International is a complex organisation operating in many geographic and market segments. The reinsurer will see this, but how does the reinsurer make rhyme or reason of the actions of ACME International in a given marketplace and how does ACME International effectively engage the reinsurer to be able to leverage the business relationship for mutual benefit?

One approach is the identification of a panel of "core reinsurers", usually no more than 10 in number. ACME International's reinsurance manager will require an account manager to liase with each of these core reinsurers. The reinsurance account manager will then embark upon a process of communicating ACME International's operations and strategies through that account manager into the reinsurer's organisation, with the explicit objective of ensuring a high level of understanding of ACME International and from a strategic perspective how ACME International wants the various pieces of its reinsurance puzzle to fit together.

ENSURING EVERYONE KNOWS WHAT THE REINSURANCE PUZZLE SHOULD AND DOES LOOK LIKE

So far, this chapter has discussed policy and communication and has explored how to engage internal constituents. However, does everyone know how these various pieces of the puzzle fit together or whether they are blank? Worse still, do important constituents have puzzle pieces that do not fit into the puzzle that you (as the worldwide reinsurance manager of ACME International) are trying to put together? This subject goes beyond policy and communication and drops down into the techniques by which policy moves from the drawing board to implementation, preferably in as few steps as possible, a subject that should not be tackled by the beginner!

Developing a reinsurance policy and the strategies with which to implement it within an organisation is a difficult process, and at ACME International, it is all the more complex as the challenge spans multiple segments, geographies and cultures.

First and foremost, clear and mutually agreed core policies and strategies have to be established in advance to ensure everyone knows where they stand. Senior management's explicit approval of the core elements of policy and strategy is essential.

Additionally, the issue of implementation can prove difficult; even with the presence of a group reinsurance board to bring about multi-constituent focus, implementation will still not be universally understood or appreciated throughout the various nodes of the organisation. Therefore, the reinsurance manager has to personally deliver the message to as many parts of the organisation as is feasible and practicable, wherever they may be.

Generic and contract negotiation skills

The reinsurance manager of the multinational insurance company is in a unique position in that effective internal and external negotiation skills are a prerequisite in order to balance the demands not only of the contractual parties, the ceding company and the reinsurers, but also of the internal constituents who will invariably argue that any solution not specifically tailored to their needs is at best a compromise and at worst a complete waste of time and money. Notwithstanding this sentiment, the likelihood of everyone agreeing the internal allocation of costs associated with any reinsurance that is shared between multiple parties within the organisation is extremely low unless they can be persuaded that the allocation is logical, impartial and fair.

Technical and general reinsurance knowledge

Technical and general reinsurance knowledge should not be taken for granted. The reinsurance department is a partner with its internal constituents, each brings something to the table, be it tax, finance, claims, underwriting or reinsurance. Each is expected to bring value to the process and in so doing each has to have the ready ability to acquire the appropriate level of skill attributed to their area of responsibility. The reinsurance department has to have the right level of fundamental reinsurance skills across a broad range and have the ability to acquire specialist reinsurance skills in the event that they are required for special projects, such as the development of an effective capital management programme. This latter skill may not be unique to large multinational companies but, whereas the skill may be called upon from time to time at other companies, this skill will be required regularly at those companies where reinsurance is used internally as a substitute for physically resident capital on selected balance sheets.

Awareness of capital market-related solutions

This area can be linked to the previous sub-section. The role of the reinsurance manager has fundamentally changed over the course of the last 10 years and will continue to change significantly as we move into the future. The role used to be narrowly defined as "reinsurance buying", and the "buyer" worked in a relatively narrow world of traditional reinsurance solutions offered up by the direct and broker market reinsurers. Little was understood of such concepts as capital allocation, reinsurer credit risk, frictional costs and other areas that, as the reinsurance industry has become more financially and technically sophisticated, we have begun to understand. It is not just the market conditions immediately following the events of September 11, 2001 that bring about the need to look at alternative solutions, but also the simple fact that for certain risks the traditional insurance and reinsurance market is simply neither big enough nor efficient enough. The trend toward continued development of alternative solutions adapted to acceptance within the capital markets will pervade both hard and soft market cycles of the future and the multinational insurance company is at the cutting edge of defining the types of products and solutions that will one day be more commonplace. Woe betides the reinsurance manager that does not keep abreast of these trends.

Market management – internal and external

Relationship management is another capability that needs to be properly understood. Credibility is an important factor both with internal constituents and with external reinsurers and brokers. The key internal and external constituents need to be identified and a plan of professional communication and relationship development should be implemented. This is the essence of building the kinds of professional relationship that provide an enduring platform of partnership based on trust, transparency and, to a certain extent, give and take.

Understanding the financial implications of the reinsurance process

How much capital is released as a consequence of a given reinsurance transactions? What is the true cost of facultative reinsurance? What are the frictional costs of proportional vs non-proportional reinsurance? Are reinsurance recoverables being aggressively pursued?

So often the reinsurance industry looks narrowly at the cost of reinsurance in terms of premium expenditure or claims recovered rather than looking at the quality of the overall reinsurance asset, often the largest "other asset" carried on the balance sheet. We should not assume that this is risk-free; our ability to make the asset perform is often directly linked to areas such as the internal claims recoveries procedures and the financial strength of the reinsurer.

AWARENESS OF REGULATORY ISSUES

The world of the multinational is a jungle of jurisdictions, each with their own regulatory requirements. These determine to a large extent some of the key parameters associated with reinsurance policy and strategy inasmuch as they are prescriptive in their definition of regulatory capital and margins. Adherence to local rules is essential, but recognition that local rules are often an impediment to broader-based operating models is also important. They are designed to protect the local policyholder (rightfully so) and to preserve the integrity of the local tax base. These are legitimate objectives, but again not always in your best interest as you try to navigate through the complex world of reinsurance purchase.

Transfer pricing skills

Clearly linked to an understanding of the regulatory environment is the demand that internal reinsurance, an integral component of most multinational's financial model, must be priced in accordance with applicable rules in respect to transfer pricing. To ignore this is to foolishly ignore the importance of tax compliance.

But how can the correct transfer price be determined? This can be achieved by using the company's assumed reinsurance underwriters (using in-house reinsurance pricing techniques) (if available), or by external benchmarking (obtaining indicative prices from the external reinsurance market). Whatever the solution, the process will benefit from a consistent programme-type approach.

Market trends

This is not a simple matter of reading industry journals but also why the development of a valued network of partners within the industry can be important. The demand relates to the requirement to feed this information back to the internal constituents to ensure that they feel "wired in" to the market through their valued internal consultant.

ANALYSING RISK

The determination of the optimum reinsurance structure, both in terms of external placement or internal transfer of risk, requires the usage of increasingly sophisticated tools such as dynamic financial analysis and stochastic modelling to analyse the impact of various structures on a business portfolio. Reinsurance financial analysis is a key competency that must be integrated into the reinsurance management area, accessed from technical support areas such as actuaries, or outsourced to a third-party service provider such as a broker or independent consultant. The use of a single tool or at the very least a complementary set of tools is imperative as the analyses are going to be required for multiple purposes. First and foremost, these tools, properly utilised, are designed to support the underwriting management process by identifying the key performance drivers in a given portfolio, yet reinsurance decisions are still too often based on perceptions of risk that are not supported by factual analysis.

The use of financial tools is the most fundamental component of the analytical process; the next step is to merge the factual base of data represented by the portfolio analysis with the output from a risk review that seeks to identify risk hazards on a forward-looking basis. Once these two steps are complete we can move on to the first part of designing an appropriate reinsurance structure for a given line of business or segment.

There is an obvious link between analysis and reinsurance pricing; knowing the impact of a structure allows you to start to develop a benchmark price for a given reinsurance placement. The benchmarking of reinsurance pricing within the environment of a large multinational insurance enterprise is a fascinating process where companies have tried a multiplicity of models with limited success. The challenge here is brought about by the simple fact that most internal units (profit centres or other units with the responsibility of underwriting the original business, commercial property, for example) believe that they can purchase their own re-insurance cheaper than someone buying on their behalf. Even if they are comfortable with the concept that their reinsurance may be purchased from another point within the group, it is likely that the method of allocating the cost of a given reinsurance cover will cause clashes of opinion.

The analytical processes described above (the use of tools and merging the factual base with output) introduce an element of transparency that is an essential component of enhancing the understanding of the true costs of reinsurance. Notwithstanding the analytical process, external benchmarking is attractive to the large multinational in that it can be seen to bring about a level of credibility that is almost never perceived to exist with any internal pricing mechanism. Companies have used their wholly owned commercial reinsurance entity operations (where they have them) to provide market and transaction benchmarks with varying degrees of success. Often the issue of credibility arises when the motivation of the internal reinsurer in developing a pricing benchmark is questionable. This will rise when there is no incentive for the internal reinsurer to undertake a complete pricing analysis. An external reinsurer will base their pricing on the probability of underwriting the treaty or risk and will therefore include market factors – the internal reinsurer may have no such motivation. Consequently, the internal reinsurer's pricing may not be indicative of the market at any given point in time.

MAKING SURE THE PIECES FIT TOGETHER PROPERLY

A key component of reinsurance strategy is a consistent and well-articulated approach to net retention and how reinsurance capacity, particularly treaty reinsurance capacity is used. There will many constituents with multiple opinions but the key to remember is that risk retention tolerance is hierarchical (in that it increases in size as the scale of the manager's portfolio increases, so the CEO will have the largest risk tolerance and the underwriter the lowest, with ranks of middle management in between), it is driven by numerous factors, including risk quality, size of portfolio, allocated capital and how performance is measured. This has to be explicitly recognised especially when internal reinsurance is being utilised to consolidate cessions from multiple balance sheets through a common balance sheet. Such a reinsurance strategy, basically stated, is to:

- Optimise financial performance by incorporating the group net retention in the design of any external treaty reinsurance structure.
- Derive economies of scale and scope through the purchasing of treaty capacity purchased on a global (or minimally regional) basis.
- Provide explicit support for the development of global and speciality businesses, as well as the development of businesses globally.

Common, group-level reinsurance buying can realise economies of scale not available to units purchasing independently, while at the same time significantly reducing group exposure to credit risk (fewer reinsurers). The deployment of this capacity from a central point within the group ensures optimal use of group capital and provides units with an economically compelling alternative to independent reinsurance purchasing.

Key to the success of reinsurance capacity secured at a group level is effective internal deployment; it is imperative that the economies of scale that are realised (through the process of buying external reinsurance based on the highest common denominator and thus creating buying power to create leverage) be passed down to operating units for performance management purposes, so that every level of the structure benefits. This requires the provision of transparent exposure-based, rather than experience-based, pricing for any internal layers of reinsurance as this could provide a stable pricing criteria that is more closely related to the dynamics of a direct insurance portfolio; the unit cost of reinsurance placed on an exposure basis is theoretically more stable than one placed based on reinsurance market conditions that will change and may well change more rapidly than the ability to adjust insurance pricing. By incorporating the pricing economies inherent in the group reinsurance capacity concept, reinsurance costs for any given unit will not only be stable but consistently competitive throughout the market pricing cycle.

Facultative (individual risk) reinsurance can be an economic form of securing reinsurance for those risks whose capacity requirements exceed net and treaty capacity or for those risks where the reinsurers' "extra pair of eyes" adds value to the underwriting process. Facultative reinsurance is also purchased to "improve" a risk by extracting volatile components (high hazard components of an individual risk such as a single property with a much larger value than all of the other properties belonging to an insured). Whatever the business motivation, facultative reinsurance is expensive to administer, often duplicates treaty coverage in place (particularly at the group level) and consequently should ideally be kept to a minimum.

In a hard reinsurance market, reinsurers will seek to return their portfolios to profitability through restricting automatic capacity (reducing the amount of reinsurance capacity that they are prepared to allow the ceding company to underwrite against without referral to the reinsurer) and offering facultative limits in their place. The cost of facultative reinsurance is often underestimated because of the hidden administrative costs and efforts are ongoing to develop an operating platform that enhances the efficiency of this process significantly and improves knowledge of reinsurance distribution. Royal and Sun Alliance, for example, have implemented a electronic trading platform for the placement of their facultative reinsurance.

Depending on the business model, facultative reinsurance purchasing can be centralised or distributed. In either case the purchaser is assuming a fiduciary responsibility to ensure that the reinsurance transaction meets all of the requirements of their local underwriting authority and any requirements laid down in the group's reinsurance policy.

It is common practice that the treaty contract is the "buyers contract" whereas the facultative certificate is the "sellers contract". What this means is that whereas there is considerable control over the contents of a treaty contract, the same cannot be said to be the case with facultative reinsurance, especially when the model chosen is de-centralised in nature.

CONCLUSION

The management of reinsurance within any company is an increasingly complex undertaking as companies become more sophisticated in the way they look at risk, while the fundamental need to provide both underwriting capacity and financial management, the traditional domain of the reinsurance department must always be addressed. Much of what has been discussed in this chapter applies to small and large companies alike. While it has highlighted the scale of some of the issues facings more complex organisations and some of their unique requirements, the purpose of this chapter has been to illustrate the fundamental keys to success in manager the ceded reinsurance function within any organisation.

1 A management matrix is a flat management structure with distinct responsibilities assigned along both the horizontal and vertical planes, the points of intersection being the key to the matrix. Often, the horizontal and vertical axis are taken by line of business and geographic management respectively.
2 A silo is a team responsible only for its own area of operation and with limited interest in the fortunes of the enterprise as a whole.
3 The use of either proprietary or commonly available analytical tools that provide the ability to perform either financial analysis with the variables of model or model components reduced to a minimum, ie, enhancing the consistency of the result. An example would be using a single model for the analysis of natural hazard exposures.

3

Reinsurance Buying Practices

Philippe Derieux

AXA

AXA is a global insurer operating throughout the world with expected operating earnings for 2002 in excess of €1.8 billion. At a presentation in London on October 9, 2002, Claude Brunet (member of the AXA Group Executive Committee) identified these advantages of being global: diversification of risk, skills/knowledge transfer, leverage scale, unique brand. He argued that in order to obtain leverage from scale and ensure efficient skills/knowledge transfer throughout the group there has to be arbitrage between local autonomy and total centralisation – total autonomy generates no leverage, total centralisation may destroy value. His alternative is: convergence with added value.

This chapter examines how that balance is achieved in the field of reinsurance and identifies the steps that are taken to make the approach a success in AXA.

GROUP CULTURE AND ORGANISATION

As a general principal the use of reinsurance is very much linked to the culture of the insurer. A highly devolved organisation will tend to have a decentralised reinsurance policy with each unit buying locally what it believes it requires. A centrally controlled organisation will retain reinsurance purchasing at the centre and will tend to be more influenced by the demands of the total group than by local or regional interests. Thus, in formulating reinsurance strategy, the reinsurance director will have a number of questions in his or her mind:

Question 1: How is reinsurance perceived within the group?
Reinsurance may be considered as a minor issue for the company or central to the group's business strategy.

Traditional insurers think about reinsurance only once a year during the renewal season, when trying to buy covers that are more or less in line with their appetite for risk. Most of the time the same people seem to profit from reinsurers, either because they have bought cheap covers or because their claims experience is bad. In their mind, a good reinsurance programme is a programme that makes the ceding company "win money against the reinsurer".

Other insurers consider reinsurance as an equity allocation tool and then use it with a risk management mind. A large number of other different attitudes can be noticed, but most companies fluctuate between those two extremes.

In the latter case, and despite the fact that treaties are renewed only once a year, reinsurance is a permanent issue, which is fully integrated in the company management.

Compared to traditional insurance, reinsurance is a world apart, obeying a different and specific culture. Not only do the technical expertise and tools differ, but also inevitably the vocabulary and habits are so far from the direct insurance world that it often happens that the company reinsurance department feels itself closer to the reinsurance market than to the company for which it works. "Reinsurance is left to experts who do what they have to do and nobody will challenge them because nobody really understands what they do and how they do it, so don't bother them with too many questions, just listen and try to understand" was recommend by a company board member to a set of young new hired employees 20 years ago.

The frequency of catastrophic events in recent years has shown reinsurance as an absolute necessity that has to be carefully managed; the culture is changing but the range of cultures between the two extremes is narrowing slowly.

Sometime after the World Trade Centre event, a European reinsurance department manager was asked by his CEO to comment on what could change in the future. The manager answered: "Of course reinsurers will try to use this event to increase their rates, but this event happened far from our country and there is no evidence it could happen here: there is no reason why we would suffer from that". Then the CEO put another question: "Yes, but in more general terms, do you intend to change your programmes in the coming years?". The manager answered: "Except if prices go up too far, there is no reason why I would change my programmes: the net contribution of reinsurance for our company has been positive for years. In case of significant price increase, I will just increase our retentions. This is always the same game with cycles, it's been the same for 30 years".

The third question from the CEO could have been: "And how will you respond to the evolution of exposures in our risk portfolio?". Or "How can you be sure this will last long?". But there was no third question, the CEO being fully satisfied with the two answers...

Most of the time, the way in which reinsurance is bought is a mirror of the reinsurance culture: in a traditional world, the experts (very few) buy their covers at the very end of the year, sometimes in a hurry, through a personalised process. Face to face discussion with reinsurer and broker counterparties is the most common method and negotiation, and the price is the centre of the debate.

When the reinsurance culture is closer to a risk management attitude, the buying process is organised at least with a schedule; the definition of targets and buying methods are set in advance with reinsurers and brokers.

Another type of culture may also influence the reinsurance buying process: the cost-cutting culture. Until the 1990s, the optimisation of buying processes had been developed in different industries for decades, but not really in the insurance industry. An explanation as to why this optimisation did not reach insurance was that insurers were too rich to consider economies of scale, and even if they were interested, they were just using it for general expenses. Since reasonable profits were more difficult to reach for insurance companies, the managements have now hired buying experts from other industries. This was mainly in order to improve IT costs or costs derived from the management of assets.

But some of the newcomers have posed the question: "Why don't you apply rationalised buying methods to all activities in your company?", or "Why couldn't we apply a central buying methodology to insurance or reinsurance?". In many cases the answer was: "Because it will not work". In some other cases, with more demanding shareholders, the answer was "let's try it".

In large groups, culture may be somewhat a patchwork though an official group culture exists. In this case, reinsurance will be perceived with significant differences among different affiliates.

Then comes the organisation.

Question 2: What type of organisation should be reinsured?

In a traditional company, reinsurance is centralised for treaties and decentralised for facultative risks. The centralised reinsurance department derives from the cultural weight on the decision process described above. So, a centralised department for reinsurance purposes is the most common organisation one can find for one company but not for a group of companies.

In many instances, major insurance groups have been built through a set of acquisitions. In such a case each new acquired company may already own its reinsurance process. Even in the case of internal growth and when the development happened in a new country, the new entity manager could claim his capacity to buy reinsurance by himself. The major argument against any group centralisation is: "If each country is specific, then each market is specific".

The big groups' organisation scheme has focussed on what was considered as essential for the group: reporting and financial flows. But a group cannot be a group if the only link is reporting: thus, most groups try to optimise their organisation in two directions:

1. Try to find the best balance in the power sharing (central/local).
2. Try to find all possible synergies that not only provide a financial advantage but also a qualitative impact.

The organisation is linked to the group culture and philosophy: letting local management have a large degree of autonomy and just driving global strategy and capital allocation from the centre implies a very decentralised organisation. Driving not only global policies but also detailed actions, imposing all underwriting policies and guidance implies a centralised organisation.

Reinsurance plays a specific role since it is a key driver of a group underwriting policy and capital allocation, thus a centralised organisation will include a centralised reinsurance process and conversely a decentralised organisation includes reinsurance local actions. However, reality is always more complex and many type of reinsurance processes are in place that do not fit exactly with this principle. Hence, a large variety of half way processes are in place within large groups.

Some groups, though very much centralised, let their affiliates buy reinsurance by themselves provided they follow a set of predefined rules. Some others, though quite decentralised, have developed a centralised tool for reinsurance, just because of its cost-cutting impact. Whatever those exceptions, we can state that no reinsurance buying process will last long in a group if it does not really fit with the group's culture and organisation.

Contrary to other activities where all actors apply more or less the same process, reinsurance buying is still an area where a large number of organisations exist and where no-one seems to lead and appear as the flagship of the race.

From all the different possibilities, AXA has chosen for its reinsurance a centralised buying process that has been called "rationalised buying process". In reality it is a full component of the group risk management strategy.

WHAT IS A CENTRALISED BUYING PROCESS?

Behind the word "buying process", many actions are hidden that are not linked to a strict buying function. Buying a large quantity of commodity goods on a regular basis obviously requires some good logistical and negotiation skills. But buying a large number of sophisticated goods that are never totally similar also requires some other capacities. These are discussed in detail below.

As far as reinsurance is concerned, a buying process for treaties starts early in the year with information and analysis.

Information collection

The first step in buying a reinsurance cover is collecting the company information that shows and quantifies the risk to be covered and shows how the insurer manages risk. Although this first step consists of gathering the best possible information to give a good perception of the risk, the problem is that no insurance IT system in the world can yet fulfil this duty.

One of the main difficulties for reinsurance is the collection of adequate information. The centralised buying process starts with a deep review of available information about the risk to be covered. In reality, the information in many cases does exist but is so painful to capture that a compromise must be found between the need for detail and the cost/time necessary to get it.

In some circumstances, information is not available because no-one thought about the need to file it. This could be because either:

- ❑ it was not supposed to be essential for business; or
- ❑ the risk was unknown – "We don't know what we don't know".

The centralised buying process then includes a full review of risk information and the creation of standards to be followed by all affiliates. It also includes a formatting process performed by the central team who review all information provided by the affiliates.

The formats apply to:

- ❑ underwriting policies;
- ❑ portfolio profiles and exposure information; and
- ❑ claims experience reports.

During the recent years, the development of catastrophe modelling (by companies such as RMS, EQECAT and AIR) has helped in the standardisation of information and the definition of the minimum information needed as far as catastrophic exposures were concerned. However, a lot of work is still needed to improve the quality of information, and more specifically for specialised lines of business.

This standardised information is the first step for a centralised buying process: most of the time, it does not only help for reinsurance buying purposes but also for internal purposes such as local technical reporting improvement and education of local underwriters.

The AXA experience shows that it takes a couple of years before reaching a sufficient level of accuracy; the acquisition of experience for the central team – even if this team is made of good experienced professionals – and the adaptation of the affiliates to the information requirements can take a minimum of two years in a large group which deals with very different areas and which has to cope with significant differences between the affiliates. Once the information is gathered, the central team makes the risk analysis.

Information analysis

The second step in buying a reinsurance cover is analysing the risk embedded in the portfolio to be covered.

This analysis includes two steps:

1. A global review of the strengths and weaknesses of the company balance sheet (equity, reserving policy, etc). This review is a light one and uses sources of information given by other group or affiliate departments. It merely clarifies the capacity of the local affiliate to take risks.
2. A deep analysis of the portfolio of risks showing what are the main constraints and quantifying the need for reinsurance protection. As far as this second step is concerned, modelling plays a significant role, not only for catastrophic exposures but for all kind of risks.

Because the tools are quite sophisticated, this analysis is driven and made by the central team, who gather the knowledge and concentrate experience. But this team works in close coordination with the affiliate's team that has provided the basic information and which will use in the conclusions of the analysis.

Experience has shown that an educational process needs to be put in place to make all this work profitable for the local affiliate and then for the group. In addition, the workflow managed by the central team needs to be carefully scheduled. Within the schedule, a final feedback to the affiliate must be organised in order to persuade the affiliate's management to accept the conclusions of the performed analysis.

Experience has also shown that the allocation of time between the first step (information collection) and the second step (risk analysis) is critical. Very often, the time for accurate information collection is understated if one takes into account all corrections needed. This is the reason why building up a centralised buying process requires not only time but also an adequate set of procedures to be put in place slowly but steadily.

At the end of the second step, one must be in a position to know what is to be covered and why. Then comes the "how?".

Programme definition

The third step in buying a reinsurance cover is defining the optimised programme structure.

In an ideal world, the second step is achieved by the end of the spring each year, leaving the summer available for the third step. In some cases, the analytical work is not achieved by the end of June and then less time is left for the programme definition. However, if the second step is very well performed, it makes the programme structuring significantly easier and then faster.

Defining programmes requires two actions, internal and external:

The internal action consists of creating a set of options for the protection of each risk/line of business that are then tested in terms of exposure efficiency, linked to the analytical work performed and to the risk appetite of the affiliate. The programme definition is challenged with the affiliates, who may ask for some changes. A check is also made on the consistency between this risk appetite and the real capacity of the affiliate to suffer from adverse scenarios. The global review as described above is used for this purpose. In case of strong disagreement with an affiliate, the central team has a duty to report to the highest level of the group in order to get a final decision.

The external action consists of the central team testing the proposed programmes with some key reinsurance partners and brokers in order to check whether the programmes can be easily placed. Some amendments may then be introduced in order to fit with the market constraints.

Even though flexibility is often valuable, the central team has to follow some technical standards that describe what is permitted and, more importantly, what is not accepted by the group. Those standards are approved at the highest level of the group and are formulated in close co-ordination with the group's chief financial officer.

In a centralised process, the knowhow about programmes' structures is optimised and expertise concentrated. The central team needs to make sure that all the specific local requirements have been recognised and, where possible, integrated in to the programme.

Buying the programmes

The fourth step in buying a reinsurance cover is selling the reinsurers the results of the first three steps. In a rational market, the cedent that provides the best information to its reinsurers and shows a good control of its risks should get the best terms. In some cases quality of information (transparency) is not yet recognised as an advantage in favour of the ceding company.

The market challenge: price, capacity, wording and security

In a soft market, buying on a centralised mode should, in theory, provide some advantage to the buyer in terms of prices. Considering cycles and the fact that it would be unrealistic to act globally when the market is soft and then change the organisation when it is hard, the centralised process has to prove its efficiency in other fields:

- It must gain capacity from a reinsurer on programmes that are not easy to place. Once the reinsurer makes a first analysis and proposal for each programme on its own merit, a discussion can take place with the ceding group central team based on the global relationship.
- More security should be given to the group affiliates by managing the risk of the counterparty on their behalf. This requires specific skills and the creation of processes such as security committee, development of a security list, etc.
- There must be an evolution of treaty wordings and the capacity to negotiate conditions with the market.
- It must gain capacity for the cedent to quote its own treaties and then be capable of negotiating at arms length with its reinsurers. A good degree of expertise from the central team on technical and actuarial aspects help in a hard market.

In the author's experience, the evolution of the reinsurance market in the recent years tends to indicate that these four issues are now quite important.

Throughout the renewal season, the affiliates are kept informed about the evolution and the results of the buying process. They have the right to give their opinion on the choice of the programme leaders but must not interfere with the placement. If the market asks for additional information, this must be managed by the central team and direct contacts between reinsurers and the affiliates are not recommended except if organised at the request of the central team.

Those restrictions apply only during the buying period (around one month); during the first part of the year (steps one to three), reinsurers are invited to visit the group affiliates in order to make their opinion of local underwriters.

A rationalised agenda

The fifth step in buying reinsurance cover is monitoring a process including an IT tool.

The centralised buying process requires the creation of specific tools to manage the renewal with the reinsurance market. The central team is therefore in charge of creating and maintaining an IT system dedicated to this purpose. This goes obviously through an internet tool which enables it to:

- ❑ provide information to the market on the proposed programmes;
- ❑ receive quotes and conditions from the reinsurers;
- ❑ exchange news and comments; and
- ❑ manage the placement.

Such a tool can be efficient only if an agenda is built with opening cessions, closing dates for receiving quotes, etc.

One advantage of such a process is the visibility given to the group on target dates for the achievement of the placement, which enables the top management to communicate on the group protections to its shareholders.

But, as before with the other steps of the centralised buying process, flexibility is required to make such a process a success:

- ❑ The agenda may change within the season because of market conditions and all the process must be designed such a way that it can be easily adapted.
- ❑ The existence of an Internet tool does not replace face to face negotiation, visits and meetings when necessary (which is often the case). In other words, the tool creates some discipline

throughout the renewal season and eases the information flow but does not replace market relations.

- The Internet tool may be designed internally and be used for some time but since IT is evolving quite rapidly and the reinsurance market is not stable, a limited investment sounds reasonable for a tool with a limited life. This enables the group reinsurance central team to renew its tool either by creating a new one internally or choosing one of the emerging marketplace tools that are now proposed to ceding companies.

Once the placement is achieved, accounts and cashflows have to be managed.

Managing a centralised back office

The sixth step of buying a reinsurance cover is managing a back office, which is a significant issue in a centralised buying process.

The centralisation of premium and claims flows have provided some gains for the group:

- it enables the group to manage global cashflow with the counterparties; and
- each affiliate within the group will have only one counterparty, the central team, which will then dispatch the flows among brokers and reinsurers.

Such an organisation requires the existence of a back office team and system that are similar to a broker or a reinsurer back office. There are two possibilities, either the central team acts as a broker, or the central team acts as a reinsurer.

In terms of back office, the two solutions are very similar in terms of workload. However, being a reinsurer enables the central team to play a full role for managing the risk of counterparty.

It also gives the possibility of creating a group retention level and then optimising the reinsurance scheme on a global standpoint for the group.

Different levels of sophistication

The seventh step is to think globally by integrating all parameters including the global balance of the group protection.

Several insurance groups (AIG and Zurich for instance) have created central teams in order to cope with this subject. In such cases, the centralised buying process is more sophisticated as there is a transformation level between the risk ceded by the group affiliates and the risk ceded to the reinsurance market.

Different processes are in place within large groups in terms of:

- the creation of internal reinsurance pools shared by the group affiliates;
- the retention of the risks through a reinsurance captive;
- the creation of a reinsurance portfolio with a mix of inward and outward reinsurance; and
- the transformation of local affiliates treaties into large group global treaties placed in the market.

In AXA, the central team (AXA Cessions, which is a reinsurance company) manages a retention pool and, as a reinsurance group captive, keeps some risks within the group.

Another development is the integration of the facultative business in the centralised buying process; having a good control on the treaty flows does not imply having a good control on reinsurance ceded by a group. Facultative risks must be included. Moreover, trying to build up global relationship with reinsurers means that all the business flows with those have to be at least known and preferably controlled by one entity in the group.

Some groups have organised themselves such a way they reach this target. As far as AXA is concerned, a specific facultative buying platform, developed by the central team is in place. Among other things, this platform enables the central team to control the adequacy between the treaty covers and the facultative covers for each affiliate.

When such tools are available in a group, the same risk transformation process as described above for treaties can be applied by the insurance group for facultative risks.

WHAT IS THE VALUE OF A CENTRALISED BUYING PROCESS?

The first value for the group is the gathering of strong expertise in one team which is at the disposal of the entire group. Sophistication of risk analysis requires expertise and experience which is expensive (for example, the cost of cat models).

Furthermore, the central reinsurance team is one major component of the risk management process of the group.

The second value is the reporting power to the group management. A central reinsurance team managing a process as described above owns a large amount of information about the group that can be shared.

The third value is the capacity to make global deals with the reinsurance market and, to some extent, improve the bargaining power of the group.

The fourth is the simplification of the back office flows within the group, with both a cost-cutting perspective and a quality improvement on the administration side.

The fifth is the education that can be provided by the central team to the affiliates, and more globally the technical synergies that can be developed.

Sixth, such a process helps the group, among other things, make its evolution from a patchwork to a network.

But, creating a centralised buying process as described above requires a certain number of conditions to be really efficient:

1. A strong commitment of the top management of the group to support the central team vis à vis the local affiliates and, when necessary, with the market.
2. Investing sufficient money and, more importantly, time. The world today is very impatient but heavy processes need time to become fully part of a group organisation.
3. Clear definition of what are the local affiliates responsibilities and what are those of the central team. These should be adhered to with almost no compromises; there will always be some grey areas but trying to minimise them is a key for success.
4. Good transparent communication from the central team to the local affiliates is essential; "the more a process is mandatory the more you have to sell it".
5. Make the necessary moves to adapt to the group culture and organisation without giving up the key drivers of the process.
6. Try to measure the value added. This is one of the most critical issues within such a process. The best way to show the efficiency would be to let another process run at the same time as the centralised one. However, this is not realistic, so the measure-

ment is partially done on a qualitative basis but also by comparing some figures in a relative way, such as, what did I get as a price compared with my peers for the same line of business and market? Though some frustration may emerge about the capacity to quantify precisely the value added of a centralised buying process, it must not stop the move. In some areas, a paradox exists: "the more value you create, the less you can show it"!

CONCLUSION

Because reinsurance is such a mixture of culture and finance it is very difficult ever to establish a definitive perfect system. The process outlined in this chapter is delivering real benefits but as always it can only ever be as good as the data that is fed in to it and the attention to detail. Equally no system can be left static as the world is changing so rapidly. However in today's climate of increasing globalisation of reinsurance markets and huge progress with information technology we at AXA are persuaded that this is a viable and sensible course to steer, helping us achieve the words at the beginning of the chapter, "convergence with added value".

4

A New Rationale for Reinsurance Buying?

Herbert Sedlmair

Allianz AG*

There have always been new rationales or approaches to how reinsurance is bought. Many of them have arisen from either internal or external constraints but in some way have been a logical step in the development of an individual company or to the whole insurance / reinsurance industry.

From an insurance or reinsurance point of view, companies are prepared to face huge catastrophes from a financial and management perspective and guidelines have been developed for who would do what in such a scenario. However, the World Trade Center (WTC) tragedy of September 11, 2001 changed the way such insurance was perceived; until this event, catastrophes were merely understood in the context of natural catastrophes caused by natural perils, but the horrific terrorist attacks of September 11 took the lives of thousands of people and caused huge structural damage. It was the world's largest catastrophe by insurance standards and a whole industry was unprepared.

Since this eye opener to the insurance and reinsurance world, comprehensive discussion has started about man-made events and the industry has widened its horizon by looking into emerging risks and urban accumulation control. The latter should also prevent future unpredictable losses, even if the cause of loss is intentional, as in the WTC terrorist attack.

*All opinions expressed herein are strictly those of the author and do not necessarily reflect the position of Allianz AG.

By looking back one could probably categorise the "ingredients" of the new unknown ground the WTC event produced as follows:

- ❑ different coverage declaration and opinions insuring the same object;
- ❑ not matching insurance and reinsurance wordings, leaving gaps not reinsured;
- ❑ coverage and limit for new scenarios outside the current spectrum;
- ❑ correlation of various classes of business; and
- ❑ default of reinsurance.

What has the insurance industry learned from this event and to what extent has it caused a rethinking of reinsurance purchasing?

INTRODUCTION

This chapter outlines how the environment has changed since September 11, 2001 and what conclusions have been drawn in terms of reinsurance purchasing. This is discussed in the context of an international operating insurance company with an industrial customer segment. The company is by size one of the top companies in the world. It has chosen an organisation with a holding company as its headquarters and financial entities underneath. With its entities the company is well represented and positioned in the major insurance areas. Its perspective is clearly international and its world-wide network also supports the writings in the international industrial business sector. The holding company is also a licensed reinsurer with the aim of writing reinsurance business from its own subsidiaries. This company is used as an example to show how the WTC event has affected the buying of reinsurance, either internally or in negotiating with the reinsurer.

CHECKING INTERNAL STRUCTURE AND RISK ASSESSMENT

The decentralised vs centralised approach

One of the principles of the company used here is that business is conducted locally and local management has full responsibility for their gross and net results. As a result, of course, reinsurance buying has also been under local responsibility otherwise it would suffer from interference from the top to local management, making measuring local bottom line performance difficult.

Looking at this decentralised approach, it seems to make a lot of sense at first glance. The people who write the business against their own guidelines and portfolio considerations buy reinsurance from partners who they know from the local market and where there has been understanding, trust and reliance over years and decades.

The weakness of this system shows, however, the more international or global aspects are added to the business. For a global insurer with one consolidated balance sheet, internal controlling and reporting requirements may clash with local independence. Such considerations can encompass:

- buying power;
- setting of deductibles;
- reinsurance guidelines (matching of coverage etc);
- reinsurer's credit risk; and
- accumulation of risks.

Outside the company environment, reinsurers have also changed over time. The local independent reinsurer has mainly disappeared and now belongs to a larger international group. What was formerly a typical conversation about the local insurance and reinsurance business has now evolved into a negotiation enriched with global aspects and constraints.

A good example of how to measure how things in reinsurance purchasing have changed is to look at the business of international industrial corporates. This kind of business is complex as most of the companies are conglomerates consisting of entities from various business sectors. Therefore, insurance needs are numerous and, if consolidated in one programme, quite comprehensive. In addition, typically, such high limits are required that the insurance programme is placed in various markets and a single insurance carrier cannot digest it without the help of the reinsurance industry.

Many corporates have discussed this issue and apparently agreed to a form that best suits their interests. Knowing how complex the business world is and how manifold businesses within a financial conglomerate, it can be assumed that the chosen form is always a slight compromise. Things do become a bit easier if only local business is written which has no interdependencies with any other business abroad. Logically, international industrial business operations are more complex as this business is predominately international.

A decentralised strategic set-up is a common choice, meaning that business is written from an entity where the client is domiciled. Corporates with international insurance needs are negotiated at the place of the domicile but transacted locally according to its world-wide subsidiaries – "think global and act local" is the slogan. Although this business segment is one of the key segments of the company, local entities have been writing the business against their own balance sheet. The only involvement from the company's headquarters was of a facultative capacity. Therefore, local management decided to use both underwriting and reinsurance. The pros are quite visible: reaction to market changes can be addressed locally and swiftly and the whole group works on a flexible basis.

From a reinsurance perspective the requirements are quite comprehensive. Because of the nature of the business, the scope of coverage has to be international and hence reinsurers have to be capable of accepting international business too. Indeed, in many cases the capability of a reinsurer to write international business is dictated by their own reinsurers, which is commonly known as the "retro" market. In a soft reinsurance market phase, some reinsurers fuel more capital or capacity into the retro market in expectation for a higher return. In this phase the market reinsurers can offer huge capacity to their cedents by generously making use of their capacity booster. This is, of course, an ideal situation for cedents with large risks in their portfolio. Due to this, the panel of reinsurers clearly dramatically shrinks although the need of capacity is huge.

But in a swiftly hardening market as seen following September 11, 2001, the situation for the cedent could become immediately dangerous. Reinsurers who themselves depended upon retro capacity are no longer provided with international capacity facilities and therefore are forced either to discontinue the international business completely, or can only afford to write geographically segmented business for their clients. International corporate clients are asking for a truly international insurance programme, with international coverage that is independent in terms of where the loss occurs and how many entities within the operation are affected; a strictly segmented reinsurance cover could leave the cedent with potential gaps in his placement process. What remains for the cedent is a diminishing number of quality reinsurers. In other words, the cedent faces a less competitive market with the result of reduced capacity at a higher price.

In most cases the cedent cannot react to this by increasing the amount of net retained business (retention rate), because the capital base is limited and may be already exhausted by its other lines of business or by shrinking returns on financial investments and, because of the typical low retention ratio (huge limits involved), any proportionate increase would disproportionately increase the volatility by only adding a minimal premium. In this situation where possibly more entities are approaching reinsurers with similar reinsurance requests, support could be provided by the group reinsurance department. It is the task of this central function to demonstrate the overall strategic importance of this business segment by presenting total ingoing and outgoing volumes as well as to put the local business relationship into a group strategic relationship. This step will also ensure that the strategic goal connected to this business segment will not be endangered by reinsurance reductions within certain countries.

In this respect the author believes that a centralised approach would allow the group to use all its flexibility and buying power to maintain the basis to fulfil their strategic goal. Figures 1 and 2 display the various merits and disadvantages of both approaches.

The need to set up uniform underwriting guidelines

It seems logical to assume that the bigger the group, the better it is to have uniform guidelines in place. This not only supports any central controlling function but also helps the risk management process and any reinsurance protection on a combined basis.

In the author's experience, any attempt to introduce uniform guidelines into a decentralised organisation has been opposed by underwriters on the grounds of local standards and peculiarities. Obviously, if the group wants to be locally represented, the local market environment, including its legal or regulatory standards, has to

Figure 1 Centralised vs decentralised reinsurance function

○ **Not optimal**
● **Optimal**

Criteria	Centralised	Decentralised
Scale effects	● • Reduction in expenses due to central reinsurance team	○ • Expenses are multiplied by having local reinsurance teams
Synergies	◕ • Pooling of know-how	◔ • Duplication of know-how in the group
Transparency	● • Uniform standards	◑ • Local standards not always congruous with group
Group flexibility	● • Reinsurance can swiftly respond to management decision	◑ • Response could be delayed if decision interferes with local responsibility
Team up with underwriting	◑ • Optimal if central underwriting strategy exists	● • Intensive contact with local underwriters
Reinsurance approach	◕ • Strategic with a panel of selected reinsurers	◕ • Varying reinsurance approaches according to local needs
Reaction to market cycles	◑ • Fast on an international basis	◑ • Fast only if local markets change

Figure 2 Centralised vs decentralised reinsurance buying

○ **Not optimal**
● **Optimal**

Criteria	Centralised	Decentralised
Diversification benefits	◕ • Diversification across all international entities results in a reduction in reinsurance expenses	◔ • Only intra-company benefits across lines of business can be achieved
Administration	● • Number of contracts are reduced to a minimum	○ • Each group entity needs its own set of reinsurance contracts
Buying power	● • Use of group's total ceded premium and consolidated financials	◑ • Only possible on the basis of local cessions and financials
Group flexibility	◑ • Limited because of central programme but possibility to set up own reinsurance fund	◑ • High flexibility is only limited by the entity's own financials
Placement	● • Central control on security and reinsurance guidelines	◔ • Limited resources to asses credit risk and reinsurance mismatch
Reinsurance capacity	◕ • Group demand might be higher than maximum available market capacity, eg, for natural catastrophe	● • Full access to local and internal reinsurance capacity
Planning and controlling	● • Central controlling and top down bottom up approach on economic capital and limits	◑ • Bottom up approach only

be considered. However, the additional assumed risk and how much of reinsurance capacity will be available must also be assessed. For truly international industrial business this process can be quite challenging and risk management can become quite complex.

In years when proportional reinsurance coverage was available for this type of business, reinsurers were willing to share the inherent complexity of the business and its full fortune. As a result, cedents could reduce their risk volatility but the intransparent risk remained just on a lower level. Since September 11, 2001, such times seem to be lost; reinsurers now disregard local peculiarities by adding that if this business is supposed to be international then the requirements should be internationally uniform. Granting coverage only on an excess of loss basis with its own terms and conditions, and pricing exposures separately and by risk element, reinsurers do not follow the fortune of the cedent as they used to.

Within such an environment where insurers have to weigh up how much risk they can accept and what reinsurance coverage is available, uniform guidelines seem to be a mandatory tool for an international company to steer its business.

The following points detail a few general criteria of uniform guidelines that are now imperative to successfully run the business and that also support any reinsurance buying for this business.

- Underwriting has to be strictly within the guidelines and treaty exclusions have to be observed.

Some companies found that their catastrophe protection was just designed for losses ensuing from natural perils, but it was perils such as terror coverage that assumed huge accumulation potential, making it imperative that they became a part of the coverage.

In another case, after the WTC event, reinsurers totally excluded terror cover, while in Canada a mandatory provision exists to include fire coverage after a terror attack.

- Additional premium for each extension in coverage has to be charged. No coverage can be granted for free.

This includes a comprehensive assessment of natural catastrophe and other potential losses of low frequency and high severity events. In this respect, neither profit sharing nor cross-subsidisation can be allowed.

After experiencing a huge loss from WTC, one company representative mentioned that he has no problem with the loss involved but with the fact that the company has failed to collect any premium for the risk.[1]

❑ Improve premium payment provisions and cashflow.

In a soft market the experienced premium payment morale of corporates is quite low (meaning that they are slow to pay their insurance premium), while insurers are generous with payment provisions. For corporates with an international insurance programme the collection of the international premium is even more delayed. When cedents are involuntarily forced from a proportional sharing of accounts into an excess of loss programme, liquidity problems immediately surface due to the advance payments of excess of loss premiums.

❑ Control local facultative cessions.

Treaty reinsurers are sensible if facultative reinsurance for either peak risks or other risk reduction purposes are done on an excess of loss basis. The main reason for this is the "compression" of the treaty, which means less premium for an unchanged frequency of losses. If facultative reinsurers are also overcharging the coverage then the reinsurer and the cedent remain with an insufficient premium.

Coverage evaluation and threat assessments

Anyone who has looked into policy forms of insurance contracts of international corporates will have noticed how the same condensed wording is used across the board. However, corporates mostly have different product lines under one roof with different business processes. In many cases business has gone abroad as well. For all of this, the corporate intends to buy full protection for any kind of eventuality that may arise from their complex business environment. It is easy to understand who wins the bargain. Even if the insurance wording addresses the major risk components there are so many possibilities of getting a loss from scenarios that underwriters have never thought of before. It seems that underwriters are constantly on the learning curve.

A good example of this is the inclusion of contingency business interruption in a property insurance contract, ie, the coverage of any financial loss to the insured corporate because of an occurrence delaying the production or delivery of any products or components, as in the prominent case of Philips and Ericsson.

As mentioned above, business is complex and interdependencies in today's world are huge. With lengthy analysis, underwriters might be capable of understanding the first tier of interdependencies, but prior to the WTC event second tier interdependencies were also given to the insureds. The assessment of risks like this seems to be a "mission impossible".

Another way in which September 11 turned out to be a devastating blow for insurance companies was the error in assessing the possible maximum loss (PML) judgement. High-rise office buildings like the WTC were considered to have a low PML, as spreading fires could be contained within several floors. The two examples illustrate perfectly that the full extent of the coverage could either not be assessed or was wrongly assessed.

In all cases the result for the insurer is huge and the question of reinsurance arises. As long as the reinsurance is structured on a proportional basis and the reinsurer follows the fortune of the cedent, the bulk of the loss is definitely ceded to the reinsurer. But what happens if reinsurance has organised loss limits? Given the previous judgement of the risk, the majority of the loss is so extreme that it falls back into the net of the company. The message here is to evaluate primary coverage before reinsurance negotiations begin.

Certainly, not all scenarios can be assessed, but if the reinsurance contract's clauses and exclusions are not congruous with the original primary policy, coverage gaps may appear which then fully reveal themselves in the bottom line result of the ceding company. In this respect stress tests or threat scenarios might help to understand what risk means in the insurer's book and for which part of the risk reinsurance coverage is needed.

And if this theory was applied to the WTC event? The WTC attack caught the insurance industry unaware twofold, firstly by its sheer size and secondly because it added a new scenario to their catastrophe set. Using such methods as stress tests or threat scenarios could not have foreseen the scenario of a terrorist attack to the WTC but perhaps the potential of such a loss in such an area could have at least been projected. Such an assumption can be made based on the fact that many insurers had been at least aware of exposure accumulation within a specific urban area or within a building. A lack of geographical information probably prevented insurers from having a precise figure. Writers of large industrial firms or financial services find their clientele predominantly in those business areas such as in downtown Manhattan. Therefore recognising the potential and supplying some realistic scenarios like a fire conflagration or an airplane crash over Manhattan would have helped to identify the risk potential and act upon it. With the simulation of such a series of fictitious events, probabilities could be assigned to the loss. The newly created set of events might show losses far larger than the one experienced, and might help to understand the full extent of future risk.

Merits of a central reinsurance function

As stated above, in the author's opinion, there are a lot of pros for a more centralised approach for the industrial insurance segment.

The sheer size and complexity of those industrial risks requires very thorough risk analysis, which could possibly be better achieved in the Home Office rather than in the individual underwriting centres. Additionally it could be ensured that different coverage declarations and opinions exist within the same group. September 11 has shown how vulnerable the industry is when coverage is agreed upon different standards. It would also prevent uncontrolled accumulation as tranches of the insurance programme might be placed on various insurance markets and offered to companies belonging to one group.

Since most of the industrial insurance business needs heavy support from reinsurers, the reinsurance function has to go hand in hand with underwriting. Otherwise, as we have learned, not matching insurance and reinsurance wordings could be leaving gaps that are not reinsured.

In the author's opinion, by looking at the reinsurance function from the top down, a great deal of synergies can be achieved on an economic scale. Notably, scale effects can be applied if each reinsurance entity has to encompass all different skills to secure and maintain proper risk management as well.

Net retention

Within risk management the discipline of net retention assessment can be considered to be a primary function of a more centralised reinsurance unit. Here, all aspects of the hierarchical levels within a group – profit centre, company and consolidated group – can be viewed and benefits could be achieved that a single company otherwise would not have had.

The assessment of net retention in a company can have many different facets. Over a decade ago, companies were either applying the net retention or net premium in ratio to the shareholder capital or using rules of thumb. Increased pressure from shareholders and regulators forced companies to use more state of the art techniques to either demonstrate capital efficiency and maximal return on equity or prove capital adequacy for risks retained by the company.

Before looking into the modern techniques of retention setting, this chapter will briefly discuss how the risk process within a company should be designed. This is a poignant discussion because notably post September 11 the time for constantly ceding financial losses to the reinsurers is passed, at least for the immediate future. In this respect, a company's management (especially those who write industrial business with all its peculiarities) will have already started to evaluate its expectations of the uncertainties they would like to address: Is the business manageable? Can the risks be qualified and quantified? Can a leading position, a better portfolio mix and diversification benefits be achieved? Above all, can profit expectations be fulfilled?

The subsequent phase should then contain the assessment of the risk position. As stated earlier, computer modelling tools using theoretical risk aspects supported by powerful Monte Carlo loss simulations allow the calculation of all possible scenarios and portfolio compositions. Once the risk assessment has been completed, the company can then determine appropriate security measurements through a systematic risk process. As we know, reinsurance is one of the more well known and widely used risk measures for a company, but, as pointed out, in today's world not always the most tolerated one. The total evaluation must reach from risk avoidance over risk reduction to an acceptable level of risk that can either be shared by risk transfer or self retained. If finally an optimal level has been achieved then the safety balance is in place.

Stronger ties between underwriting, controlling and management could be beneficial to a company especially if the company is squeezed between shareholder expectation and tough reinsurers not willing to accept bad risks. Indeed, this concept is already practiced by some specialised risk takers, such as monoline catastrophe reinsurers in Bermuda or companies dealing in alternative risk transfer (ART). The methods they use are quite simple and old fashioned but seem to be very effective. Basically, they only provide insurance coverage on named perils, perils in which they have experience and which they can fully assess. In case of any grey areas that may appear in contract wordings, coverage will be addressed in a positive form but restricted by loss limits. The only sophisticated methodology seems to be in the portfolio management where individual risks are measured and correlated against the total portfolio.

By applying such a systematic risk process, the ultimate goal must be to keep as many of the profitable risks net in the company.

This is even truer for an international group where net retained risks can be further diversified and where there are more possibilities to retain risks. This can be established by using a group reinsurer. Principally such a reinsurer could take the next level above the group company's self-retention. (The company determines its own deductible and the group reinsurer takes the next layer over and above deductible. The size of the deductible and group layer will be determined by the volatility and risk return aspects.) An internationally diversified book of business will help the group reinsurer to ultimately apply a lower risk capital than would otherwise have been achieved if the company had kept the business.

The question might arise that if the group is one of the biggest insurers in the world, does it still need to buy reinsurance at all? The answer much depends on the underlying business, the international spread and risk appetite of the group. Given that the group reinsurer still does not have the diversification potential of a larger professional reinsurer, reinsurance is still necessary to achieve the necessary economical benefit.

A risk management and retention policy within a group could be delineated as in Table 1. The shaded areas highlight the addi-

Table 1 Group retention

Level	Size of risk			
	Small	**Medium**	**Large**	**Catastrophic**
1: Profit centre	Self retain	Internal stabilisation	Internal stabilisation	External stabilisation
2: Company	Self retain	Internal stabilisation	External stabilisation	External stabilisation
3: Consolidated group	Self retain	Self retain	External stabilisation	External stabilisation

tional amount of business a group reinsurer could potentially keep within the insurance group once a systematic risk process has been initiated.

It is important to recognise that the bundling of reinsurance functions on a group level without having a central underwriting responsibility under the same roof could cause problems. If underwriting and net bottom line responsibility is with the local insurance company, any group-level reinsurance decision will interfere with the net bottom line responsibility from local level. Of course, underwriting judgement shall be made on a gross basis but the financials of the company are measured on a net basis, as is the remuneration of the management.

REINSURANCE BUYING

Developing guidelines for outgoing reinsurance

September 11, 2001 demonstrated to some cedents that there were some weaknesses in how they bought reinsurance. In particular, it has been experienced that the exposure in urban areas or in a business building was not calculated or was done so insufficiently, insurance and reinsurance wordings were not matching and therefore left gaps not reinsured and reinsurance companies defaulted after the event.

It is not that managers for outgoing reinsurance were not doing a good job, but extreme events and the resulting loss thereof show how important it is for a ceding company to have proper and comprehensive guidelines in place. These should give the reinsurance manager a good indication as to whether the goals of reinsurance placement have been achieved but should also demonstrate correct business practices for the board of directors and officers (which can also be audited).

To secure the quality of design and placement for outgoing reinsurance the following tasks can be considered to be critical:

- Exposure evaluation should be made in three dimensions: per risk, per event and in the aggregate. The evaluation should contain exposure from historical experience and unknown exposure elements that result from probabilistic modelling. As mentioned before, the modelling should also contain new scenarios like the emerging risks of electro-magnetic fields, genetically modified organisms or cyber risks. Disaster scenarios across different lines of business as well as other financial exposure analysis of the company will also help to get a comprehensive exposure picture of the company.
- Based on the exposure analysis, retention setting and capacity need should be considered next. With appropriate tools in place the retention should be calculated under risk return aspects and measured against capital solvency requirements. Mismatching limits between what was granted in original policies and what the total reinsurance capacity provides falls immediately back to the net, and in case of a loss, causes extreme losses to the company. This needs to be done for each of the three dimensions.
- The forth dimension, time, is even more important as it often gets overlooked especially when reinsurance structure or terms and conditions are changed. When reinsurance structure is changed a seamless continuity has to be achieved from the old to the new so no gaps in reinsurance coverage will appear. However, this is not always the case. After the WTC event, terrorism was suddenly excluded from reinsurers' contracts with coverage on a losses-occurring basis leaving the cedent with all the exposure until the natural expiration date of the original policy. In such cases, aggregated exposure could easily get to an unacceptable level for the company. To avoid such unprotected run of exposure, correct time matching between original risks and the reinsurance capacity must be ensured.

It goes without saying that in addition to these tasks a concurrence of provisions and clauses has to be achieved to avoid any gaps. Further guidelines regarding the placing, administration and execution would also help the company to maintain a proper placing process.

Consideration of a group vs a local reinsurance structure

Starting with a top down approach the primary goals of each group can be assumed to be:

- better control/planning of exposures;
- to reduce reinsurance costs;
- to achieve a high level of transparency; and
- to guarantee cover to support strategic goals.

Concentrating on these issues allows us to qualify the aspects for a group vs a local reinsurance structure.

Again starting with a decentralised structure where some entities are positioned in the same business segment, the former discussion of the internal structure has shown that it can hardly be achieved.

What arguments remain from the ceding company's management to keep the local structure? Probably those that underline the local independence of the group companies, ie, reinsurance practices that prevail in their market. Some of these arguments deal with the fact that reinsurers are prepared to grant a lower retention level than they would otherwise do to a big group. Indeed, once a transformation of business is done to a group level, reinsurers immediately start to factor in the financial strength of the whole consolidated group. Other remarks refer to the fact that reinsurers are keen to have direct contact with the origins of the business and where business is not already aggregated on a group basis. It seems that reinsurers like to do their own diversification games on their portfolio and that they are prepared to accept the resulting reduced transparency. Local leverage is also often used, meaning that cedents can better convince reinsurers to participate in more volatile business for a share in their "bread and butter" business.

In comparison to the local and decentralised approach what would it mean if business were purchased on a group level? Definitely some form of internal organisation has to be achieved first. In brief, groups could decide to:

- pool the business;
- cede 100% of the reinsurance to a group vehicle on which reinsurance is then bought; or
- use the group reinsurance function for structuring and negotiating reinsurance for their individual companies.

What all these three options have in common is the use of the total group buying power when they negotiate the contracts with the reinsurer. In this respect, buying power can be interpreted as the quantum of ceded premium that attracts the reinsurer as well as a reduced chance to participate in the group's reinsurance programme. It should be kept in mind that reinsurers no longer have the choice to select clients within the same group.

This group leverage could result in substantial reinsurance reduction, possibly even beyond any diversification effects the grouping may have generated; if the underlying risk has a high potential for concentration and exposures can add up over the individual insurance companies, like for example in catastrophe business, the likelihood of getting peak exposures is high. Here, the risk of losing the pricing benefit might outweigh any additional margin to attract full market capacity.

Undoubtedly a centralised reinsurance programme offers a high level of transparency for the group. Therefore, after a loss the group can swiftly determine its net position. The highest value could be the strategic value of having a strategic capacity that can be used to write the risks.

To the best of the author's knowledge, reinsurers seem to accept this idea. They probably realise the chance of being either in or out and they like the transparent set-up as well. They also like the idea that after substantial group retention, reinsurance capacity is used for the peak risks rather than for the low-risk high-frequency money exchange programmes. However, reinsurers do seem to be sceptical about the reduction in cost derived after the group has taken all the diversification benefits into account.

Pricing assessment by economical benefit

In this chapter, the exploration of this subject will concentrate on the pure risk premium rather than actually considering the actual market premium. This prevents reinsurance premium from being lower than the expected loss under the reinsurance contract in phases of a soft market cycle. Under these circumstances, of course, with any cession a profit is automatically added and the conclusion must be to cede off all business and live with the risk-free premium. That said, reinsurance premium is still considered to be the number one measurement to judge the benefit of reinsurance to the cedent. Reinsurers themselves with their many tools and in their experience of advising cedents have also mainly focused on how much additional premium could be kept in the company and what amount could be saved. However, whether this expected additional profit benefits the cedent has in most cases not been tested, as any correlation to the additional amount of retained risk has not yet been conducted.

To overcome this deficit, sophisticated tools have been invented which are based on the loss experience of the underlying portfolio. Theoretical risk aspects were added to allow for measurement of the risk-based capital and the confidence intervals for losses. Connections to the overall financial situation of the company, including other lines of business and risk categories from financial risks to operational risks, generally have not been taken into account.

In today's world where companies are forced to demonstrate their business performance to their shareholders, a holistic view of the operation has to be applied. Therefore, only reinsurance simulation tools that interface with the company's overall risk analysis have the capability to provide the full set of answers. In this context any reinsurance structure can be evaluated and the remaining net risk can be correlated against other risk categories, eg, reserve risk, reinsurer's credit risk, financial risk, operational risk, etc, within the company. The compound risk evaluation allows the company to measure the impact of reinsurance against its total company result. This technique also allows the reinsurance manager to work as a profit centre as he/she can demonstrate to management how much return or economic value added (EVA) was generated by exploring alternative reinsurance structures. However, EVA alone might not always be sufficient for finding an "optimal" reinsurance. One proposal may maximise EVA in terms of a higher self-retention but at an unacceptable risk. Probably a better way is to look at the risk and return. The definition of an efficient frontier shows the boundary of possible results.

Buying reinsurance for the unknown

Obviously, it is difficult to assess the unknown and from the perspective of a reinsurance manager it is difficult to find support from management to spend money for coverage of a scenario that may or may not occur. However, the events of September 11, 2001 clearly demonstrate that reinsurance managers have the duty to look beyond historical experience and explore the previously inexperienced/unknown in order to prepare management and ultimately prevent the company from a major (re)insurance impact.

These days, statistics show that the WTC claim is by far the largest for the entire insurance industry; it is two to three times larger than the previous largest event, Hurricane Andrew in 1992. For some European companies the magnitude of loss is even five to six times larger than the 1999 European storms. However, to put the WTC claim in perspective, some modelling firms for natural catastrophes outlined that from a market perspective the WTC loss is consistent with previous industry natural catastrophe loss estimates with a probability of 1% (ie, a 100-year return period). And, one must not forget that companies are knowingly exposed to potential natural catastrophes larger than WTC, albeit with extremely low probability (eg, the US New Madrid Earthquake).

Not only do insurers face a higher severity, but there also seems to be an ever-increasing number of catastrophic scenarios in specific areas all over the world. Once meteorologists or seismologists have assessed the event and applied a return period to it, how many 100–500-year events happen within such a short observation time can only be speculative. Scientists of course always have a good reasoning but also do not fail to adjust the underlying model immediately with the result of a heavier tail in the distribution of losses and the extrapolation into new extreme scenarios. In this respect, companies who buy reinsurance up to the level of losses stemming from the reinsurer's latest reference loss seem to be constantly unprotected for the top scenario. Reinsurance within the scope of expected losses could almost be carried within the company or, to a larger extent, within the group reinsurer. Unexpected losses need protection as they could destroy a company's stability. If exposure is identified and not reinsured a high capital charge will be applied as well.

Simulating inexperienced catastrophic events is not only done to protect the solvency of the group, but also to reduce the volatility of results and assure sufficient risk premium in policy pricing. In addition, the insurance must expect pressure to increase from rating agencies, regulators and reinsurers to demonstrate its competence in this area. To do this, the primary goal is to implement basic catastrophe management practices such as proactive exposure steering, exposure planning, development of catastrophe budgets and post-exposure management such as risk transfer and financing.

With these practises in place reinsurance managers should be in good position to propose a strategy of what type of catastrophe losses could be faced from the underlying portfolio and what reinsurance could do to reduce risk and ultimately relieve the company's risk capital.

Determine the reinsurance partners' sustainability

In all business cases, be they in the private or commercial world, nothing is more unacceptable than paying money for no return in service. In the insurer–reinsurer relationship, the insurer normally pays a premium in advance to the reinsurer with the expectation that the reinsurer will take over any eventual losses that may arise within the scope of the contract. In some lines of business, such as liability or professional indemnity, the loss might appear many years after the contract was made. Also in risks that have a low frequency but a high severity, eg, exposure from natural catastrophes, insurers could pay premium over many years before the loss happens and the contract would give relief. Some brochures of professional reinsurers actually emphasise their appetite for business that is out-of-the-money.

But what happens if the reinsurer defaults at some point in time? Is there any chance for the insurer to recover some of the losses? If the reinsurer can pay all its balance sheet liabilities, what happens then to the future losses for which the reinsurer is obliged to pay according to the contract with the insurer? Experience tells that fortunately the cases of reinsurers defaulting are rare. However, they do exist, notably after big events where the correlation of risks causes an aggregated loss to the reinsurer. Whenever such a case happens, the result on the balance sheet of the ceding insurer is severe. Not only the one contract year defaults but all business historically ceded to the reinsurer is affected. Hereby insurers may not just look at the amount of ceded liabilities but the total exposure picture, which also includes future losses to the reinsurer. Recoveries, in general, are low and the run off process is cumbersome and time/cost consuming.

What can be done to avoid such a scenario? As we know, crystal balls in insurance/reinsurance are always desirable but unfortunately unavailable to tell about the future stability and claims paying ability of a reinsurer. However, there are considerations that could at least help to minimise credit risk. In this respect, a specialised security vetting could help the reinsurance manager to better understand the quality of the envisaged reinsurer and better control the respective credit risk. The task of the vetting team is to look into the reinsurer's soft and hard fact information available from internal companies and external sources that may provide quantitative and qualitative information on financial strength and claims paying ability and willingness. Lastly, market environment, legal framework and underwriting philosophy will also be taken into account to assure that placements are made at an acceptable risk level.

Another tool to minimise credit risk, especially by dealing with poorer reinsurers or unrated captives is to ask for a letter of credit on the amount of ceded exposures. This instrument, which in some countries is required for unauthorised reinsurance – the USA requires 100% of ceded technical reserves including incurred but not reported losses and Canada even requires 110% – replaces reinsurer's risk of default with the credibility of the issuing bank. Besides the technical aspects of rating reinsurers, companies may have their own philosophy on how to determine their panel of reinsurers. Some of them may lay their business in the good hands of only the best rated reinsurers in order to secure stability and collection of losses, others do not like to put all their eggs in one basket and are looking for a more diverse source of coverage, with the chance of a higher collectability after a major event occurs. There are pros and cons of each strategy and every company has to chose on which suits best.

In any case transactions should highlight the sophistication and security of the buyer in the eyes of its stakeholders. In the author's opinion this means also that the company has to determine the level to which they believe reinsurance creates economic benefit.

Typically a reinsurer creates an economic benefit to the cedent by assuming risks on the basis of less capital than the cedent's capital otherwise would be. However, since the key is diversification of risks, a strong concentration in peak risks puts the reinsurer into the same situation as the cedent. For these extreme scenarios the mechanics of reinsurance are obviously no longer working. Even if reinsurers offer an economically attractive premium, cedents should be aware that peak risks like severe natural catastrophes cause a strong loss correlation between reinsurers and increase the default probability dramatically. At the end of the day, the cedent's relief in premium risk may be more than offset by the huge credit risk to the reinsurer.

These examples show that ceding companies must therefore not only decide from where they start to buy reinsurance but also decide up to what level they buy it. In general, international insurance groups with a well diversified portfolio with less peak risk and backed by a strong financial balance sheet might choose a lower ceiling than other companies. Here solutions of a self-funding mechanism could be better applied.

CONCLUSION

So, is there a new rationale for buying reinsurance? The answer could be either yes or no. In the author's opinion, the events of September 11, 2001 and the subsequent huge loss for the whole industry has changed the industry's perspective of reinsurance quite dramatically. Of course, not all of the views on reinsurance have been newly invented but have been made more sophisticated to take into account the more complex business matters. Insurance buyers are becoming more demanding and insurance groups in their attempts to satisfy their demands have had to broaden their range of products and operate on a more international basis. In this process risk assessment becomes ever-increasingly dominant for the insurance company and for the reinsurance buyer in order to fully evaluate the sustainable amount of loss.

With this ever-increasing amount of risk and its inherent complexity it remains to be seen what role reinsurers will play in the future. The answer might be to have a more concerted approach to risk to secure the sustainability of both insurers and reinsurers after a mega event happens again – and it is sure to.

1 Personal communication with the author.

5

The Evolution of American International Group Inc.'s Reinsurance Strategy

Christian M. Milton

American International Group Inc. (AIG)

INTRODUCTION

American International Group Inc. (AIG) was formed towards the end of the 1960s as a result of a corporate reorganisation following the death of its founder, Cornelius V. Starr. During the 1970s, a series of mergers within AIG took place, culminating with the reverse takeover of American International Reinsurance Company, Inc. in the autumn of 1978.

This chapter will provide an insight in to the development of AIG's reinsurance strategy and the key role it has played in the group's success. It begins with an analysis of the issues that faced AIG in its early years and the subsequent reinsurance organisational structure that emerged, which has endured to this day. It will also examine the development of the central pool, the role of quota share and the critical importance of the aggregate stop-loss covers. Last but not least it examines the importance of result stability and the role that reinsurance plays for AIG in achieving this.

In 2002, the following questions may appear to be naive. However, AIG was still evolving in the mid to late 1970s, and these issues were in the forefront of the group's thoughts:

1. What was the minimum capital and rating needed to become a reinsurer of the group? In 1975 the thought was that US$5

million and an "A" rating was good. Fast forward to 2002, and such a reinsurer would not even hit the group's radar screen, as a minimum capitalisation of US$250 million is required and an S&P rating of AA is looked for.

2. Did the group want to buy reinsurance through a central reinsurance function or locally? How do you manage reinsurance relationships and ensure a consistency throughout the group?
3. Is the group's contract language the same for all reinsurance contracts and does the group need to bring order to the process?
4. How is the group measuring the purchase of reinsurance and where is that process reviewed?

REINSURANCE DEPARTMENT

Change within the group was necessary to even start to address some of the issues in the previous section. In 1976, AIG appointed its first reinsurance officer, an actuary, to bring order to the group and to provide tools with which to evaluate the reinsurance being purchased. In quick succession, departments or positions were created to do the following:

- ❑ monitor and approve reinsurance security;
- ❑ monitor and approve reinsurance contracts;
- ❑ measure major reinsurance relationships;
- ❑ determine the group's needs to better utilise the group's capital; and
- ❑ build reinsurance systems to account and report reinsurance.

By 1980, the reinsurance department of AIG had evolved and was making inroads into resolving many of the issues that had previously given rise to some of the concerns that had been voiced by senior management. Many of the issues had not been resolved, but at least they were being discussed.

For example, there was a recurring internal debate as to who should be responsible for purchasing reinsurance within the group. The country and profit centre managers were concerned that they were being asked to retain more risk on a specific allocation of capital than they could tolerate if they were to be held accountable for producing a compounded return on equity, year after year. On the other hand, the central management group recognised that the allocation of capital to subsidiaries and on a notional basis to profit centres increased the amount the group spent on reinsurance and did not efficiently utilise the group capital. What became evident by 1982 was that there was no real direction as to how the group purchased reinsurance. The infrastructure of the group had always relied on the fact that its reinsurance was profitable and a source of potential recapture as its capital grew. This worked well for AIG; as its capital grew, it became easier to expand the income to meet an increasing capital base by reducing reinsurance rather than returning to the producers and seeking more business. The changes that were occurring within the markets, however, required more thought as to not only how to buy reinsurance but also from whom the group should buy and on what terms.

The result of this introspection was the creation of various areas within the reinsurance department that had significant power to veto a placement or a contract term. This caused all manner of disputes both internally and with reinsurers and brokers who were accustomed to having a free rein in the purchase and decision making processes. Reinsurance security was the first major area to encounter resistance. The emerging markets of South America, for example, all wanted to participate in reinsurance, which would provide them significant amounts of hard currency that would be paid back over time. The problem was that they were not equipped to adjust to the turn in the market. Who would have thought back in the 1980s that the state reinsurance company of Argentina would eventually be liquidated? Sovereign risks cannot go out of business, right? Reinsurance security vetting became more focused and intense. Insurance is a unique product, inasmuch as a risk that is assumed and paid for in year one may generate losses that do not materialise until 40 years later (asbestosis being the classic example). If the risk was reinsured but the reinsurer becomes insolvent before all the liabilities are apparent then the risk returns to the insurer. As the list of insolvencies grew, special termination clauses dealing with cancellation of business on a going forward basis were introduced. Clauses were introduced to address this problem.

On the contract side of the business, issues of claims control, declaratory judgement expenses and bad faith were emerging in the context of whether they were the province of the ceding company or reinsurer. Precisely what was the reinsurer responsible for and how was it articulated in the reinsurance contract? These issues were beginning to be dealt with in a systematic and uniform way. As far as measuring reinsurance relationships, numerous questions presented themselves, including to what extent should a ceding company take into account the cashflows and investment income (remember that we are talking about 1980) and whether to consider facultative business in the mix. The reality is that the sum of all economic activity at all levels should be counted, as that naturally raises the issue of reinsurance systems and their ability to capture the relevant information. The systems were not efficient, but improvements were being made. Systemic analysis and support became more focused. In order to account for reinsurance to any reinsurance contract or reinsurer, a code number was assigned to accumulate all types of data (cessions, claims, commissions, fees, premium, reserves and balances). The person who controlled the codes had all the power!

INTERNAL REINSURANCE POOL

In 1981, AIG introduced the compulsory cessions account (CCA). The CCA became the central vehicle to better manage reinsurance and gather essential information. The CCA required that each operating unit cede 5% of every treaty and facultative cession up to US$1 million per risk. By taking a sliver of each and every risk, the group quickly built a central repository of information that was used to make informed decisions. Previously the group relied on static information that was invariably stale by the time it reached central management. In addition, the group could systemically account to the CCA, saving the expense of booking results and accounts from sources around the world.

CATASTROPHE PROTECTIONS

Having now commenced the process of centralisation, the next question was how the group wanted to revamp its protections and capacity. The first area that drew attention was the purchase of catastrophe protections. The foreign operations had existed under the auspices of what is generally known as the "association", shorthand for American International Underwriters Overseas

Association (AIUOA). AIUOA had always purchased global catastrophe covers covering all classes and territories except the United States; any risk that had United States exposure had to be reinsured to a domestic carrier. Until 1982, the domestic companies had not given any credence to buying for the group. In 1982, as a result of the information collected in connection with the CCA, senior management realised that a global catastrophe cover for the domestic companies made sense. The question, however, was whether this purchase should be part of the foreign covers or kept separate. Surprisingly, the answer was both.

The key was exposures. The foreign operations had the Caribbean, with its yearly exposure to hurricane, as did the US. While it would have been easier to put the Caribbean with the United States, from a reinsurance pricing perspective that did not make sense; the foreign operations had built up a large credit with reinsurers, and changing the exposure base would not necessarily have resulted in the pricing reductions that one would think should follow.

Domestic catastrophe reinsurance pricing is significantly different and more expensive than international catastrophe pricing. In part, this is due to the greater concentration of risks on the east and west coasts of the US, which are exposed to either wind or earthquake damage. The other factor that had to be considered was the frequency and potential intensity to both of these perils when coupled with the values at risk. So what was the solution?

The solution was to buy three catastrophe protections:

1. A Foreign General catastrophe cover that would respond to the first US$100 million of loss.
2. A Domestic General catastrophe cover that would respond to the first US$100 million of loss.
3. A Super Global that would respond to losses over and above (1) and (2) up to a further US$100 million.

CAPITAL NEEDS

Prior to 1978, AIG had operated principally as a managing general agency under the management of American International Underwriters, which was headquartered in Bermuda. As 1978 approached, the group transformed itself into a risk bearer.

Moreover, the group retained a significant portion of the risks it wrote. However, AIG's capital was in short supply. There was a "mismatch" of capital in the sense that the group's overseas companies had capital but the domestic companies had the business opportunities, principally as a result of its developing casualty portfolio during the hardening market at this time.

The solution to this mismatch came in the form of the reserve takeover, which placed control of the overseas capital within the grasp of the domestic companies, and reinsurance. Reinsurance was seen as a way to build capacity as well as to control the pricing, terms and conditions of large risks. Around this time, numerous reinsurers were forming in Bermuda, South America and other emerging countries. These new markets had different thought processes and were eroding the monopoly of the European and London reinsurance markets. (As time has shown, no vacuum exists for long before being filled!) Companies in these countries were searching for opportunities to increase their revenue, and reinsurance captured their imagination. The capital base of these new entrants to the global reinsurance market was small, and their operations were locally concentrated, unsophisticated and in need of diversification, especially when compared to European reinsurers such as Munich Re or Swiss Re. Nevertheless, interest rates were rising, and the expected investment income from the cashflows that would be generated by writing reinsurance were thought to be more than sufficient to realise a modest return for the risk being run.

Captives (wholly owned subsidiaries formed to self insure the retained liabilities of the parent company) also provided a source of reinsurance. It seemed that a new captive was being formed every month, and they needed non-parental reinsurance income to justify their tax position and demonstrate that they were true reinsurance companies writing a diversified portfolio of risks. While their own parental business formed an economic base, they were searching for more business. The creation in 1983 of the Bermuda subsidiary Overseas Partners Ltd by United Parcel Services is a good example.

CASUALTY VS PROPERTY BOOKS OF BUSINESS

During this time, AIG believed that large commercial accounts, which were the principal client base AIG wished to service, had increased insurance and – due to their captives – reinsurance needs, and that those needs could be serviced in a way that also served AIG's needs. The group became heavily involved in US casualty business, providing primary insurance, excess casualty insurance and specialty casualty products, such as directors and officers, pension trust and error and omission insurance. Thus, unlike many of its overseas peers, the group's portfolio tilted much more toward casualty than property business.

To put this in context, it should be recognised that prior to this time, Europe, unlike the US, was relatively free of significant catastrophe losses, the first real wake up call for Europe coming with the storms in 1987. That is not to say that insurers and reinsurers ignored the fact that there were significant catastrophe exposures around the world, but since there had not been any major losses, the degree of weight given to the likelihood of a catastrophic loss in the underwriting process in any particular portfolio was minimised. In contrast, underwriters writing US property business were still focusing on the horrific losses of the 1960s.[1] However, even here, the focus was fading. Time has a way of eroding the true impact of losses, particularly as new underwriting talent is introduced into the marketplace; experiencing the loss and being told about the loss have two very different affects on the thought process!

The result of this development was less reliance on excess of loss reinsurance for the property portfolio and more focus on proportional covers, principally with a view to minimising the potential catastrophic risks of wind and earthquake. The lead property underwriter in the group, American Home Assurance Company, wrote "difference in conditions" and subsequently "all risk" business, embracing a wide range of perils. This business needed significant amounts of catastrophe protection, which American Home could ill-afford. Quota share and surplus treaties were the answer to this need as they followed the original conditions and provided valuable catastrophe cover.

In the meantime, the landscape was fluid on the casualty side of the business. For example, the legal environment was changing. New laws were being passed by the legislatures and the courts were giving new interpretations to existing laws, most of which favoured insureds. For example, the California courts, in particular, assumed a generally pro-policyholder view of the law, which increased the frequency and severity of insurers' losses. In addition, large domestic commercial companies became risk adverse, which caused them to buy increased limits of insurance coverage. Placements of excess liability coverage with US$300 million limits were not unknown. As a result, the leverage for insurers was significant. However, casualty capacity in both the insurance and reinsurance markets was plentiful, and it did not take too long for the adequate pricing of the late 1970s to erode quickly. Supply and demand rules took hold! Finally, the growing casualty business needed excess of loss reinsurance, which was rated on loss frequency as opposed to exposure. It was quite easy to structure a programme up to US$25 million.

FACULTATIVE REINSURANCE

With reinsurance needs increasing, facultative reinsurance was also required. However, this frequently caused a problem relating to the statutory penalty that insurers incur for using non-admitted reinsurance. Moreover, by definition, facultative reinsurance is specific to each transaction, and requires significant human intervention at nearly every stage of the process (eg, placing, binding, endorsements, accounting, claims), creating great expense. The cost of maintaining large volumes of facultative reinsurance is not generally appreciated.

The reinsurance strategies of today were taking shape during the early 1980s. AIG needed mechanisms to consolidate its buying power, and harnessing facultative buying was, in part, the key. The other key component was the establishment of internal reinsurance pools to share premium and losses. What was not fully appreciated at the time, however, was that reinsurance pools simply increased the total available capacity within the marketplace. Other facultative capacities did not vanish when these pools were created; the pools simply diluted the market until the market figured out that they were sitting further up the food chain still providing limits, albeit at rock bottom prices.

AGGREGATE EXCESS OF LOSS COVER

In the early 1980s, AIG anticipated the collapse of the market and took steps to adapt to the changing environment. AIG's philosophy up to that time had been shaped by the growth of relatively inexpensive reinsurance, but with the impending collapse of the market, security concerns came to the fore. In addition, the view emerged that if the group were to survive the impending storm, with its substantial decrease in reinsurance capacity, a change in focus was needed. The group decided on its strategy: the purchase of aggregate excess of loss reinsurance, protection against the accumulation of losses in a year rather than individual events.

Implementation of this strategy started in late 1982 and culminated in 1984 with the purchase of a three-year aggregate excess of loss cover. The thinking behind the cover was relatively straightforward: the group should be able to project the ultimate values of any casualty reinsurance portfolio and its cashflows. If that holds true, the group can predict at what level a reinsurer will break even and the capital needed to support the transaction. The reinsurance buyer should be able to determine the cost of renting a reinsurer's capital, which should entail no more than a modest fee if it can be demonstrated that the portfolio lacks any real adverse loss experience.

In addition, when a reinsurer writes a casualty book of business, he presumably takes into account some element of investment income to justify his result. If that holds true, the reinsurance buyer should be making the same calculation when purchasing reinsurance, so as to measure the reinsurer's expected return.

Finally, net retained premium growth was not an issue for AIG as the group was already generating good top line (before reinsurance) growth, even after the stop-loss protections. For the casualty business, the lesson was quickly learned that the need for individual excess of loss protections decreased when one considered the value of aggregate excess of loss protection. Such protection can be more transparently priced using net present value techniques with a good degree of risk added for risk transfer.

An individual excess of loss reinsurance requires each loss to be established, documented and negotiated with the reinsurer. An aggregate excess of loss contract is driven simply by the financial outcome of the year. Thus, the constant arguments between insurers and reinsurers over the definition of a loss event and delays in recovering reinsurance from reinsurers vanish with aggregate excess of loss protection. In addition, claims recovery allocation disputes, which haunt many casualty writers even today, became less contentious with aggregate excess of loss covers.

Different accounting regimes have a role in determining the method that is used in making these calculations. For example, companies operating within the US account for their operations to the regulatory authorities on a statutory basis, ie, the regulator needs to be able to answer the hypothetical question, "if this company were to cease trading today and therefore receive no more premium, would it have sufficient assets to meet its liabilities?". From the shareholders' perspective, shareholders see results on a Generally Accepted Accounting Principle (GAAP) basis, ie, as if the company were an ongoing business with revenues and costs earned and incurred over the expected life of the product. These two types of accounting, plus the tax code, which is not harmonised with either set of rules, oftentimes influence reinsurance buying decisions.

At the end of the day, the driver is the need to use capital efficiently for shareholders' benefit. Long-term shareholder value can only be delivered if managers are able to deliver consistent compounded rates of return year after year. The market and shareholders prize this above all other qualities. The goal of the reinsurance buyer therefore has to be to maximise the efficient use of capital while eliminating the inherent volatility of the insurance portfolio.

MARKET COLLAPSE

By 1984, the landscape was changing due to a number of different factors:

1. Interest rates were declining as underlying inflation abated.
2. Loss frequency was rapidly increasing, eroding the cashflows and consequently the investment income that was expected to cover the shortfall.
3. Asbestos and environmental losses were growing at an alarming pace, overwhelming results for many insurers and reinsurers at home and abroad.
4. Emerging reinsurance markets were becoming aware of the risks that they had assumed, as were captive reinsurance markets.

Nevertheless, nobody really suspected that the market was about to collapse. 1984 still exhibited the appearance of a soft market, getting a little harder but by hardly noticeable degrees. By 1985, however, the cat was out of the bag and insurance and reinsurance markets were starting to panic. The US reinsurance market was in disarray. Reinsurers woke up to the seriousness of the losses that they were facing. Insolvency followed insolvency, while solvent reinsurers either withdrew their capacity, vowing never to return, or imposed terms and conditions that pushed up insurers' retention and expected loss levels. Techniques such as loss ratio caps, loss ratio corridors, reduced commissions and guaranteed profits were among the tools that reinsurers employed in re-underwriting their portfolios to replenish their weakened profit and loss accounts as well as their balance sheets.

Insurers (who were cash starved, as reinsurance recoverables were not being collected fast enough to replenish the cash being paid out for claims), began liquidating their investments, thereby reducing their investment income. Reinsurers, aghast at the results, started to audit actively and rigorously books of business, searching for ways to deny liability. The problem of collecting reinsurance recoverables in a timely manner was aggravated as reinsurers insisted on conducting an audit before payment, a problem further compounded by the fact that there were insufficient auditing firms with the ability to perform this task.

Rates, terms and conditions for every class of business moved by leaps and bounds and, by the close of 1985, net retained business had grown 100% over the prior year. By year-end 1986, the retained income had been driven up by 100% again. So in the space of two years, AIG had quadrupled in size. In part, the ability to stabilise reinsurance capacity at the group level had assisted the group's ability to deliver capacity and achieve higher than expected results from the operating units. Responding to a changing market is somewhat akin to fighting a war; the ability to provide battle-worn troops with new ammunition to go back to the front and to incite them to give their all is still an important facet of business life that few companies understand.

The results of these efforts were not without some turmoil within the group companies. Average retentions for the group had always been low, with the surplus lines operations retaining in some instances less than 5% of the total income base. To suddenly change direction and retain risk meant that the subsidy previously provided by commission income was no longer available, which placed underwriting mangers at risk. To temper the increased risk retentions and loss volatility at the profit centre level, the internal pool was utilised to take advantage of the full balance sheet of the group. This internal pool was an integral part of the group's reinsurance strategy. The pool, as well as the nets of the operating units, was then protected by the group aggregate stop-loss contracts.

CONCLUSION – WELL POSITIONED FOR THE FUTURE

By 1985, the group's reinsurance strategy, while not entirely integrated, was becoming well established. Reinsurance was perceived as an essential tool to enhance the returns on capital. Moreover, reinsurance could be used to create internal growth when necessary rather than relying exclusively on increased production (and therefore increased exposure) at less than satisfactory pricing.

With the turn of the reinsurance markets in 1986, AIG was well positioned to take advantage of market pricing. Reinsurance capacity had been stabilised through the use of:

1. aggregate excess of loss covers;
2. the compulsory cessions account; and
3. catastrophe purchasing, which was centralised to minimise the loss of earnings and to contain overall reinsurance costs.

In fact, it could be said that the ability to maintain and deliver reinsurance capacity to the operating units at this time was a key ingredient in the growth of AIG. It did not matter whether the capacity was derived from external or internal sources; the importance of having capacity that was unencumbered by dictates of reinsurers was the critical point.

1 A combination of underpricing and an increase in claims frequency and severity as courts awarded much higher settlements, coupled with major loses from areas such as flooding and hurricanes.

Part II

Risk assessment

6

Can Reinsurance Credit Risk be Priced?

Chris Klein

Benfield Group Ltd

The risk inherent in buying reinsurance is perhaps the most serious potential credit risk faced by ceding insurers and reinsurers, because a defaulting reinsurer may have an impact upon the cedent's ability to meet valid claims when they fall due. A spate of reinsurance failures since the mid-1990s, most notably in Australia, highlighted this credit risk. The terrorist attacks on the USA on September 11, 2001 also threw into very sharp focus the importance of reinsurers' ability to pay claims and to pay them in a timely manner. A notable feature of many of the statements from insurers and reinsurers following the attacks was the disclosure of their estimated gross and net losses coupled with a broad analysis of the credit quality of reinsurance receivables due. This usually took the form of showing reinsurance receivables by commercial agency rating grade. Many insurers and reinsurers emphasised the fact that the majority of their receivables were – and, in many cases, remain – due from reinsurers with ratings of A or higher. The intent was clearly to reassure nervous policyholders that their claims would be paid and shareholders that their investments were safe.

All of this comes at time when exposure to reinsurance credit risk has been increasing. An analysis of the regulatory returns of almost 2,700 US non-life insurers revealed a steady increase in insurance and reinsurance receivables and recoverables as a proportion of the total assets of insurers and reinsurers. Between 1997 and 2001 reinsurance receivables increased from 7.4% to 9.6% of aggregate total assets.[1] The gearing also increased, but at a faster rate. Reinsurance receivables were equivalent to 20.6% of consolidated surplus at December 31, 1997. By December 31, 2001, this ratio had increased to 32.1%. The sharp decrease in equity values in the first nine months of 2002 will have further increased these ratios. This is a serious issue as, in addition to the risk of direct loss arising from a default, liquidity and investment income potential are impaired; the latter is a not insignificant matter at a time of low interest rates and falling stock markets. Furthermore, unlike bonds or equities, when the credit risk of reinsurers increases, it is not possible to trade the receivables for cash. Excessive exposure to reinsurers was a material factor in the collapse of the US-based Reliance Group Holdings in September 2000. Its ratio of reinsurance receivables to consolidated surplus exceeded 600% at a time when no liquid assets were held in the holding company and several tranches of sub-investment grade debt were imminently due for repayment.

INTRODUCTION

Despite the increasing credit risk faced by cedents, the seemingly arcane method of reinsurance pricing does not include an explicit component that reflects the relative credit risk presented by reinsurers to their reinsured counterparties. Conversely, those reinsurers that offer stronger balance sheets do not necessarily receive an explicitly enhanced premium necessary to provide an acceptable return to shareholders. This absence of a credit risk component in reinsurance pricing appears to be unique in the capital markets and this chapter argues the case for a more sophisticated approach to reinsurance pricing that includes credit risk spread.

REGULATORY INTEREST

Reinsurance credit risk also attracted increasing attention from regulators and commercial rating agencies. Risk-based capital models are including the assessment of reinsurance credit risk and imposing consequential capital loadings, thus effectively increasing the cost of capital, especially for highly-geared cedents. During 2002, the UK's Financial Services Authority (FSA), which is, among other things, responsible for the regulation of insurance, issued new draft prudential regulations.[2] These include a requirement for insurance companies to take "reasonable" steps to ensure that credit risk management systems are adequate for their intended purpose. Reinsurance counterparty credit risk is addressed specifically. Each insurer must formulate a policy that includes an "adequate description" of how it selects reinsurers, how it assesses and monitors reinsurers' creditworthiness, how it identifies actual and contingent exposure and whether and how it uses loss mitigation techniques such as premiums withheld, trust funds and letters of credit. Contingent exposure should identify amounts that might become due from reinsurers if the reinsured event occurs.

In Australia, regulation has also been tightened following the implosion of the domestic reinsurance market between 1999 and 2000 and the collapse of the HIH insurance group in 2001, at the time Australia's second largest insurance group. The Australian Prudential Regulatory Authority (APRA) now requires non-life insurers to develop a high-level reinsurance management strategy. Each insurance company's reinsurance strategy is required to address counterparty diversification and creditworthiness, include controls on the use of financial reinsurance and set out clear processes for reinsurance decision-making. APRA also requires internal controls to ensure that so-called financial reinsurance is used for bona fide purposes only.[3] The revised APRA regulations also include an assessment of reinsurance receivable credit risk in the model used for calculating minimum capital requirements.

PRICING CREDIT RISK

As mentioned previously, the FSA's draft prudential regulations require insurers to identify and measure actual and contingent reinsurance credit risk exposure. The measurement of actual and contingent credit risk presents different problems, which we shall consider later. However, in both cases some means of quantifying the credit risk is required.

The traditional tool for assessing the creditworthiness of counterparties is the commercial agency rating. The specialised rating process has been in existence for over 75 years and is dominated by the principal credit rating agencies: Standard & Poor's (S&P), Moody's Investors Services and Fitch. Analyses of the very large universe of corporate, government and sub-sovereign issues have enabled the rating agencies to produce and publish bond default rates and their correlated ratings. A M Best & Co, a US-based monoline insurance rating agency, recently entered the bond rating market, though its exposure and market share to date are modest.

There exists many types of financial obligation that are assessed for credit worthiness by the rating agencies. These include:

- medium and long-term notes;
- surplus notes;
- subordinated debt;
- commercial paper;
- convertible bonds;
- preferred stock;
- debentures; and
- collaterised debt obligations and other asset-backed securities.

Definition of a default

In the capital markets, a default, or credit event as it may also be described, is recorded on the first occurrence of payment default on any financial obligation, rated or un-rated, other than an obligation subject to a bona fide commercial dispute. The principal default occurrences are:

- The failure of the issuer to pay its coupon interest obligation by the due date. Note that the rating agencies make an exception when the payment is missed, but is made within the agreed grace period.
- The payment of only part of the coupon interest that is due.
- The failure to redeem the obligation on the due maturity date.
- The failure to redeem the full principal value of the obligation on the due maturity date.

Other defaults include filing for bankruptcy, insolvency and compulsory restructuring. An example of a distressed restructuring occurred in Argentina in December 2001 when foreign denominated investments held by various domestic financial institutions and investors were compulsorily appropriated and exchanged for domestic government bonds.

Figure 1 Standard & Poor's average cumulative default rates

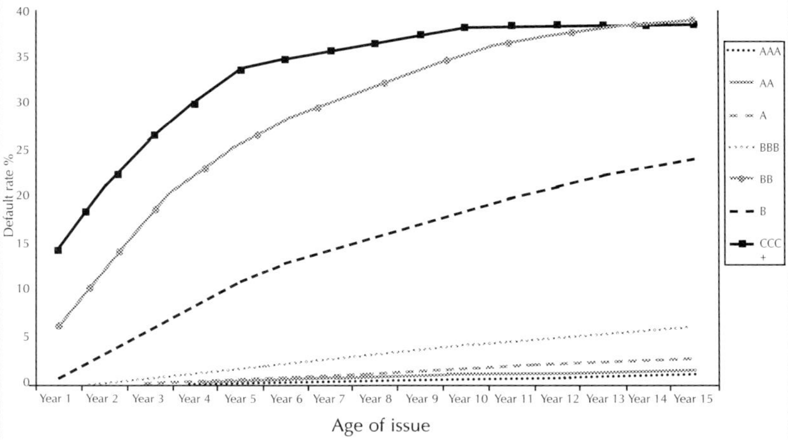

Rating grades

Rating grades fall into two principal categories. Issues assigned an S&P BBB rating (or equivalent) and above are classified as "investment-grade" ratings. Issues rated by S&P at BB+ (or equivalent) or lower are classed as "speculative-grade" ratings and are better known as "junk bonds" or, more recently and less pejoratively, as "high-yield issues".

The ratings of the different types of obligations emanating from a single issuer will reflect the seniority of the obligation through differential grading and notching within grades. Typically, preferred stock and subordinated debt ratings will be rated one notch lower than investment-grade senior unsecured debt ratings. For speculative-grade ratings, the rating is usually two notches lower, though the spread may increase as the senior debt rating is lowered. Thus, an AA issuer's senior debt rating may rank just one notch above the AA subordinated rating, whereas the BB+ issuer would probably carry a BB preferred stock rating.

Default rates

Average static cumulative default rates over a 15-year period as published by S&P are shown in Figure 1. A key feature to note is the large step from BBB to BB where the threshold from investment- to speculative-grade rating is crossed.

Recovery rates

So far we have looked at the default probability risk component of credit risk. However, the credit risk implicit in holding bonds has two components. In addition to the probability of default, there is also the risk associated with any expected recovery after the default event. Recoveries are often estimated on the basis of the prices that the defaulted securities fetch at some point after default. Although attractive in concept, this approach is problematic as in practice defaulted securities are either not traded or only traded in small volumes. Pricing data is therefore limited. Nevertheless, S&P has analysed a significant sample of defaulted securities and concluded that:

- The average recovery shortly after default was 40 cents per dollar.
- Recoveries are greater on average, the higher the seniority and rating of the issues affected.

PRICING ACTUAL REINSURER CREDIT RISK

"Actual" reinsurer credit risk exposure for the purposes of this paper may be defined as that which arises from reinsurance receivables that have been crystallised and appear as a real asset with a value on a cedent's balance sheet. Such assets would include the un-recovered reinsurers' shares of paid claims and associated expenses and the reinsurers' shares of specific reported claims, IBNR (incurred but not reported) claims provisions, unearned premiums and contingent commissions.

Some insurers and reinsurers, rating agencies and regulators use bond default rates as a proxy for quantifying reinsurance recoverable risk. Indeed, the capital adequacy ratio (CAR) that is calculated by S&P as part of its insurer rating process employs default rates for reinsurance receivable capital charges that are derived from the rating agencies' general bond default rates. The S&P charges are shown in Figure 2 and represent the nominal capital provision required to absorb potential losses arising from defaulted reinsurance receivables.[4] By applying the S&P CAR rates, or similar rates employed by other agencies, it is possible to compute a theoretical default risk for reinsurance receivables. Thus, a reinsurance receivable with a BBB rating grade has a 4.7% risk of

Figure 2 Standard & Poor's capital adequacy model charges for reinsurance recoverables

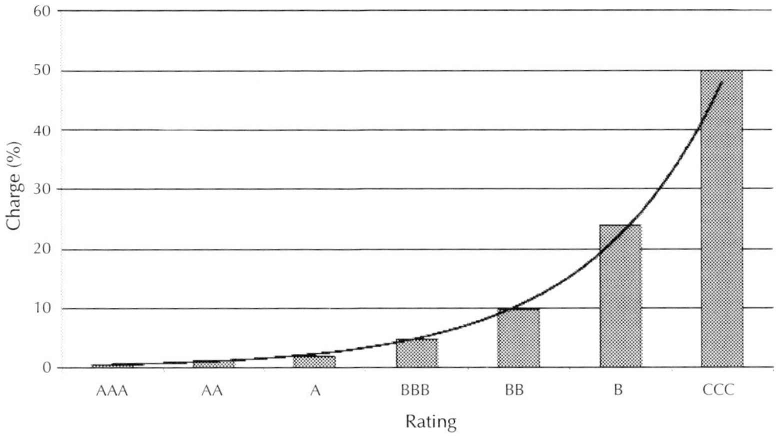

default over a 10–15 year period. This methodology is most easily illustrated with two case studies.

Case study 1 – Lloyds of London reinsurance receivable credit risk September 11, 2001 loss

At the time of writing, Lloyds had announced the largest estimated gross and net losses of any insurer or reinsurer arising from the terrorist attacks on the US on September 11, 2001. The current gross and net loss estimates are £7.5 billion and £1.9 billion respectively.[5] Reinsurance recoverables at £5.6 billion represent 75% of the gross loss estimate, an exceptionally high level of gearing. Aware of the sensitivity of this gearing issue and its associated credit risk, Lloyds disclosed the composition of the receivables by rating grade. Lloyds reported that approximately 35% of reinsurance receivables were due from Munich Reinsurance Co, Swiss Reinsurance Co,[6] Employers Reinsurance Corp,[7] Berkshire Hathaway, all of which carried S&P AAA ratings at that time, and Hannover Reuckversicherung AG, which carries a S&P rating of AA.

Using the information disclosed by Lloyds about its reinsurance receivables and applying the S&P CAR default rates it is possible

Table 1 Analysis of Lloyds of London's reinsurance receivables

S&P rating	% of total	Receivables (£ million)	S&P default rate (%)	Provision (£ million)
AAA	35	1,960	0.5	9.8
AA	38	2,128	1.2	25.5
A	23	1,288	1.9	24.5
BBB	3	168	4.7	7.9
Other	1	56	25	14
Total	100	5,600		81.7

to calculate a theoretical amount at risk. The calculations indicate that the theoretical weighted credit risk exposure is £81.7 million. The weighted average default rate is 1.5% indicating a weighted average rating in the range of A+ to AA on the S&P scale. The calculations are shown in Table 1. It should be emphasised that this default calculation was based on the S&P criteria and took no account of any systemic spiral risk of reinsurer default that might arise due to the magnitude of the September 11 losses.

Case study 2 – A major North American financial services group

For the second case study the report and accounts of a major financial services group with substantial insurance and international reinsurance operations were reviewed. Analysis of the company's report and accounts from December 31, 1996 to December 31, 2001 revealed that the amount of unsecured reinsurance receivables as a proportion of total assets and in relation to the group's shareholders' funds (SHF) had increased very rapidly. The ratio of reinsurance receivables to SHF had increased from 138% in 1996 to 360% by December 31, 2001 as is shown in Figure 3.

Clearly, the reinsurance credit risk had increased to a potentially dangerous level, with implications for solvency and liquidity. The composition of the group's unsecured reinsurance receivables as at 31 December 31, 2000 is shown in Table 2. From these data a weighted average default risk of 4.8% or BBB was calculated. The implications of writing-off 4.8% of these receivables would have been an 11% decrease in the amount of consolidated SHF and a decrease in the solvency margin ratio from 74% to 65.8%.[8]

Figure 3 Reinsurance receivable gearing of a financial services group

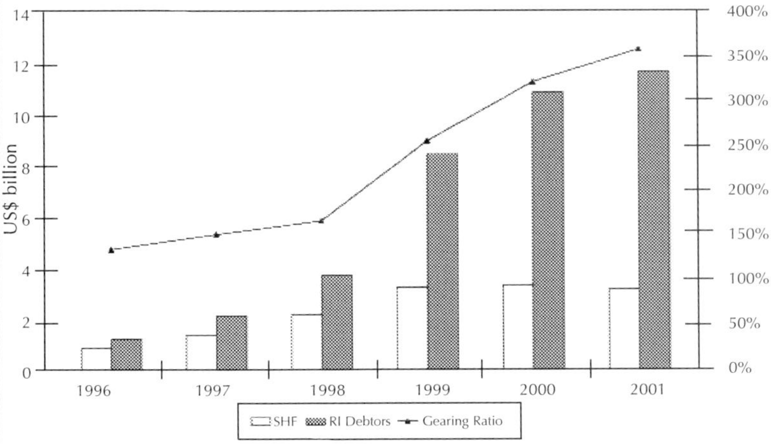

METHODOLOGICAL PROBLEMS

The method used to compute the theoretical default risk of the reinsurance receivable portfolios in the two case studies detailed in the previous section is problematic for a number of reasons. The rating of insurers and reinsurers by the commercial rating agencies differs from that used for all other entities. Uniquely, insurers and reinsurers are assigned an entity rating, usually called an "insurer

Table 2 Analysis of the reinsurance receivables of a major financial services group

S&P rating	Amount	S&P default rate (%)	Provision (US$ million)
AAA	3,036	0.5	15
AA	1,169	1.2	14
A	1,768	1.9	34
BBB	290	4.7	14
BB	9	9.6	1
CCC	43	49.7	21
Unrated	416	25.0	104
Total	6,730		203

financial strength rating" (IFSR) or "claims-paying ability" (CPA) rating. However, the concept is more nebulous than that which applies to the credit rating of other corporations and specific issues. In essence, the IFSR/CPA ratings aim to provide a prospective evaluation of an insurer's financial security to its policyholders. Normally, the IFSR/CPA is ranked one notch above the senior long-term unsecured debt rating of the issuer in recognition of the seniority of policyholder obligations. However, there are problems in extrapolating a default rate for policyholder obligations from, say, the senior debt rating, not least the problem that many insurers and reinsurers are not issuers.

At the heart of the problem is the definition and identification of a default occurrence on policyholder obligations. A defaulting issue can be easily identified because there are precisely defined obligations with respect to timing and quantum. Furthermore, the majority of rated bonds and other types of rated obligations are publicly traded, which aids transparency.

In attempting to define a default on a policyholder's obligation we are faced with several problems. Firstly, when is claim default deemed to have occurred? The issue of timing is difficult because solvent, going-concerns may legitimately take several years to dispute the liability and/or quantum value of claims. This gives rise to the problem of applying differentiated default rates to take account of the time factors. The S&P CAR and the APRA (Australian Prudential Regulatory Authority) minimum capital requirement models apply a flat rate to each grade irrespective of the likely duration of the settlement process.

Secondly, cessation of underwriting is not a satisfactory definition as it may not be synonymous with insolvency or necessarily result in default. Many firms cease underwriting all or some classes of risks voluntarily for business reasons. A notable example was the decision of the Bermuda-based reinsurance group, Overseas Partners Ltd, to stop underwriting new reinsurance business in February 2002 because its shareholders, who were the 98,000 employees of the United Parcels Service of America Inc., wanted to liquidate their investments. Indeed, not even the insolvency of an insurer or reinsurer would suffice as a universal and technically correct definition since the policyholders' obligations may be adequately covered by provisions that are subject to regulatory control and protection that prevents their use for other purposes, thus leaving only non-insurance obligations in default. That said, IBNR claims provisions are often early default casualties when a reinsurer is forced to cease underwriting and go into run-off whilst commutations offering partial settlements tend to become more aggressive and less favourable to the creditor as time passes.

Thirdly, how does the credit risk assessor, ie, the rating agency, know when a reinsurance default occurs? The claims settlement process is usually a private matter that is handled either directly between the counterparties or through an intermediary.

Perhaps for the reasons explained above, is not surprising that no detailed study into the quantification of reinsurance default and recovery rates exists. S&P specifically exclude from its default studies and tables insurers and reinsurers that do not have debt ratings.[9] It is also important to note that the published default rates for each rating grade are derived from a broad range of industries, which do not face the same risks as reinsurers. An analysis by S&P of rating performance reviewed 9,769 issuers grouped into 12 sectors.[10] Of these, insurance and real estate, which were grouped together for the study, accounted for only 9.8% of the total number of issuers surveyed. In particular, the various sectors do not face the same correlation of economic cycles, catastrophic events and insurance pricing cycles. Consequently, it is quite possible that there may be no correlation between published default rates and the true default experience of reinsurance receivables.

PRICING CONTINGENT REINSURER CREDIT RISK

So far we have looked at the issue of pricing the credit risk of actual receivables and the establishment of appropriate provisions. Unfortunately, the higher cost of these provisions and the concomitantly higher regulatory and rating agency capital loadings were almost certainly not reflected in the original premium, ie, a cedent may not have received what might be considered to be an appropriate discount on the premium paid to higher risk reinsurers. This is because the reinsurer sets the price to be paid. When a ceding insurer or reinsurer buys reinsurance, it is effectively buying a "put" option that allows it to put a loss into the reinsurance market with a view to making a recovery. The assuming reinsurer underwriting the "put" option analyses the risk, sets the conditions under which the option may be exercised and charges a price for the option. Conversely, the lower-risk reinsurer may not have received what it considered to be a fair enhancement to its premium in consideration of the lower credit risk and lower capital loadings.

So is it possible to factor credit risk into the pricing of a reinsurance purchase? Contingent reinsurer credit risk is the risk that the reinsurer may be unable to fulfil its contracted obligation when a claim is presented. Attempting to price this contingent risk is more problematic for several reasons. The first problem to address is the determination of the contingent exposure. Here, the proposed UK prudential regulations might provide some guidance. The regulations require insurance companies to monitor their contingent reinsurance counterparty risk exposure as well as that arising from actual receivables. The FSA effectively defines contingent exposure as those amounts that might become due from reinsurers if the reinsured event occurs. For a simple excess of loss (XoL) treaty the amount of contingent exposure might be the maximum limit of a particular layer or layers. For a simple quota-share (QS), the contingent exposure might be the reinsurers' shares of the estimated or probable maximum losses of the portfolio of risks covered by the treaty.

Having established the amount of the contingent exposure, it is a relatively straightforward matter to apply the S&P default rates to determine the level of credit risk. A simple example will suffice. Let us assume that a cedent's property catastrophe XoL reinsurance programme includes a layer with a limit of £50 million excess £10 million. The maximum contingent exposure on the layer is £40 million. Several reinsurers of differing credit risk as measured by commercial ratings participate in the layer. The breakdown of their shares is shown in Table 3 together with the maximum, nominal amount of contingent credit risk by rating grade.

The method just described is subject to the same methodological problems as those applicable to the pricing of "actual" credit risk described above. A new problem arises when considering how to reflect the relative credit risk in the premium. A simplistic approach might be to make pro-rata deductions from or enhancements to

Table 3 Contingent reinsurer credit risk pricing (limit £50 million, excess £10 million)

Rating grade	Share (%)	Maximum contingent credit risk	S&P default rate (%)	Nominal provision (£ million)
AAA	25	10	0.5	0.1
AA	30	12	1.2	0.1
A	35	14	1.9	0.3
BBB	10	4	4.7	0.2
Total		40		0.6

the agreed premium rate for the layer based on the subscribing reinsurers' ratings in relation to rating of the lead, price-setting reinsurer. Whilst higher-rated reinsurers might be happy with such a situation, those facing deductions most certainly would not. In any case, traditional reinsurance pricing practices might militate against this, particularly where "most favourable terms" clauses are included in the leader's terms.

A theoretical solution to this problem is to separate the underwriting risk price (URP) and then to add a separate credit risk premium (CRP) that would, in effect, generate a credit risk spread. The URP would be received by all reinsurers subscribing to a share of the proposed risk. The URP would be set at a floor level and those reinsurers with a credit rating above the floor level would receive an additional CRP based upon their credit rating grade. This might overcome the theoretical problem of "most favourable terms" as this would only apply to the URP, though problems are likely to arise over the agreement of the correct URP.

For this concept to work, a number of problems would need to be solved. First of these is the proxy for pricing the CRP. The simplest solution would be to be employ agreed commercial ratings subject to the caveats discussed previously in the pricing of receivable default risk. Assuming agreement on this point, the floor rating would then need to be agreed. A convenient floor might be BBB on the S&P and Fitch scales, representing the lower threshold of generally accepted investment-grade ratings. This of course assumes that the URP does not already include an additional pricing component to reflect higher ratings, a practice that some of the top-rated reinsurers have been trying to impose on the market for some time. Indeed, certain top-rated reinsurers have sought to obtain what they consider to be an acceptable return on their capital by refusing to participate in subscription treaties and setting their own unilateral price. This would work to undermine the concept of a credit risk spread.

The second problem is the formula for calculating the CRP spread. One method is a simple linear scale for the CRP spread where an equal increment of, say 50 or some other agreed number of basis points (bp), is applied to each rating grade. This is unlikely to provide a sufficiently attractive CRP spread where the URP is set at a relatively high rate on line. An exponential CRP scale derived from the S&P default rates might offer a solution and would be fairer and more logical given that the capital charges applied to recoverables are calculated exponentially. Table 4 shows the S&P default charges and indicates a simple arithmetic CRP spread of 420bp from the BBB–AAA rating grades. Again this does not address the problem of the size of the spread in relation to the base URP. An alternative is to calculate the arithmetic spread as percentage of the base S&P default BBB rate using the following formula:

$$\frac{(\text{S \& P BBB bp charge} - \text{higher rating bp charge})}{\text{S\&P BBB bp charge}}$$

This formula generates a CRP spread ranging from 60% for A to 89% for AAA. Such a wide spread, whilst obviously very attractive to the higher rated reinsurers, would probably struggle to gain acceptance by the market. Dividing this raw CRP by a chosen factor might produce a more acceptable spread and Table 4 shows the result of dividing by five. Alternatively, if a single A range rating is chosen as the floor, the spread would be tighter for the two higher grades. However, for sub-single A reinsurers a negative spread would be implied, which would, logically, have to be subtracted from the URP thus undermining the base concept that the URP is the correct price for the underwriting component of the risk. In addition, the formula does not account for the likely length of the reinsured tail. Adapting bond default rates, which provide

Table 4 Reinsurer credit risk spread

Rating	S&P	Difference from rate (%)	Difference from BBB rate (bp)	Difference /5 BBB rate (%)
AAA	0.5	420	89	18
AA	1.2	350	74	15
A	1.9	280	60	12
BBB	4.7	0	0	0

incremental rates out to 15 years for each grade might provide a solution, though a method for defining and calculating the estimated duration of the contingent liabilities would also need to be agreed. This is a matter for further debate, but additional discussion here would be nugatory until certain other obstacles are overcome.

Other obstacles to introducing a CRP mechanism arise from the structure of the reinsurance market. All market participants, ie, reinsurers, cedents and intermediaries, would need to agree to the CRP concept. This would also require all parties to agree that the rating agencies, which tend to follow rather than lead reinsurance cycles, are the most suitable organisations to price credit risk. A high degree of discipline would be required, particularly during the phases of the cycle when supply of capacity exceeds demand, to ensure that the CRP was not discarded.

The absence of any financial recognition of reinsurer credit risk at the time of purchase remains a significant omission in the pricing of contingent reinsurance capital. Reinsurers with strong balance sheets have long been a keen to obtain a credit risk premium as a reward for offering a lower level of default risk. Efforts to obtain such recognition may be confined to the highest-rated reinsurers demanding an enhanced premium. Under the current, arcane reinsurance pricing mechanism, such a position is likely to persist only when demand exceeds supply.

1 Benfield Group Analysis of NAIC Returns, Thomson One-Source.
2 Financial Services Authority (2001).
3 http://www.apra.gov.au/General/General-Insurance-Reforms.cfm.
4 Standard & Poor's Rating Criteria for Property/Casualty Insurers.
5 Source: Lloyds website: html://www.lloydsoflondon.com.
6 Swiss Re's S&P rating was lowered subsequently lowered from AAA to AA in September 2002.

7 Employers Re's S&P rating was subsequently lowered from AAA to AA+ in February 2002 following a change in agency's group rating methodology.
8 Solvency margin ratio = shareholders' funds/net premium written.
9 Standard & Poor's (2002).
10 Standard & Poor's (2002).

BIBLIOGRAPHY

Financial Services Authority UK, 2001, *Integrated Prudential Sourcebook, Annex C: Draft Rules and Guidance,* June.

Standard & Poor's, 1999, *Rating Criteria for Property/Casualty Insurers.*

Lloyds of London, http://www.lloydsoflondon.com.

Standard & Poor's, 2002, *Ratings Performance 2001,* February.

7

Catastrophe Modelling

Dickie Whitaker[1]

Guy Carpenter plc

The reinsurance buying process has evolved considerably over the last few years and a key part of that evolution has been in the utilisation of catastrophe (cat) modelling. First, simple deterministic models became available in the 1970s, which evolved into the production of more sophisticated probabilistic models in the early 1980s available initially for the USA. These early models increased in number and in coverage and now cover all main economic regions globally. Catastrophe modelling has become an intrinsic part of the reinsurance buying process in all major economic regions.

There is however inconsistency in the ways in which these models are used and indeed several options exist as to how they can be incorporated into the reinsurance buying process, whether this be from an intermediary, company or reinsurer perspective.

INTRODUCTION

The following chapter will attempt to define some clear strategies in the use of these models and some of the issues that need to be addressed in the reinsurance buying process. This understanding has to be built on a number of separate components: first, an understanding of the construction of models is needed. Second, one needs to understand how uncertainty is handled and finally one needs to understand the outputs from the model. This first step in this process is to have a clear understanding of how these products are constructed.

HOW CATASTROPHE MODELS ARE BUILT

Catastrophe models are a complex series of mathematical functions, algorithms and engineering assumptions usually embedded in a software architecture that allows easy introduction of exposure data in order to estimate losses from a natural hazard that can be characterised as a catastrophe. There is no universal definition for the term "catastrophe model" and anyone could theoretically produce an extremely simple model that is so called. For the purposes of this chapter we assume that some minimum standards have been applied and that we are dealing with a credible model such as those produced by the main global catastrophe modelling companies, RMS, AIR and EQECAT. No global standards have been established for what catastrophe models should contain other than that commissioned by the Florida Insurance Commission. Here all the models used by these companies are stochastic but if required are capable of deterministic output.

The main components of cat models

Fundamentally, all catastrophe models are divided into three distinct sections:

1. hazard module;
2. vulnerability module (otherwise known as the engineering or damage module); and
3. actuarial module.

Hazard module

This component is used to establish simplified representations of the complex physical characteristics that are being modelled. For example in hurricane modelling this process would initially involve the collation of historical experience of hurricanes for the area concerned. If we looked at the USA there are approximately 150 years of data available with varying degrees of accuracy. These historical events would be represented spatially in sections of the coastline that are split into segments or "gates" or "bins"along the coastline. The difference in the size of bins varies by modelling company but can be from 10 to 35 miles on average. For every modelled hurricane a number of characteristics would be defined. These characteristics can vary from model to model but would include most of the following:

- forward speed of the hurricane (the speed over land);
- radius to maximum wind speed (distance between the eye of the hurricane and the maximum wind);
- central pressure;
- hurricane size, usually measured on the Safir–Simpson Intensity (SSI) scale: this integer-valued scale ranges from 1 to 5 and depends on the maximum wind speed and pressure;
- landfall location (where offshore hurricanes hit land);
- peak wind speed;
- direction of hurricane track;
- wind profile (asymmetric due to Coriolis force caused by the rotation of the Earth);
- surface roughness (used to estimate the slowing effect of the terrain on the forward speed of the hurricane).

Once this information has been collated and a conclusion (by modellers) reached on the appropriate use of the data, probability distributions are then fitted to these parameters. This representation of historical events is statistically insufficient to populate the model. "Synthetic" events are then produced by sampling from the probability distributions with the fitted parameters.

These synthetic events form the event database and are the backbone of the hazard component of the catastrophe models. The size of the event databases required vary by peril and by country but start at a few thousand for simple models for small countries, up to approximately half a million for the USA.

The same principles apply to the modelling of other perils, such as earthquakes, tornadoes, flood, etc. For example, the following parameters are used in an earthquake catastrophe model:

- seismic fault geometry (location, length, depth, dipping angle);
- fault type;
- frequency and severity of events on a fault: earthquake severity is measured by various types of magnitude (body-wave, surface-wave, moment, etc). Moment magnitude is the most objective scale since it is proportional to the seismic energy released during an earthquake; and
- soil characteristics.

The result of this component of a catastrophe model is the estimate of "site hazard", which is the intensity of shaking (in case of an earthquake) or wind speed (in case of a hurricane or other wind) at the sites of interest.

There is a variety of measures of site hazard intensity, especially for the earthquake peril. The simplest one is Modified Mercali Intensity (MMI). This integer-valued scale (from I to XII) is descriptive and not quantitative (for example, MMI = II is described as "felt by persons at rest, on upper floors, or favorably placed"). A better way of measuring site intensity level is peak ground acceleration (PGA) which is the maximum acceleration caused by an earthquake at the site of interest (quantity directly measurable by seismic instruments). Yet a further improvement in intensity measure is the Spectral Acceleration (Velocity or Displacement) that takes into account the amplification or weakening of vibrations due to the soil and building characteristics at the site. Although this measure is hardest to estimate and there is not much historical data on it, most of the catastrophe modellers are moving towards using of Spectral Acceleration in site hazard analysis. All the measures of earthquake site intensity are estimated using the so called "attenuation functions", which are relationships between the earthquake size (magnitude), distance from rupture to the site and soil type.

Some modellers consider the following earthquake-induced phenomena that can cause losses and are part of seismic hazard:

- Liquefaction: liquid-like behaviour of saturated soils due to loss of their bearing strength. Buildings situated on such soils can topple or sink in a liquefaction event.
- Landslide: downslope movement of a soil mass due to loss of soil strength along the sliding surface.
- Fire following: fire triggered by an earthquake due to broken gas lines that can spread quickly because of the earthquake-caused disruption to the emergency response system (water supply, transportation).

These are the general principles applied to most catastrophe models. For flood the same concepts apply but the issues in some ways are more complex due to the nature of the risk; not only is there the interaction of the hazard on the insured property but also there are the effects of the terrain, the antecedent conditions and defences already in place. To compound the issue there are poor levels of data generally available. This and the fact that flood is not covered by the insurance industry in many countries may be the reasons why there are so few stochastic flood models available in the market.

Vulnerability module

This component is where the model uses the hazard estimates to calculate damage, given some details about location and construction type (steel frame, concrete shear wall, etc). In many cases the information available might be limited as this data is not always recorded and assumptions become a necessity. There are also practical limitations on the resolution required by each model to ensure a reasonable assessment of the risk. In practice, CRESTA zone (an internationally recognised method of accumulating exposures generally along recognised political boundaries) data is a practical minimum ex-USA, and county or zip code within the USA. Generally speaking if the data is coarser than this the uncertainty of the results will be considerably increased to a level that may be considered unusable. In all cases the industry is moving towards an agreement that location data should be kept at zip/postcode level with commensurate improvements in results. Vulnerability function (or fragility curve) is a relationship between the site hazard intensity and the damage to the building, contents or time element. The damage can be expressed as a percentage of the building value or the replacement/repair cost. Vulnerability function is established by addressing the three essential components of structural analysis. In the first instance, what the building is designed to withstand (Design Codes & Practice). Second, which are likely to be the dominant failure modes (this would encompass their causes and the likely resultant damage – loss of roof covering, wind loading exceeding dead weight, partial roof repair required, etc). Third, what the resultant loss for this damage would be (15–30% of roof cost, for example).

These functions are results of using three different types of information in combination:

1. *Empirical information*. For a number of years the scientific and catastrophe modelling community have collected detailed data following catastrophic events. To be of use this needs to contain

information on such factors as wind load or intensity, with detailed information on damage and building type. Information thus collated has considerable value as it not only avoids some of the uncertainty seen in the more theoretical approaches but also contains information on issues such as post-loss inflation. Unfortunately, in a lot of cases, empirical information consists of claims data "contaminated" with application of limits and deductibles, which makes it difficult to adequately extract the damage values.

2. *Engineering consensus*. Here, expert opinion becomes the mainstay of the production of vulnerability functions. For many years the main source and derivation of earthquake vulnerability curves came from the "Applied Technology Council for the State of California" (ATC 13), (who were one of the few organisations to provide generic information on damage). These curves were created by leading engineers estimating the damage resulting from specified local intensity characterised by MMI. This method is required where there is an absence of data either for a specific type of structure or hazard load.
3. *Engineering reliability analysis*. Here, computer-aided design (CAD) models analyse specific components of buildings to ascertain the probability of loss under specific circumstances. This information is combined at a building level and reliability analysis is used to estimate the probabilities of various failure modes. This method is the most sound one from the theoretical perspective, however, the resulting fragility curves still have to be calibrated using actual loss data which in many cases is not sufficient. Another drawback of this method is that it estimates the damage of an "average" structure, while the buildings in question may be constructed better or worse than average. Because of its expense this method is mostly used for complex commercial or industrial structures.

Actuarial module

This last component calculates the loss resulting from given levels of damage deriving from building structures that have been analysed. This section also calculates the effect of policy conditions such as deductibles, attachment points and limits. Some of the models have the additional ability to calculate the effects of a number of types of reinsurance, including excess of loss, facultative and some types of proportional.

Data requirements

Cat models are all designed to take a variety of resolutions of data, but obviously the more data available, the less the uncertainty in the results. In essence however the models need the following information to be used effectively:

- location;
- value of risks;
- type of coverage, ie, buildings, contents or business interruption;
- classification by commercial, industrial and residential;
- policy conditions as applied at both policy level and site level to include limits, deductibles and attachment points; and
- construction and occupancy.

SENSITIVITY AROUND THE COMPONENTS OF MODELS

At each stage in the course of developing a catastrophe model, it is important to see if there is some separate calibration available, and also to determine the sensitivity of modelled results to each element of the model. Ultimately catastrophe models are focused on quantifying the probability of loss and its correlation across a portfolio within a single event. Therefore, sensitivity tests are undertaken on the principal elements of a model, as described previously, to determine the impact on loss results. Some examples of such sensitivity analyses include exploring the impact on different sampling windows and smoothing algorithms on the spatial disposition of risk, and of alternative assumptions about maximum magnitudes on a fault, or minimum central pressure of a hurricane within a given region. Sensitivity tests help the modeller identify which parameters are most critical in affecting results and hence where to focus specific attention on setting parameters for the model.

UNDERSTANDING UNCERTAINTY

Understanding how catastrophe models are constructed and the relative sensitivity of the components enables users to begin to learn how the results can be used and what judgements to make as

Figure 1 Recorded accelerations and those calculated (median ± 2 s) using the relationship of Seed and Idriss (1982)

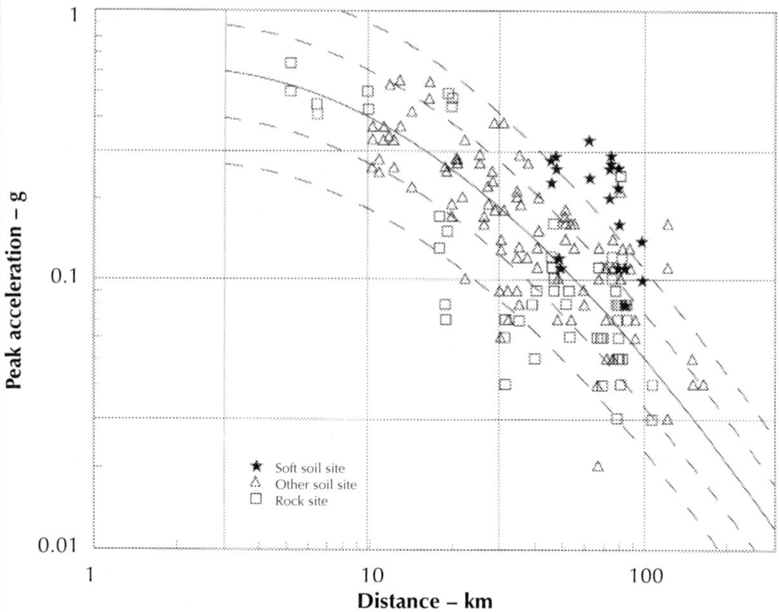

Source: Office of Planning and Research, 1990, p.96. Supplied by Risk Management Solutions.

a result of these. However, probably the single most important factor in the use of catastrophe models is an understanding and recognition of the uncertainty inherent in catastrophe modelling.

Intuitively we understand that we cannot predict any specific event that may occur in the future and we also understand that it is unreasonable to expect modellers to be able to predict the exact financial loss arising from that event. We do of course expect that the models should be able to produce better estimates with greater certainty than we can ourselves produce. Before we analyse the degrees of uncertainty let us first examine the areas in which the most significant elements of uncertainty exist.

Hazard uncertainty

For Earthquake the main parameters that modellers use are usually similar between the models. However, all these parameters (discussed in a previous section of this chapter) are modelled differently because of the uncertainty in the data used to estimate them.

The event catalogues on which each model is based will be generally derived from published data available in the public domain. For this reason there is usually a reasonable consistency between the varying models. New research is always being undertaken which refines these catalogues and this needs to be incorporated on a regular basis. However, for some geographical areas, especially ones that are relatively inactive, such as the New Madrid area in the USA, expert judgement plays a significant role.

The uncertainty in ground motion (the reduction in seismic energy over distance) will always contribute significantly. Figure 1 plots the peak ground motion acceleration against the distance in miles from the epicentre of the Loma Prieta earthquake.[1] It demonstrates the difficulty of predicting the ground motion of a potential earthquake. Regarding soil amplification, alluvial soil for example greatly increases the amplification of shock waves compared to solid rock. The appropriate algorithms to define this introduce significant uncertainty both from the ability to define the level of appropriate shaking and from definition and resolution of soil types (see Figure 2).

To model windstorm risk, a main component in the uncertainty comes from the limited historical catalogue available. For most parts of the world there are only 100 years of data available and the early parts of that have limited amounts of information. For the US there are approximately 228 hurricanes listed and only two SS5 on the Saffir–Simpson scale events that form part of these. Given that we are particularly interested in the tail of the distribution where reinsurance is particularly important, this lack of data can cause some problems. In addition, the effect of terrain on the wind speed is also unpredictable.

Vulnerability uncertainty

In this chapter, we are concerned with variability of damage that occurs either as a result of a specific wind speed affecting one insured property or the ground motion resulting from an earthquake. The uncertainty in building performance comes from a number of different sources, such as type of building or construction quality.

Figure 3 plots building damage ratios against wind speeds for Hurricanes Andrew, Hugo, Opal and Erin. A damage ratio is the

Figure 2 Difference in premium by location in Mexico City due to soil differences

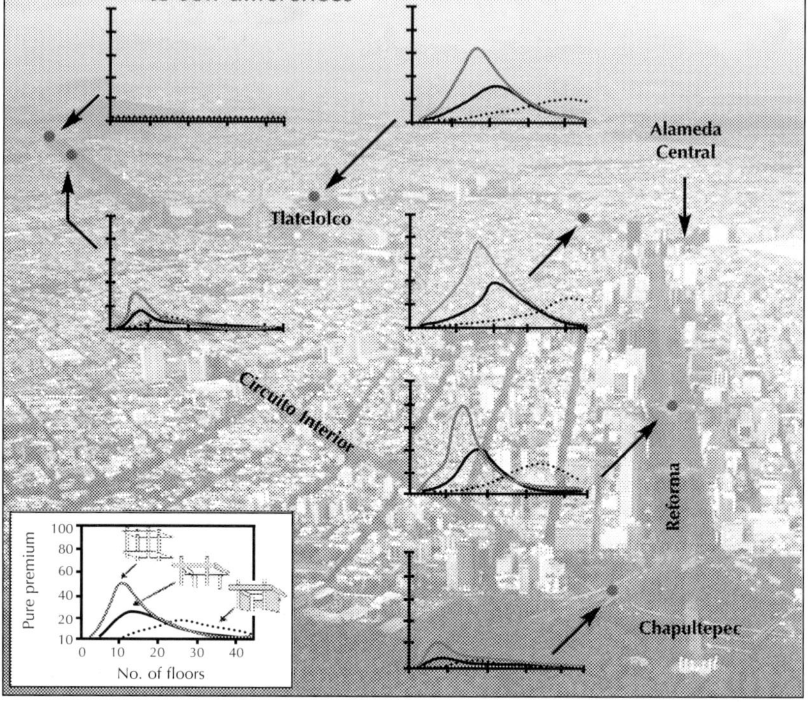

Source: Ordaz, Miranda and Reinoso (2002).
Supplied by Instituto de Ingeniería de la UNAM.

per cent of the building that suffers a loss. Each data point represents the performance of wood-frame single-storey dwellings for a zip code in the path of one of these hurricanes. The graph shows a general upward trend in the damage ratio with increased wind speed. Significant variation in the trend can be observed demonstrating the uncertainty.

Uncertainty is also caused by the lack of data under extreme loads; where there is limited extreme event experience, inevitably there is little data from which to construct damage functions.

Data

The resolution (ie, the level of geography data that is collected) of the input data will also have a significant effect on the uncertainty. Zip or postcode data will produce different results with lesser uncertainty than county or CRESTA zone data. However, to understand

Figure 3 Hurricane damage uncertainty for single-family wood frame structures

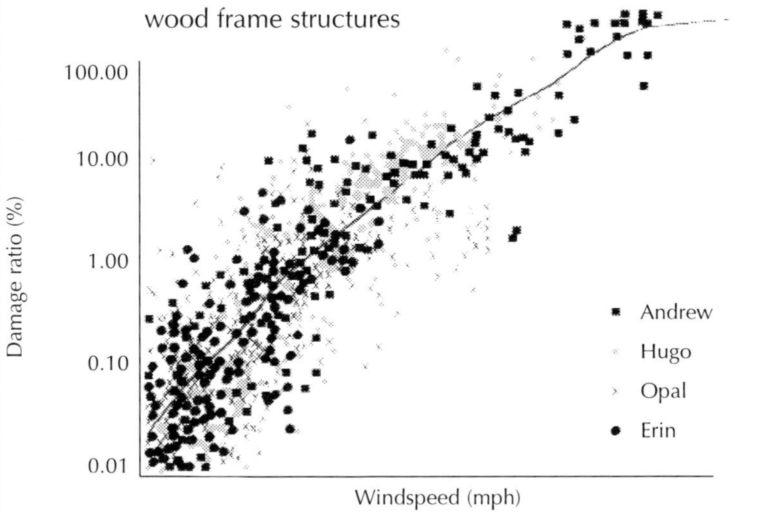

Source: Risk Management Solutions.

the full implications one also has to bear in mind the resolution to which the hazard is addressed on the model being used. For example, for the US, address or zip code is common, whereas for many other parts of the world the hazard is addressed at a higher level, such as CRESTA zone or country.

Attempts to standardise the data available, such as the recently launched standard "CRESTA plus", should greatly assist in this process and should make this process much less tortuous.

What uncertainty should we therefore expect from catastrophe models?

The true evaluation of uncertainty is a complex procedure, however there are elements of catastrophe models where we can use statistical techniques to calculate confidence bounds. This approach, although not statistically perfect, allows us to gain some understanding of the inherent uncertainty within these tools.

Dr David Miller studied this issue (Miller, 1999) and concluded that, for a USA national portfolio, we should expect to see variability around the mean to be in the region of between 2 and 2.8 times. Although this research was done in 1998 based on the data that was then available the degree of uncertainty could be expected to be broadly similar today. In essence, regardless of the progress in scientific research (paleo-seismicity, forensic hurricanology), the shortness of event catalogues, especially in case of earthquakes, relative to the return periods of occurrence of the largest events (hundreds of years) will inevitably produce significant uncertainty.

How do modelling companies explain uncertainty?
To begin with uncertainty can be split into aleatory uncertainty – associated with intrinsic randomness, and epistemic uncertainty – related to our level of knowledge. (The boundary between these categories remains, however, open to movement as scientific knowledge changes.)

Only a part of this uncertainty inherent within models is, however, explicitly calculated. There is also a lack of unanimity or transparency by the modellers as to what elements of uncertainty are calculated. However, there is increasing acceptance of the following definitions of uncertainty within the models.

Primary uncertainty
This is the uncertainty (or volatility) around whether an event will occur within a given time period and what size or location of event it will be. The randomness of occurrence of hazard events is considered aleatory (unless there is in fact some way in which an earthquake prediction, for example, could have forewarned the event).

Secondary uncertainty
This is the uncertainty in the size of the loss given that a specified event has occurred. Secondary uncertainty contains both aleatory and epistemic components, as it results from both inherent uncertainty in the randomness of the hazard parameters (such as speed of the wind at a location) as well as lack of knowledge of the specifics of a building in the path of the storm.

Parameter uncertainty
For any component of the model parameter uncertainty reflects uncertainty in what the mean value of that parameter should be. This could include the mean activity rate, or the mean vulnerability

of a population of buildings subject to a specific wind speed, or even the mean resolution at which the hazard is itself sampled. As such it is associated with epistemic uncertainty. Parameter uncertainty can be particularly difficult to quantify, although it is clear that the more high quality data available to determine each element of a model, the lower parameter uncertainty is likely to be.

Process risk/model risk

Process and model risk results from the choice of modelling methodology, which parameters are considered critical to the result, or the choice of a specific mathematical expression to characterise some behaviour. Process and model risk can be explored by trying to find whether there is an improved representation of loss by incorporating additional parameters, rival distributions or an alternative modelling methodology.

EVALUATING THE MOST APPROPRIATE MODEL(S)

An understanding of how models work and the inherent uncertainty within them gives a solid grounding as to what models are able to do. There are a number of other key questions that need, however, to be considered before a decision is made.

First, the territorial coverage needs to be matched with each of the available models. The extent of coverage available from the modelling companies varies enormously and it would obviously be important that the relevant key territories are covered.

Second, details of the insurance structure should be borne in mind since not all models cover policy level data which may have to drive the decision making process.

Ease of use and run-time also play a part but may be of less concern for something as fundamental as reinsurance purchasing. It should be noted however that under current conditions the model run-time for particularly large programs can extend to weeks even on the fastest machines.

Benefits of a multi-model approach

So, given that we wish to use catastrophe models to assess requirements for reinsurance pricing and structuring, and assuming that we have ascertained the suitability of available models and have an understanding of the associated uncertainty what do we now need to do? We need to understand that there is substantial variability in the results and this has to be kept in mind when the model results are handled (as discussed in the next section dealing with pricing and the subsequent use of catastrophe models). It is useful at this stage to use more than one model to begin to understand the range of results available. To the inexperienced user this often produces a degree of consternation. The end of the reinsurance buying process is usually the purchase of a fixed limit of cover. Given that this will usually have been derived at least in part from the output of a catastrophe model it is worrying for some to have to consider that this fixed limit may not actually protect the insurer from a fixed return period loss but may merely have a probability of doing so.

One way to assist in the final decision is to use another model with differing assumptions to compare results. This may be particularly true where the underlying portfolio has been optimised based on one particular model. If the same model that has been used to build up the portfolio is then used to understand its accumulation, this over-reliance could lead to risk management problems for the company concerned.

USING THE RESULTS

Being informed in how models are constructed we are now in a position to use the results that almost all models have as standard output.

As indicated above there are two main purposes for using catastrophe models; one is to provide information for a cedent to calculate the amount of cover required, and the other is to provide the cost of this cover to the insurer/reinsurer. Model output can be categorised into two main headings; deterministic and probabilistic. Below is an explanation of these outputs and how they help in the insurance/reinsurance buying process.

Deterministic

In simple terms this is one event applied to a client portfolio resulting, therefore, in one loss. This model assesses the impact of a hazard by investigating the severity of a single possible outcome. Currently models have three main types of deterministic events:

1. historical (real events from a catalogue);
2. postulated (hypothetical events with features, such as location and size, specified by the user); and
3. Lloyds Realistic Disaster Scenarios.

Historical

This is where a significant historical event is applied to the portfolio. For example it could be the 1923 Tokyo Earthquake, Hurricane Hugo or 90A in the UK applied to a current portfolio, thus generating an approximate loss to that portfolio.

Postulated

These can also be called "worst case" scenarios and here again a single possible outcome is calculated. An example would be a Category 5 hurricane hitting a large part of the Florida coast.

Lloyds Realistic Disaster Scenario

These are scenarios that Lloyds of London suggest would cause a significant loss to the insurance/reinsurance market. A Los Angeles earthquake, Tokyo earthquake or Florida hurricane are examples of these.

Deterministic analysis can offer some comfort and give an indication as to the performance of the model but in essence they do not offer the user significant value compared with a probabilistic analysis; if there is one thing that we can be sure of it is that the same event with the same characteristics will not happen in the same place again.

Probabilistic

A probabilistic model output would assess the impact of a hazard and assign probabilities to a whole range of possible outcomes. The model is populated with a group of events that simulate multiple events for a single peril, such as a series of earthquakes and windstorms, and account for the probability of these events over time.

Probabilistic model outputs are the most often used in determining how much reinsurance should be bought and at what cost. Different probabilistic outputs are now discussed and how they are used for the objectives of insurance/reinsurance.

Event sets/event by event and scenario output

This is the output that allows for the calculation of "exceeding probability" (EP) curves and is used as the basis of pricing reinsurance treaties. The event set is a powerful tool and is often used in actuarial analysis.

An event set is made up of:

1. *Event number*. A unique number given to a set of discrete events from the probabilistic event set simulated in the model. Events from the probabilistic set are mostly "synthetic" (a combination of simulated variables) and are there to give representation of the types of events that may occur.

   The number of events used in the models will be determined by a number of factors including the size of the country, the complexity of the hazard, the ensuing run time and sensitivity to the results.
2. *Frequency*. Also known as event rate. This is the expected frequency of an event to occur annually (number of events per year). For example if the number is small (eg, 0.00001) then we would not expect the event to happen often. If it is large (eg, 1) then we would expect the event to occur more often. Frequency can also be reported as a percentage. These numbers can also be translated into return period; frequency of 0.00001 would mean that we would only expect the event to occur once in 100,000 years.
3. *Exposure*. This is the exposure of the portfolio being analysed. This can be evaluated in one of two ways, either with the full exposure of the portfolio to all stochastic events (probabilistic) or with the exposure of the portfolio to a specific event (deterministic). What value is reported in the exposure will depend on the type of distribution used by the models.
4. *Mean loss*. The mean loss is the average loss to a portfolio from all catastrophe events causing any loss to that portfolio.
5. *Standard deviation*. The standard deviation is the square root of the variance around the mean loss. Both variance and standard

Figure 4 Exceeding probability loss

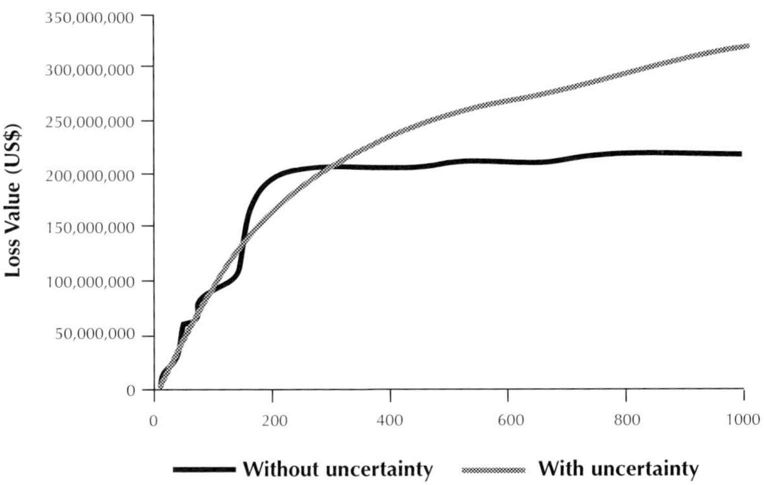

deviation are measures of the scatter (uncertainty) of a probability distribution around the mean. The higher the standard deviation, the larger the dispersion around the mean loss.

6. *Exceeding probability*. The exceeding probability (EP) curve can help determine how much reinsurance should be bought. The curve represents the probability of exceeding specified loss thresholds at least once in a year and defines the probability of various levels of potential loss for a defined structure or portfolio of assets at risk of loss from natural hazards. The EP curve is usually defined as a value of each return period. Figure 3 is a graph of a portfolio including secondary uncertainty and a curve without secondary uncertainty.

The return period is the expected length of time between recurrences of two events with similar characteristics. The return period can refer to hazard events such as hurricanes or earthquakes, or it can refer to specific levels of loss (eg, a US$100 million loss in this territory has a return period of 50 years). Therefore, this curve in Figure 4 can be used to determine what retention or limit would be the best for the company's objectives.

Another way to look at the curve in Figure 4 is to say that for the 100-year result (approximately US$100,000 loss value with secondary uncertainty in this case) we are 99% confident that we will not exceed US$100,000 in one event of one year. Therefore, when buying reinsurance, the capacity, the model, the quality of data and experience should be taken into account. For this, the return period can be used. A 100- or 250-year limit is often chosen as it represents a common global risk appetite.
The exceeding probability loss curve can either shown from various perspectives

- *Ground up (damage) value*. The total amount of loss occurring to an insured and subject to the insured's insurance policy, beginning with the first dollar of loss and prior to the application to the deductible or deduction, if any, required by the policy.
- *Gross loss*. The amount of a ceding company's loss irrespective of any reinsurance recoveries due. It is calculated by taking the ground-up loss less any deductibles, limits and proportional share. When making the decision to buy insurance, the gross loss is usually taken into account.
- *Net loss*. The amount of loss that an insurer keeps for its own account and does not pass on to another insurer (or reinsurer). This is calculated after a reinsurance treaty has been applied to the gross loss.

The other financial views that we get from the models are:

- *Aggregate exceeding probability*. A measure of the probability that one or more occurrences will combine in a year to exceed the threshold.
- *Occurrence exceeding probability*. A measure of the probability that a single occurrence will exceed a certain threshold.

Traditionally, occurrence exceeding probability has been used (as was the example used in Figure 3). Since reinsurance is usually bought with one event triggering payout then a per occurrence approach is useful. Aggregate exceeding probability is useful for reinstatement reasons; as the aggregate exceeding probability is for one or more events in a year then it will either be the same or greater than the occurrence exceeding probability. If the aggregate exceeding probability is a lot greater than the occurrence exceeding probability then this means that the frequency of the events are high, while if the aggregate exceeding probability is the same as the occurrence probability then the frequency of the events are low. For example, the aggregate exceeding probability for "California Earthquake" will be higher than the occurrence exceeding probability because the event of an earthquake occurring in California is higher than what? The aggregate exceeding probability and the occurrence exceeding probability would be very similar for UK Earthquake.

Probable maximum loss

This is a general concept applied in the insurance industry for defining high loss scenarios to be considered when underwriting insurance risk. The exact probability or return period associated with a probable maximum loss (PML) can vary based on the company's policies, objectives and risk aversion.

The concept of PML goes back to the days before models were available, when an insurance/reinsurance company used aggregated methods to determine their loss. For example, the PML for Japan Earthquake was calculated on the aggregate of Zone 5 (Tokyo) to represent 9% probability of occurrence. Models have expanded this method and therefore a return period that meets all the decision criteria of a company for buying reinsurance is now used to represent PML.

APPLYING REINSURANCE STRUCTURES

So far, this chapter has discussed some of the output relating to the purchase of reinsurance. Here, it will discuss how the model output can help with pricing reinsurance. As discussed above, the exceeding probability curve helps in assessing how much reinsurance may be required. Another important output, mean annual loss (also referred to as pure premium or pure loss cost) is also needed to price reinsurance coverage. This is the insurance rate or premium intended to pay for insured loss, ie, for the cost of repairing or rebuilding the damaged property. If a treaty has been applied, then the pure loss cost can be calculated for each layer. When the pure premium is divided by the limit of the layer this is said to be the "loss on line" and is the basis of calculations for the rate on line. The pure loss cost does not include adjusting expenses, underwriting expenses, profit and other contingencies, or inflation, which insurers add to the loss cost to obtain a final rate.

To calculate all the expense adjustments, the risk models (simulation models) take the output of the event set and calculate the rate on line by taking the mean loss and adding a percentage of the standard deviation to it, then adding amounts for expenses and other costs.

CONCLUSION

This chapter has demonstrated why models need to be understood and how, with this understanding, they form such a vital part in the reinsurance buying process. Of course it is not only here that they have use. They additionally form an important part of many other key functions within the insurance and reinsurance industry such as investor data, rating agency information and regulatory submissions. Considerable investment is being made in many areas such as hazard recurrence and vulnerability assessment that will produce benefit to the users of catastrophe models.

The functionality and geographical scope of models is being increased from year to year with additional ability to handle detailed policy data being rolled out to more diverse locations. More emphasis is being placed by the modelling companies on using recent research and finding ways to reduce uncertainty, all of which will be of benefit to the user.

1 The author would like to thank the contributions made to this section by Robert Muir Wood from Risk Management Solutions, and Jillian Williams and Maya Belubekian from Guy Carpenter.

BIBLIOGRAPHY

Miller, D., 1999, "Uncertainly in Hurricane Risk Modelling and Implications for Securitization, Casualty Actuarial Society Discussion Paper Program.

Office of Planning and Research, 1990, "Competing Against Time – Report to the Governor George Deukmejian from the Governor's Board of Inquiry on the 1989 Loma Prieta Earthquake", May.

Ordaz, M., E. Miranda and E. Reinoso, 2002, "Earthquake Damage and Loss Estimation for Mexico (City)", Forthcoming in the *Earthquake Spectra Journal*, EERI.

8

Identifying and Controlling Emerging Risk

Reto Schneider[1]

Swiss Re

INTRODUCTION

The desire to predict what is to come can be traced back throughout the history of mankind. Astrologers were always welcome guests at the courts of the aristocracy, and prophets such as the great 16th century French seer Nostradamus enjoyed tremendous popularity. To predict the future, to be able to prepare oneself and to even wield power over the future, is a dream all of us undoubtedly share. In the same vein, reinsurance companies have a long tradition of employing people who endeavour to develop reliable tools and systematic approaches with which to map the landscape of the future.

Attitudes towards risk vary over time. What was seen as a great opportunity last year might be considered a threat today. We must ask ourselves whether there is more opportunity in risk or more risk in opportunity. As long as the world changes at a slow pace, reinsurers have little difficulty applying what was gleaned from the past. To conduct successful and profitable business in that climate, we build upon well-known, proven patterns. Even then, of course, losses will occur occasionally. However, we can count on our extensive loss experience, calculating an adequate risk premium for risks we have known over many years.

But what happens if the rate of change in our business environment suddenly accelerates and our experienced-based models for business no longer apply? Ongoing technological change rapidly invalidates loss experience. This scenario has in fact become a reality in virtually all areas of business, and the insurance industry's traditionally reactive approach, ie, of waiting until losses have occurred before charging an appropriate price, has become a risk in itself.

One novel type of exposure, "cyberquake", serves as a good example. Internet virus attacks could threaten to affect the global economy in a matter of hours, thus generating huge economic losses for insurers with an uncontrollable accumulation potential. Insurers cannot afford to wait for such an event to occur, and then adjust premium to recover. By the same token, they will be unable to indemnify losses for incidents for which no premium has been previously charged. Actuaries are hard put to price newly emerging risks such as cyberquake because they have no historical insurance data. Traditional rating methods, such as gathering claims information by accident and underwriting year, cannot be applied to emerging risks such as these easily, for technological progress alters the risk landscape in real time and a burning cost-based pricing approach is simply too sluggish to cope with change.

TECHNOLOGY: ONLY PERCEIVED AS A FASTER PROGRESSION?

Based on the findings of Intel co-founder Gordon E. Moore who predicted that the number of transistors per integrated circuit/ computing power, would double roughly every 18 months (Moore's Law 1965), we can assume that the application of new technologies automatically creates new risks, one must also expect those new risks to develop at a speed which corresponds to that of technology.[2]

Technological development is usually linked to an increase of order. As a result it can be assumed that the more mature a structure is, the shorter the time period between significant events will be. Referring to Moore's law, the next significant event in computing power to be expected is the change from the two-dimensional to the three-dimensional chip architecture. However, information technology in our daily life is still yet to come. Even less advanced in technological evolution is "nanotechnology", which the National Nanotechnology Initiative defines as research and technology development at the atomic, molecular or macromolular levels, in the scale length of approximately 1–100 nanometer range, to use structures, devices and systems that have novel properties and functions because of their small or intermediate size. Nanotechnology has not yet reached the structured level marked by rapid progress and exponential growth, while the pharmaceutical industry has reached its boundaries with traditionally synthesised compounds and is about to cross into new frontiers: mapping the human genome. More than a thousand new targets for future protein-based drugs can thus be identified. In the pharmaceutical industry, we anticipate more structure and the corresponding speed of developing and launching new drugs (eg, lifestyle drugs) to increase. If our assumption is correct that technological progress and the appearance of new risks run in parallel tracks, a risk landscape, which changes even progressively faster, will be challenge for our industry in the future.

Proving today what will be a causal link in the future, however, is simply impossible. Virtual proofing may emerge as a new discipline, but rather than wait for science, economics and politics to establish a cause and effect relationship, we have to learn to make decisions based on probabilities and scenarios that are reasonably true and logical. For this reason, Swiss Re's risk managers engage in scenario exercises to visualise the future risk landscape and test assumptions about risks.

Two examples serve to illustrate this scenario-based approach:

1. *Mad Cow disease*. While early reports of BSE/Mad Cow disease date back to the late 1980s, politicians – beyond those in the UK – successfully ignored all warnings that scientists had raised for many years. Following the first human vCJD casualties, however, the public was sufficiently alarmed for the authorities to act. They should have done so much earlier! Today, 20 years later, insurance experts have been heard to state that "BSE is not an insurance problem up to the point of the first loss .... In the case of mad cow disease, cause and effect relationships are hard to establish, and as such, traditional liability covers are not exposed." In fact, transmitting vCJD via surgical instruments to a multitude of patients may be the scenario just waiting to happen in the first of many hospitals.

2. *The Starlink case in the USA.* In September, 2000, genetically modified (GM) corn approved for animal feed showed up in the human food chain. Rather than the obvious bodily injury scenario, the problem was that a GM product appeared in an unexpected context. As a result, food manufacturers had to recall products containing GM corn that had not been approved for human consumption. Up until this case, the manufacturing and insurance industries had been reluctant to accept new risks in the context of GM products. Swiss Re had begun dialogue around this topic as early as 1998.[3]

These two examples illustrate how long it actually takes for policyholders, industries, brokers, insurance companies and reinsurers to react to already existing problems. By applying a purely *reactive* approach to new risks, it can take several years for all involved parties to reach a common understanding of the new risk and to adjust prices and conditions or create new products for that risk, respectively.

To shorten response time to something less than one year, the reinsurance industry must devise new internal processes and create new disciplines. To assess the risk of new technologies, the application of simulation techniques, scenario modelling and scenario-based thinking will help compensate for the lack of experience. Learning from the analysis of comparable systems and applying this knowledge in a new context will be the core competency in handling future risks successfully, if, after all, "the best way to predict the future is to invent it".[4]

While analysis and application of the know-how gleaned is key, it is of limited value when turning to coping with future risks. There, risk perception is of paramount importance. To capture, manage and control emerging risks the principles discussed in Figure 1 in the context of a new drug are valid and should be consistently applied.

RISK PERCEPTION: DEFINING FUTURE BUSINESS

As Swiss Re is a global leader in managing capital and risk, a crucial part of the company's mission is to anticipate, identify and understand the developments that are shaping the future risk landscape. Risk perception, in helping define the focus of future

Figure 1 Swiss Re's suggested systematic approach to capture emerging risks (new drug example)

Perception of "hazard"
News article about a new slow release drug application (a new implantable medical device to lower blood pressure) is published – "The once a year pill".

Recognition of patterns
Analogous to acute over-dosage cases leading to death.

Creating scenarios
Implanted medical device ruptures after physical impact shortly after implantation. Subsequently the content (entire yearly dosage) is released at once resulting in the death of the patient.

Quantification of risk (probability and severity)
How many people are at risk, How likely is a physical impact that can cause rupture of the implant? How many patients are at risk?

R = 10EE-2 (per person per annum) * 10EE4 Patient = 100 Patients are at risk.

Mitigation of risk
- Changing the implant design to make it more resistant to physical impacts.
- Avoid deadly concentration of the active ingredient.
- Tolerate risk due to an acceptable risk:benefit ratio.

business, can ensure the company's very success. Yet controlling emerging risks presupposes in-depth knowledge about the risk landscape; as it changes continuously, so too does the challenge to manage these risks.

New developments and paradigm shifts must be monitored closely to make adjustments in the focus of future business. Identifying both technological and perception-driven emerging risks at a very early stage cannot be done by a few internal specialists only; it depends on specialists from various fields establishing interdisciplinary teams. Collectively, and thanks to the magnified scope of their observations, these teams are in a position to detect trends or patterns within the issue-specific oscillation of public perception.

Reinsurance applications

The number and magnitude of large losses have increased in recent years, mainly due to the changing technological and industrial environment. Today's risks have shifted from regional to global, from simple to complex and from observable to hidden. Risks develop faster, involve more countries and many lines of business simultaneously, and represent markedly increasing accumulation potential. It is essential that insurers envisage the risk landscape and recognise emerging risks in good time, so that they can react in an appropriate manner. Early detection of risks creates opportunities and reduces the adverse impact any risk might have.

To risk managers, of course, perception is a loaded word; they argue that some people see only what they want to see and that others do not see what they choose not to see. Moreover, unaware of the situation, some do not see what they do not see. But perceiving risks depends on more than just wanting to see risks; in many cases, one has to have the professional or scientific skills to interpret the signals received.

In order to perceive risks, we also have to apply business-relevant information associated with them. Once a risk is perceived it must be decoded, or broken down to have relevance. Finally it must be interpreted: What political or social implications could this risk have? Who stands to be most affected by it? What opportunity might open up to the insurance industry? How can we protect ourselves from new and unpredictable risks?

Local perception of potential threats

To further explore the nature of risk perception, Swiss Re launched a multistage risk perception survey (Delphi study). One key finding was the significant variation in risk perception according to global region, the differences particularly marked among North America, Europe and (East) Asia. The same potential threats may be observed and valued differently in various locations. Sometimes due to diverse cultural and societal backgrounds, certain threats are overlooked altogether, or not perceived as risks *per se* since no one feels threatened by them. Taken elsewhere, the very same threats risks may be subject to an entirely different degree of awareness.

Further, risk perception changes according to knowledge, background and experience, and we can only observe risks we are able to value. To be considered a risk, an issue has to trigger a mental scenario. As everyone has a different perception of emerging or future risks, a catalogue cannot depend on a limited number of persons. Everyone in the insurance industry should participate in the processes of observation and reporting.

Reporting notions associated with risk

Given the importance of systematic risk perception confirmed by the outcome of the Delphi Study, Swiss Re implemented its own risk perception platform, "SONAR" (Systematic Observation of Notions Associated with Risk). The SONAR methodology has been established to systematise the gathering of risk perceptions across the Swiss Re Group with the aim of identifying significant risk trends at an early stage.

SONAR is a risk perception network dedicated to detecting weak signals and tracking their potential impact on the insurance business. Backed by a network of reporting agents in the (re)insurance industry and a central steering unit located within Swiss Re's Risk Engineering Services, SONAR is a gateway to a systematic, interactive risk perception and development platform.

SONAR systematically screens evolving risks and changes in the risk landscape. It serves as a platform for the exchange of observations, thereby helping to forecast Swiss Re's future business. Every member of Swiss Re's staff is encouraged to recognise the risks within their area of work and responsibility, and to actively communicate their related comments and concerns to the central SONAR database. For the new generation of SONAR, a gadget was designed on the Swiss Re intranet portal to web enable input or comments on risks descriptions.

Once received by the SONAR project team, the information on emerging or future risks then runs through an iterative information process. In it, Swiss Re's risk engineering service experts evaluate the information and propose further research or action on selected topics. Finally, risks entered are then displayed to users again on the SONAR gadget in the Swiss Re portal for further comment.

To qualify as an emerging risk, several features have to be fulfilled. Swiss Re defines emerging risks as developing or already known risks or threats that may cause claims with a high loss

Figure 2 SONAR process

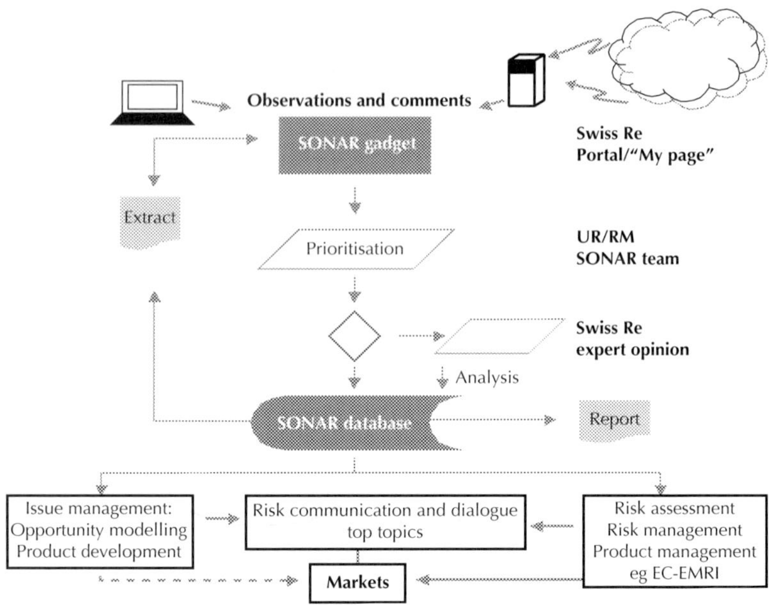

potential to Swiss Re's risk adjusted capital and are thereby deserving of underwriters' attention. In this respect, emerging risks may be the consequence of totally new risks (new technology, for example). On the other hand, emerging risks may result from well-known risks that – due to increased awareness (public perception) or changing conditions – take on a new dimension.

Given this definition, even an "old" problem such as asbestos can appear on Swiss Re's list due to changing conditions and public awareness.

Generally all risk perceptions are filed in the SONAR database. Subsequently, Swiss Re applies filters to select specific topics to sort out issues that might have an impact on insurance. Topics are rated using criteria such as:

- ❑ being new;
- ❑ being an old topic in an new context;
- ❑ a headline article, with a high level of uncertainty;
- ❑ missing sensors, where only inaccurate measures are available;
- ❑ long latency involved;

Figure 3 The losses of tomorrow

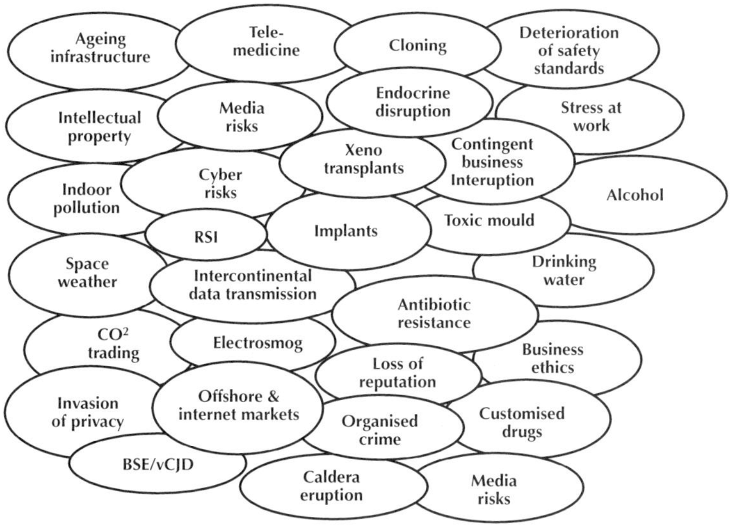

❑ lack of experience, affecting various lines of business in different industries (accumulation potential); and
❑ rare events of the highest degree of severity.

From risk perception to run off

The perception of emerging risks is only the first step in a long information process to follow. To take advantage of its early warning system, SONAR, Swiss Re must ensure that notions that have turned into emerging risks with potentially high impact on the company are addressed by underwriters. Its goals are to provide the insurance technical basics to render risks more predictable, to control Swiss Re's financial exposure and to develop the appropriate products.

To do so, Swiss Re has created an expert circle for emerging risks, called EC-EMRI. The core team of EC-EMRI exists of an interdivisional panel of experts who develop recommendations and guidelines for the underwriting of emerging risks. The panel can also initiate the development of new products. Some of the topics recently handled by the EC-EMRI are genetically modified organisms, electro-magnetic fields, Mad Cow disease (BSE), toxic

Figure 4 From risk perception to run off

mould and "new asbestos". The EC-EMRI reviews all topics annually and defines cornerstones of underwriting for the risks listed in Figure 3 and other risks for renewals.

RISK COMMUNICATION

Controlling emerging risks consists of more than issuing guidelines and defining underwriting measures. Initiating a risk dialogue is also imperative. Swiss Re's executive board views SONAR as a major contribution to its corporate responsibility: "We add value to our clients' business by anticipating societal trends. We provide in-depth analysis on the nature of risk and make this information available to decision makers and to the public."

To control emerging risks requires three interconnected processes:

1. The SONAR process perceives and identifies new risks.
2. The EC-EMRI process translates its findings into new products, prices and conditions.
3. Swiss Re informs the public of its findings.

Top topics

Since communication of "hot issues" should be consistent and reliable, Swiss Re recently launched the "top topics" process, designed to support its efforts in shaping the business environment and to inform relevant decision makers of Swiss Re's news. "Top topics" relate to natural and man-made risk issues. To foster the exchange of topic-related expertise, Swiss Re organises conferences both at its Rüschlikon Centre for Global Dialogue and in the world's major financial centres. Swiss Re relies upon its specialist research teams to develop topic-related knowledge. Equally important, it promotes an approach throughout the company to balance systematic thinking with a flexible knowledge of management culture. Among current topics are the issues of sustainability (water and climate change), terrorism, mortality trends and the convergence and management of the reinsurance cycle.

By way of example, sustainability leverages three domains – society, environment and economy – to create a progressive business model targeted at the key drivers of the 21st century global economy. Swiss Re is committed to building issue-specific awareness among major climate and water stakeholders. In keeping with this effort, Swiss Re currently chairs the UN Environmental Programme Climate Change Working Group.

CONCLUSION

Identifying and controlling emerging risks is a complex process that comprises interdisciplinary teams as well as interdivisional teamwork. The SONAR database enables Swiss Re to identify significant risk trends at an early stage by systematically gathering risk perceptions across the entire Swiss Re Group. Risk recognition is then followed by the Expert Circle of Emerging Risks, which either designs and develops new products or issues underwriting guidelines and recommendations. However, controlling emerging risk amounts to more than merely focussing on underwriting risks. A state-of-the-art risk management process includes other risk categories as well. Control of accumulation potentials and cross-category exposures will become increasingly important in the future. Both the fast-developing technological environment and changes in public risk perception force Swiss Re to supplement a traditional loss-based actuarial approach with scenario modelling techniques. Coping with future risks takes a joint effort dialogue about emerging and future risks, which should be intensified and improved among the industry, insurers, governments and non-government organisations.

Sharing common knowledge about emerging risks and having others participate at the very start of the risk perception process positively affects an insurer's competitive strength. When it comes to translating the findings into business, there will be enough freedom to create competitive solutions that vary from insurance company to insurance company. To spot and capture business opportunities – and to anticipate potential sources for future losses resulting from changes in the risk landscape – are important elements of a long-term strategy of assuring sustainable benefits for all stakeholders.

1 The author would like to acknowledge and thank Annabelle Hett and Marcel Bürge for their contribution to the chapter.

2 For further information on Moores' Law, see http://www.intel.com.

3 For more information, see the Swiss Re publication, "Genetic Engineeering and Liability Insurance – The Power of Public Perception" (1998).

4 Alan Kay, Palo Alto Research. See http://www.research.apple.com.

9

Dynamic Financial Analysis – The Answer to Rational Reinsurance Purchase?

David Simmons

Benfield Group Ltd

INTRODUCTION

As a mathematician working in insurance in the early 1980s, it seemed natural to move towards reinsurance, as surely the greater the risk, the more the money involved and therefore the greater the demand for mathematical analysis of risk? Well no, at least not in the London market of 1985. Reinsurance was more a matter of relationships, a subscription market demanded shared knowledge and good underwriters were born not made. But even so, how could the efficiency of reinsurance be assessed? How much should reinsurance cost, and stepping back, how much should be bought?

Dynamic financial analysis models (DFAs) now seem to hold the answers to many of these questions. Indeed their scope goes rather beyond the issue of simple reinsurance purchase, properly putting reinsurance into the core of capital and result management. This chapter seeks to look at the growth of DFA modelling, how it is being used, how it *should* be used and, as importantly, how it could be misused.

TRADITIONAL REINSURANCE-RATING METHODOLOGIES

A number of rating methodologies were used in the market back in 1985, all flawed to varying degrees. For example, burning cost methods (comparing current reinsurance programmes against historical loss information) normally relied on very few years' data. Top layers

Figure 1 Lloyds first loss rating scale

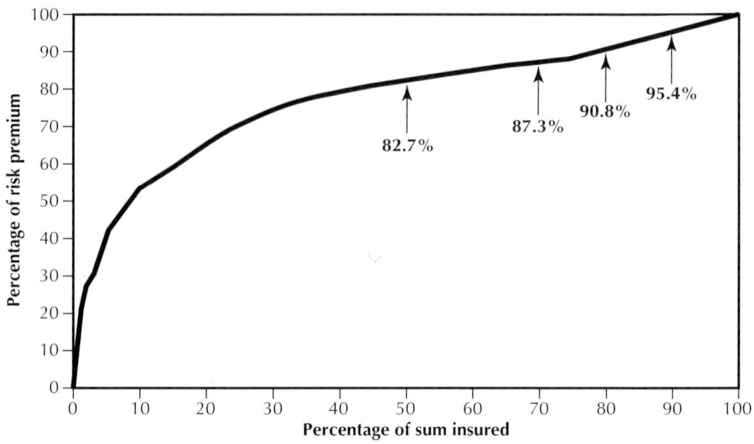

in the programme often were loss-free in the period and large losses were often ignored on grounds that "business is not written any more" (strangely no parallel allowance was ever made for losses emerging from new written business). Exposure rating methods, distributing risk premium based upon rating curves, were similarly flawed. Rating curves were in theory derived from heavy statistical analyses of claim and exposure data from similar homogeneous businesses. In practice, "standard" curves were circulated in the market and were used in an arbitrary way, the choice of which curve to use being a subjective process. Often the same curve was used for many different types of business despite clearly different loss behaviour. The method made no explicit allowance for reinstatement conditions or the assessed probable maximum loss (PML) of a risk and/or the safety of that PML estimate. A further issue was, like the burning cost method, an arbitrary expense load must be applied to allow for brokerage, reinsurer expenses and, perhaps, profit. Typically a flat expense load of 100/70 (ie, an additional load of 43%) was applied to the premium across the whole programme, which did not allow for the greater capital cost of larger upper layers. Some curves, such as the "Lloyds curve" tried to get around this by having a kink in the tail of the rating curve, a mathematical nonsense which gave rise to some very unusual results. Figure 1 shows the Lloyds curve. The curve reflects the fact that most claims will be small claims, therefore the price of, say, a layer of 50% in excess of 50% of the sum insured will not be 50% of the risk premium, but rather 17.3% (the first 50% of sum insured is shown by the curve to require 82.7% of the risk premium).

But the Lloyds curve breaks down when we compare the cost of a 10% xs 70% layer to a 10% xs 80% layer. The cost of the 10% xs 70% layer can be determined from the curve above, ie, the total risk premium allocation for the first 80% of the sum insured minus the allocation for the first 70%, ie, 90.8% minus 87.3%, giving 3.5% of the risk premium. But the cost of the 10% xs 80% layer is 95.4% minus 90.8%, 4.8% of the risk premium – clearly an absurdity as to have a loss to the second layer there must be a loss to the first.

Of course, in practice, smarter underwriters used the tools available intelligently and developed methodologies to fill in the gaps, eg, using regression methods to price layers across a programme consistently where there is no recent loss experience, or fitting a power curve to burning cost-rated layers and perhaps a top layer priced by minimum rate on line considerations. Similar methods were used to compare the costs of layers for different cedents, using adjustment factors to compare different companies, eg, premium, peak zone aggregates, reference loss amounts (eg, 90A), etc.

So, arguably, it was possible to assess whether a layer was cheap. However, was it right for the customer?

HOW MUCH REINSURANCE SHOULD BE BOUGHT?

In 1985, decisions on how much reinsurance to buy and how much to retain were often made upon comparative measures. How much do competing companies buy and retain compared to premium income and capital? Arguably this is a very rational reinsurance strategy for the reinsurance manager. There used to be a cliché in the IT industry "nobody got sacked for buying IBM". The major sin is less to suffer a loss, but more to suffer a bigger loss proportionally than your peers. To step outside of the market hegemony can be lonely in the glare of 20/20 hindsight.

Efficiency of reinsurance was measured by how it reacted to a few loss scenarios, with little formal assessment of the relative probability of these scenarios. This was the only way to compare, say, a proportional programme to a risk excess of loss (XoL) one.

There had to be a better way.

STOCHASTIC RISK MODELLING

In the late 1980s, following the financial markets, the application of risk theory to reinsurance began to gain ground. However, initial take up of these ideas was slow. There were comparatively few actuaries and mathematicians in the general insurance business, but also the practical application of these methods required considerable computing power, beyond that available on the desktop at the time. The methods relied upon describing the variables of insurance risk not by a single "best guess value" but by a probability distribution representing all possible outcomes. The choice of the appropriate statistical distribution to use is not trivial. Insurance risks are rarely well described by a normal distribution (as often used in the financial markets); they are normally highly skewed. The risks are also often correlated. It can be difficult or impossible to represent the final joint distribution by a formula; we have to use other methods – Monte Carlo simulation.

Monte Carlo methods were developed during the Manhattan Project atomic weapons programme in the 1940s. They rely on chance, just as gamblers do in the casinos of Monte Carlo. Any successful gambler must understand the game he is playing and understand its consequences. The rules of the game may not be obvious. In perhaps less salubrious casinos than the Café de Paris, a wheel may be biased. It is necessary to observe historical patterns and draw inferences about the underlying risk behaviour, deriving non-standard distributions where necessary. The strength of the method is that if we understand and can describe the probability of all possible outcomes for a number of variables, and can describe their inter-relation, we can then estimate not only the average overall result but also the probability of extremes. This can be done without resorting to complex mathematics. Indeed we can solve many problems that could otherwise be unsolvable by number crunching methods.

Stochastic method example – catastrophe XoL

For example, to model catastrophe (cat) XoL business we need to understand how likely a particular event is (frequency) and, if it happens, how much damage it will do (severity). For frequency, we need to understand the pattern of losses, for example the probability of suffering no losses in any year, the probability of one loss, two

Figure 2 Example of peril model data imported into a DFA

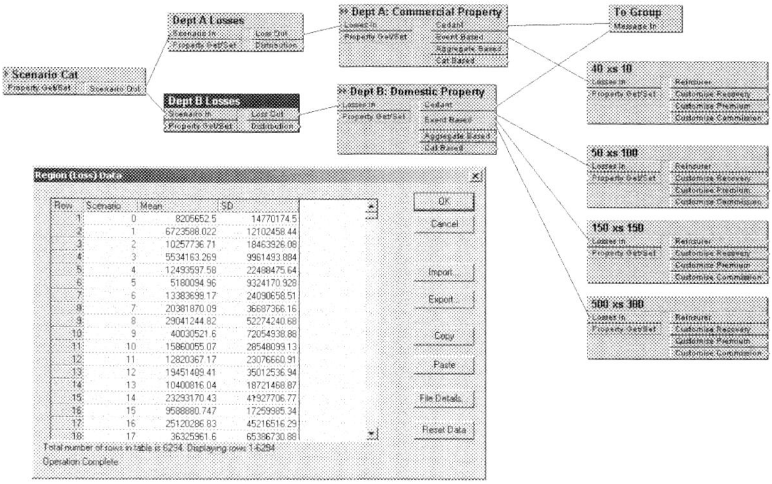

losses, etc. For severity, for example, there may be a 50% chance that an event loss is greater than US$100 million but only a 10% chance that it is greater than US$500 million. If the treaties cover more than one territory, then distributions are required for each, together with rules describing their correlation and dependencies. An example application is shown in Figure 2 – an event set (scenario cat) driving losses from two departments. In this case, each department has its own reinsurance programme, though the losses could be recombined and reinsurance assessed on the joint loss.

With this information, we can run, say, 50,000 simulated years of losses. We can then calculate associated reinsurance recoveries and reinstatement premiums. We can estimate not only the average recovery, but also how the contract behaves in the extreme; it is possible to estimate the worst result that can be expected every 100 years and see how reinsurance reduces that loss. By extension, similar methods can be used to estimate the impact of reinsurance on required capital and the cost of this surrogate capital priced. Clearly, the process is very dependent upon the assumptions made. In the current market, for natural catastrophes third party peril models are often used to derive probabilities, loss amounts and correlations. We will return to this issue later.

Development of dynamic financial analysis

The rapid improvement in personal computer speed and capacity, and the growing availability of software tools, brought the ability to do this type of stochastic analysis to the desktop by the early 1990s. This coincided with a series of market losses that saw the demand for more rigorous analysis of risk grow. Mathematical modelling was set to become core to the management of insurers and reinsurers.

Initially, this analysis was mostly focused upon individual programmes and lines of business, reflecting the way reinsurance was purchased and lines of responsibility within insurance groups. However, increasingly, the need evolved to view reinsurance purchase not just in terms of the department but also the company and the overall group. Insurance risk itself had to be viewed in the context of other risks run by the company, particularly asset risk and counterparty risk (eg, reinsurer failure). This whole company, or holistic, risk modelling is often called dynamic financial analysis (DFA). The term DFA is now loosely applied to any stochastic financial risk modelling.

DFA modelling used to be the preserve of consulting actuaries, but growth in availability of software tools such as @Risk and Crystal Ball (both add-ins for Microsoft Excel), brought the modelling to the desktop of a broader range of insurance professionals. As with peril modelling before, leading reinsurance brokers particularly embraced and developed the technology as a means to add value (and to demonstrate added value) to their customers. The driver for their investment was initially to offer a means to rationalise reinsurance purchase, but increasingly its scope became broader as its potential value in broader business and capital management became apparent.

DFA's current market position

At the end of 2002, there can be few major insurance groups who do not have a DFA model, or who are at least working on producing such a model. Even smaller operations are seeing the value and using stochastic analysis, perhaps with the assistance of reinsurance brokers and/or consulting actuaries. Advanced customisable DFA modelling tools, such as Benfield Group's ReMetrica II, allow for the rapid development of robust, fast, transparent models and allow the results to be presented in a way that is accessible to the non-actuary.

The reinsurance industry is very fashion led – is DFA just the latest passing trend? The answer must be emphatically no. Development and use of a DFA model goes hand in hand with an integrated risk management strategy. For example, insurance regulators are moving towards a risk-based capital regime. In the UK and elsewhere, regulators have indicated that they may allow the results of an admitted in-house DFA to override their standard ratio-based capital assessment and so reduce regulatory capital load. Similarly, rating agencies, arguably the real regulators of the capital levels of the (re)insurance industry, have also said that they are open to persuasion by an audited DFA model, rather than rely on their own, necessarily rather more simplistic, capital models.

DFA models, if properly applied, bring a transparency about the assumptions being used within the business and their consequences. Once introduced (and properly applied) it seems unlikely that management will be happy for DFAs to go away. But there are risks: DFAs do not take away the need for good management; there is always the need to combine qualitative judgements with the quantitative DFA output. DFA models are an aid to decision making not the decision maker.

MEASURING THE VALUE OF REINSURANCE WITH A DFA

Focus on objectives

A DFA project cannot succeed unless it has clear objectives and unambiguous support throughout the organisation. The introduction of DFA within an organisation may not be universally welcomed by all. Some will feel threatened by a process they do not understand. Others will feel it is yet another head office imposition on their business. Many will not welcome a focus on their business assumptions and motivations. The only way to counter this is to make the aims of the process clear, emphasising the benefits to each user department.

For modelling purposes, measurable objectives are required. Motivational objectives such as "Be the most profitable and innovative insurer in our market" or "Have a low cost, efficient reinsurance structure with best security" must be translated into

Figure 3 Risk vs reward over a three-year period

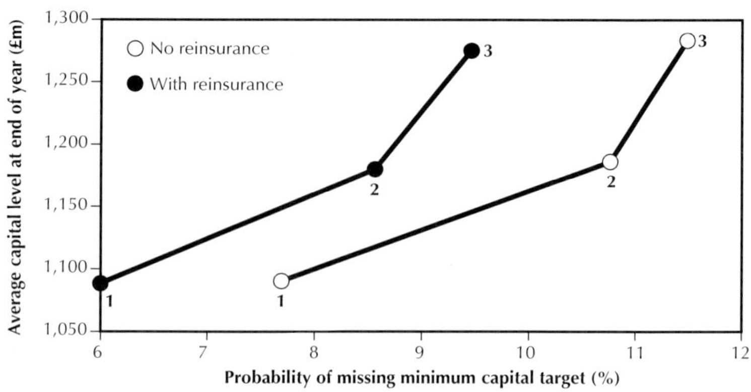

equivalent financial targets against which success or failure may be judged.

Risk vs reward

Broadly, company objectives fall into main two categories:

1. Make as much money as possible.
2. Stay in business (or on a more personal level, stay in a job or meet targets).

Objectives such as "have a market share of at least 10%" are subsidiary to these. Reinsurance decision-making must be made in this context.

But these two types of objective are mutually contradictory. To make the most money you need to take risks. To avoid risk costs money. Reinsurance is one of the major ways that an insurer can reduce his risks. But is the cost (and reinsurance should be a cost over time, although recent market experience may contradict that) worth the benefit?

One way to view this dynamic is through a risk–reward chart, as illustrated in Figure 3, which focuses on the capital level of a company over a three-year period. The graph compares the average growth in capital before and after reinsurance on the vertical axis with the probability that the capital in the company will fall below a certain threshold level on the horizontal access. The minimum capital level may perhaps be driven by regulatory capital requirements or the capital required to support a given Standard and Poor's rating.

The line with white circles, shows the position without reinsurance. On average over the three-year period capital grows strongly in this organisation, but the risk of capital dropping below the critical level is high and growing by the year. After reinsurance, (illustrated by the line with black circles), the average growth in capital is slightly lower, but not by much, this reinsurance looks very reasonably priced. But does it work to reduce the risk? Yes it does, but probably not by as much as the company would wish. This looks like a cheap reinsurance but, on its own, not the right one.

The DFA can be used to demonstrate the dynamics of the deal to reinsurers. In recent years this has led to deals being placed that were previously thought to be unplaceable. A good example is "Project Coffee", the reinsurance of the central fund of Lloyds of London. Before a financial model was built, the probability of the fund's failure was a matter of wild conjecture. After the model's completion, the argument focussed upon the model's assumptions. Once all agreed that the assumptions were robust, the consequences of the assumptions could be modelled and a deal structured that met the risk appetite of the cedent and re-insurers.

With fewer top-grade security reinsurers, cedents are keen to establish firm relationships with chosen reinsurance partners. Such relationships are best built upon transparency and trust. DFA models offer the opportunity to design structures based around common assumptions that work for both parties.

Efficient frontier theory

In the more generalised example (Figure 4), 13 different business strategies and/or reinsurance solutions have been tested against the chosen risk and reward measures. Each can be radically different; some may be proportional covers, some excess of loss; some could be based upon departments buying their own reinsurances, others by centralised group purchase; some could be traditional single-year deals, others non-traditional solutions. The DFA model can and should be able to compare any risk mitigation (or business) strategy.

Figure 4 Balancing risk to reward – identifying optimal strategies

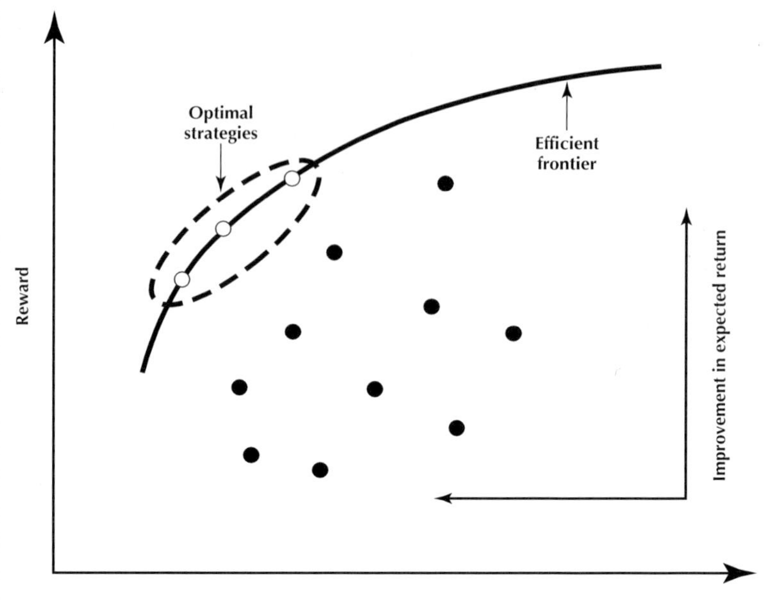

The ideal is to operate at the top left of the chart, giving maximum return for minimum risk. Unfortunately this cannot be achieved in the real world. But we can say that three options are measurably better than the other 10. For each less-optimal strategy there is at least one more optimal one that offers less risk and better return against these risk measures. Figure 4 shows the efficient frontier – the best deal available in the market for any given level of risk transfer. Clearly the role of the reinsurance buyer and his broker is to get that best deal. The role of the senior management is to determine the risk appetite level appropriate for their company.

In practice of course, things are not as black and white. A number of risk measures may be required; what is optimal to one may not be optimal to another. Also it must also be remembered that a number of important considerations cannot be modelled. For example, one of the dots representing a less-optimal strategy could be the current reinsurance structure with existing reinsurers, with whom a relationship has been built up over many years. One of the 'optimal' dots could represent an offer from a new start-up company to write that programme in full. A decision may be made to stay with the current programme and market, but the DFA model will clearly highlight the cost of that decision.

Clearly the optimal solution is dependent upon the assumptions underpinning the model. As we discuss later, it is vital that sensitivity to assumptions is assessed and the robustness of a given strategy tested. What may be optimal based upon one assumption set may not be under another.

Risk/reward measures

A number of performance indicators may be used by the company. They may include one or more of the following:

- ❑ Underwriting profit.
- ❑ Capital growth/level.
- ❑ Return on capital.
- ❑ Loss ratio.
- ❑ Combined ratio.

Typically the company will want to make the most money possible on average (the return measure) whilst staying in business (the risk measure).

Thus, the return measure would be to maximise the expected value (ie, average) of one or more of the performance measures (or minimise for loss or combined ratio).

The risk measure would normally be a measure of the variability of one or more of these performance measures. That variability may be expressed statistically as a standard deviation, but more commonly would be expressed in terms of a meaningful target, such as a particular percentile value (eg, if capital was the chosen risk measure, the lowest level that capital could be expected to fall every 100 years, often called the "1 in 100 value" or the probability of failing to meet a particular target.

Typical risk measures could be:

- ❑ 1 in 250 underwriting result;
- ❑ 1 in 100 retained capital;
- ❑ 1 in 10 loss ratio;
- ❑ 1 in 5 combined ratio;

- risk of failure to protect certain level of capital;
- risk of failure to meet management/parental targets; or
- risk of failure to maintain agreed level of result smoothing over a five-year period.

It is very possible for a company to use two risk measures; perhaps one relating to capital protection, the other the result smoothing. It is unlikely that the ideal reinsurance solution for one, is the same as for the other, again the trade off between these measures can be modelled and a management view taken.

Care needs be taken when using terms such as 1 in 100. Do we mean the predicted minimum 1 in 100 loss or the expected value of a loss that we may see every 100 years? For example, the model may predict that every 100 years we will see an aggregate loss of US$1.2 billion, but perhaps it would be more interesting to know the average total annual losses we could expect every 100 years, likely to be a significantly higher number (eg, US$2 billion). This difference, between a percentile point and an expected value is often overlooked and misunderstood.

Issues in practical DFA modelling

Assumption dependency/sensitivity

All DFA models, indeed all models, are heavily assumption-dependent. A small change in the assumption of average large loss frequency, for example, can radically change the assessed cost/benefit of a particular reinsurance strategy. Similarly the choice of a peril model from one supplier to another can change the view of the efficiency of a catastrophe reinsurance purchase. So does this undermine DFA modelling? No, but it does demonstrate that these models need to be used intelligently as decision aids, not the decision maker. Understanding the dynamics of the business, including the sensitivity of the business to such issues as claims behaviour, inflation growth, investment performance and climate change is a prerequisite for proper business management. DFA models, provide the mechanism to test a company's sensitivities to these assumptions and so ensure that appropriate risk mitigation strategies are in place. At a minimum, the assumptions upon which a risk mitigation strategy, or indeed overall business strategy, are open to view and comment in advance – providing transparency through an organisation and giving comfort to regulators and stakeholders.

Lack of data

Lack of data, or lack of data of appropriate quality is often given as a reason why a DFA project should be delayed. This is clearly wrong. Indeed if data is lacking the need for a DFA model increases. Data is used to develop or validate assumptions about the future. If no data is there, assumptions are still being made, implicitly or explicitly. If these assumptions are not supported by actuarial study, then there is all the more reason to expose them to the light and test how sensitive the business is to these assumptions. It may well be found that different business areas are making contradictory assumptions about key drivers of the business.

The tragedy of September 11, 2001 showed us again that no amount of historical analysis can predict what the future will bring. Indeed, relying purely on numbers derived from historical data is a major and possibly extremely dangerous assumption and a sign of poor management. The management of a company must own and accept the assumptions being made; they should not abrogate this responsibility to others, however well qualified. Data analysis should be used to guide and challenge assumptions made, not dictate them.

A current example is terrorism. A number of agencies are attempting to build a model of terrorism risk. Clearly it is impossible to do this with any degree of confidence. In reality it is anybody's guess which terror groups will arise, what their strategy will be, which targets they will aim at, what their success rate will be and the ability of the authorities to meet and reduce the threat. But if writing terrorism cover, some idea of the likely frequency and severity of loss is required. The only real solution is to use transparent assumptions based on the best estimates of leading experts, not to rely on a complicated model based on numerous spurious assumptions and dependencies, no matter how clever the mathematics. The DFA model can then test how sensitive the strategy is to these assumptions and how the structure modelled reacts to a number of best estimates and worst-case estimates.

Figure 5's questionnaire would be completed by front-line staff, normally the underwriter/manager responsible for the account

Figure 5 A sample Benfield Group loss behaviour questionnaire

ReMetrica II DFA
Loss behaviour capture

BENFIELD GROUP

Class: .... Completed by: ....
Year: .... Date: ....

Overall objective is to capture a view of expected loss levels together with anticipated volatility – what could go wrong (or right) and how likely this is.

Planned premium: [ ] → **Planned loss ratio:** [ ]

Attritional loss ratio [ ]

Losses below the chosen large loss threshold and excluding specified cat events/scenarios

VARIABILITY
9 years out of 10 attritional loss ratio expected to be between:

[ ] and [ ]

99 years out of 100 would expect attritional loss ratio to be between:

[ ] and [ ]

NOTE ALL LOSS RATIO ESTIMATES SHOULD REFLECT EXPECTED ULTIMATE COST.

ANY ISSUES OVER UNDER OR OVER RESERVING OF PRIOR YEARS WILL BE CONSIDERED SEPARATELY.

Large loss ratio [ ]

Non-'cat' large losses – over a size threshold of:

[ ]

FREQUENCY
How many 'large' losses are expected on average (need not be a whole number):

[ ]

Note, the above forecast should be based on the forecast exposure for the year concerned

SEVERITY
What is the estimated average size of a 'large' loss:

[ ]

If you had a list of 10 large losses the largest is likely to be at least: [ ]

And if a list of 50 large losses: [ ]

And if a list of 100 large losses: [ ]

And if a list of 500 large losses: [ ]

Maximum possible large loss size: [ ]

Cat loss ratio [ ]

Losses from events impacting on multiple risks including scenarios which may impact other classes of business within the group

Please estimate proportion (total 100%) of above ratio for each of the following scenarios:

1. Scenario 1
Proportion % [ ] PML [ ]
2. Scenario 2
Proportion % [ ] PML [ ]
3. Scenario 3
Proportion % [ ] PML [ ]
4. Scenario 4
Proportion % [ ] PML [ ]
5. Scenario 5
Proportion % [ ] PML [ ]
6. Scenario 6
Proportion %PML [ ] [ ]
7. Other – unspecified
Proportion % [ ] PML [ ]

and for the submission of the business plan for that account. This does mean that the model will use assumptions consistent with the company's internal planning assumptions (or perhaps challenge these assumptions).

The answers will then be used as a basis for defining probability distributions and establishing key risk aggregation dynamics. They can also be checked against historical company or market data, to test for veracity and robustness.

Peril model linkages

Peril models have proved to be an increasingly important tool in the underwriting process of insurers and reinsurers. They contain much cutting edge science and understanding of the risk of event occurrence and its impact upon an insurance portfolio. But, they also include a lot of assumptions and expert opinion. Peril model licence agreements often include clauses prohibiting direct comparison with other models. In territories without regulatory influence (which can constrain the amount of variability between models), there can be significant differences between the estimates of one model to another.

Modellers, to their credit, are becoming increasingly willing to discuss the assumptions used within their models. But there is still a distressing tendency amongst the (re)insurance community to accept peril model results as gospel. Clearly they are not and cannot be. The "never sacked for buying IBM" principle perhaps applies again, but it would be hoped that insurers and reinsurers would use peril model data rather more intelligently. A DFA provides the means to do this.

Rather than just import an exceedance curve as a given, the DFA models should allow the user to import the entire event set of the peril model. The event set is typically made up of many thousands of observed and hypothetical scenarios, each with a given probability of occurrence and estimate of damage to the modelled portfolio. The damage estimate is usually subject to "secondary uncertainty", reflecting that there is uncertainty about the size of loss if an event occurs.

If this information is imported into a DFA the user may see how sensitive the peril model is to:

- Assumptions about loss frequency – for example most peril models do not allow for trends, annual variability and seasonality. But we know that in El Niño years, hurricane numbers are likely to be lower than in La Niña years (see http://www.tropicalstormrisk.com). A DFA model can allow the user to test how sensitive the peril model is to changes in frequency assumption and perhaps modify the assumptions for any given year based upon a forecast by leading research groups, TropicalStormRisk at the Benfield Greig Hazard Research Centre or Bill Gray's team at Colorado State University for example.
- Assumptions about loss severity – modellers have very different views about handling issues such as business interruption and the correct level of secondary uncertainty to apply. Small changes in these assumptions can make near order of magnitude differences at the extremes of a probability distribution.
- Assumptions about event correlation – it is clear that windstorm events are not independent although most models assume that they are. For example, European storms tend to cluster, driven by prevailing climatic conditions (eg, the North Atlantic Oscillations). As discussed, tropical cyclones are largely driven by El Niño/La Niña conditions.

It is also important to model at this level of detail in order to properly understand event clashes over portfolios and territories. Most peril models now work on a regional basis, so can give loss estimates for any number of different territories and portfolios for a given modelled loss event. It is important to preserve this detail when importing the information into a DFA model. Unfortunately many DFA's are not sufficiently sophisticated to do this. Often they rely upon the peril model's overall loss exceedance curve output for each territory and make assumptions about how the exceedance curve information by territory may be split between frequency and severity. Separate broad assumptions are then made about how event and seasonal correlation may be handled. All this is unnecessary if the right information is captured initially, ie, event frequency and severity for each scenario in the event set.

Holistic vs distributed

When looking at the efficiency of a particular reinsurance structure, very different results can be derived when looking at its impact on a department or company as a whole. As an example, the author knows of an instance where an insurer wished to look at the efficiency of their catastrophe reinsurance purchase in one geographic area. This particular company used a variant of the 1 in 100 rule to determine their required capitalisation. When the catastrophe reinsurance was looked at in the light of how it reduced the 1 in 100 catastrophe loss for that territory, it was, as expected, spectacularly successful, reducing the worst case by more than US$200 million. But, when assessed in terms of its impact upon that territory's overall 1 in 100 result for all lines of insurance business, the difference was rather lower, around US$100 million. Clearly catastrophe reinsurance was one of the main influences on very bad years' results, but not the only one. The value of the reinsurance was looking less clear-cut. When looked at in the context of the underwriting result for the overall group over all territories and all lines of business, the catastrophe cover on that one territory looked marginal in the extreme. The reduction in 1 in 100 result barely covered the cost of the cover. If asset variability was then added into the mix, the picture became even worse.

So what is the rational reinsurance purchase? On a group level, clearly there was little or no value in buying the reinsurance, if reduction in the worst case 1 in 100 result was the aim. But at a local operation level the cover clearly has value. Perhaps the cover may reduce the internal capital allocation to that operation and so increase the chance of the underwriter meeting his return on capital targets. Also the cover certainly provides the underwriter with the comfort that he/she cannot post a significant loss to the group. Group management may say that removing local reinsurance will have no difference on how large local losses are perceived. However, many examples in history attest to the fact that such pronouncements are often forgotten post-loss.

So is the main reason to buy local covers just behavioural? Would the removal of external reinsurance make the underwriter more risk adverse, to the overall detriment of the group? There are ways to replace the prop of external reinsurance, for example through a system of internal reinsurance arrangements where the group centre, perhaps via an offshore captive, provides reinsurance of local operations. But if a local underwriter posts a loss covered by the internal arrangement, the balance sheet may be protected, but everybody will know who caused a loss to the group and so his/her reputation and/or bonus will suffer. Also, perhaps more cynically, no amount of internal cover can replace the lure of invitation to reinsurers' and reinsurance brokers' golf days.

Again the "never sacked for buying IBM" principle applies. If there is a large market loss, this is accepted, it is in the nature of insurance. But if your company, with 10% of the market, suffers a net loss greater than your rival with 50% of the market, then your company looks poorly managed and questions will be asked. Rational reinsurance purchase necessarily goes beyond what is modelled to be rational to the customer; it also must be driven by what is seen to be rational by investors, analysts and regulators.

Arguably, the answer is the education of investors, analysts and regulators into the realities of the insurance business. DFA will help this process, but in the medium term the dangers of stepping out from the pack to follow what the model says is right will be a brave act. Also management will need to convince staff that they understand the realities of the insurance business. Large losses are a random process; it can take years to determine if a run of bad losses are bad luck or bad underwriting. If underwriters and local managers are to be judged on their gross results then a bad result must be viewed intelligently. An example of potentially poor management practice would be the decision of one group to judge their local operations on their results after facultative covers but before treaty. The result: massive amounts of facultative covers are bought, to the detriment of the group result as a whole.

Almost invariably a central group cover will, dollar for dollar, show more modelled benefit to the group than local purchases. If this is so, the human part of the equation has to be managed. How can local management be convinced that the new structure is fair to them and that they (and their bonuses and ultimately career) will not be subject to the vagaries of chance? DFA can help with the former, developing transparent cost sharing algorithms, but the latter is a challenge of management.

Asset/liability dynamics

To an actuary, a dynamic financial analysis model necessarily includes all aspects of the company's business assets as well as liabilities. But with the gloriously inexact terminology of insurance,

DFA is now taken to mean any financial model relying on probability. As discussed earlier, asset variability can dominate underwriting variability for an insurance operation. Indeed, insurance companies have been described as investment trusts with an expensive underwriting hobby. Now with lower investment returns and significantly lower asset values, the focus on the asset side of the balance sheet is even more pronounced.

Modelling asset returns and values is certainly outside of the scope of this book, but clearly, as the earlier example demonstrated, asset variability can have a profound affect upon the perceived value of reinsurance purchased.

In practice, few insurers take asset variability into account when deciding upon the level of reinsurance purchase. Given the current fashion to not stand outside the pack, this is perhaps understandable. But increasingly, as model sophistication and investor education about insurance grows, it seems inevitable that reinsurance will be judged within the context of all risks that the company faces. Current regulatory change, in the UK and elsewhere, confirms this trend. UK regulators have suggested that capital might be allocated at around a 1 in 200 level for insurance risk, market risk, credit risk, group risk, operational risk and liquidity risk. In practice the regulatory capital requirement will be dictated by the clash of these six heads of risk. A DFA will not only need to determine, say, the probability of a major Tokyo earthquake, but also its impact on the local and international stock markets. Clearly this is a matter of conjecture; as the old joke goes if 10 economists are asked a question, you will get 20 answers. The company will also need to estimate what proportion of their reinsurers will be likely to fail following this extreme market event. A well constructed DFA model will be able to test how a company would react given a major loss based upon a certain assumption set. It does not supply the answer but gives guidance about the robustness of differing strategies to these assumptions.

CAPITAL

Assessing capital requirement

A separate book could easily be written about how capital adequacy for an insurer should be assessed and how capital should be allocated between different business lines. However, more often than not, capital requirement is assessed in terms of guaranteeing a certain minimum level of capital over a certain return period. DFA models are the ideal tools to undertake this process. As regulators (and de facto regulators such as rating agencies) move to risk-based capital systems, and begin to admit the results of internal DFA models, the motivation to build and use DFAs will grow. Having a fully functioning DFA model will also give comfort that the business is well managed and risks properly identified.

More fundamentally, reinsurance can only be properly judged in the context of its value as a capital surrogate. A good reinsurance is not necessarily the cheapest reinsurance. Even in the hardest markets, a half decent reinsurance broker can find a cheap deal, but is it a deal that gets the insurer closer to its aspirations?

Renaissance Re has made great play about its approach to business. Acceptance criteria are based not only upon expected profitability but also the likely affect on group capital and return on capital. Renaissance Re's story has been upheld by its excellent results, now everybody wants to be the same.

This is easier to say than do. The main issue is correlation. How likely is this book/treaty likely to go bad with the rest of my portfolio? For predominately natural peril writers this is arguably not an issue. Peril models will explicitly model these correlations (subject to earlier caveats about peril models and linkages to DFA models). But for other classes it is a major problem – there will almost certainly be insufficient data to properly assess the degree or nature of correlation. Frequently reinsurers use a rating methodology that bases reinsurance premium upon modelled expected (or average) recoveries to the contract, a capacity charge factor and, often, an expense load.

The key issue here is the capacity charge. Usually a load factor is applied to the standard deviation of the recovery amount, typically 40% for catastrophe business. This load factor, known as the "reluctance factor" or "variability load", should be determined by the reinsurer's cost of capital, their risk appetite and the correlation of the presented risk to the rest of the book. A stochastic model is normally required to perform this analysis.

Leaving aside arguments about whether standard deviation is an appropriate measure given the asymmetric nature of insurance risk, arguably this methodology is being simplistically applied by many reinsurers seeking a "technical" rating method using DFA theory. The 35–40% load customarily used in the current castrophe market assumes near perfect correlation of the presented risk with the rest of the business and/or an extraordinary high degree of risk reluctance by the reinsurers. So is this another example of "technical" theory wrongly applied? Probably yes, but at least it does show an industry willing to embrace DFA modelling and its possibilities. The challenge, as always, is to use this knowledge intelligently, not just unquestionably following the herd.

Allocating capital

Again, this is a subject broad enough for a separate book. There are many capital allocation methodologies in the market and the actuarial literature. The key is to have a methodology that is not only mathematically coherent (ie, it adds up and makes sense) but also that is understandable and acceptable to non-actuaries.

Capital allocation is perhaps best illustrated by looking at a theoretical company with three risk portfolios A, B and C (representing different classes of business of different subsidiaries – each having similar loss distribution characteristics). A is highly correlated with B (perhaps both cat exposed property accounts) but C is largely uncorrelated (say, a liability account).

Assume a decision is taken to set the overall capital for the company equal to the expected loss every 100 years, ie, the 1 in 100 expected exceedance.

Tables 1–4 show four capital allocation methods for the theoretical company. The company as a whole is assessed as having a capital requirement of US$148.67 million, but how much capital should be attributed to each business unit to reflect the risk each brings to the overall company? Four methods are considered:

1. "first in" or independent;
2. "last in" or marginal;
3. Shapley; and
4. Aumann–Shapley.

The simplest methods, "first in" and "last in", are readily understandable but fail the coherence test. The alternative methods, Shapley and Aumann–Shapley pass the coherence test, but arguably only Aumann–Shapley is readily understandable.

Table 1 Independent allocation method ("first in")

	Independent	Implied allocation (%)	Implied capital
A	67.64	33.46	49.74
B	67.54	33.41	49.68
C	66.96	33.12	49.25
sum	202.14	100.00	148.67

Table 2 Marginal method ("last in")

	Portfolio ex class	Class contribution	Implied allocation (%)	Implied capital
A	92.41	56.25	44.61	66.32
B	92.83	55.84	44.27	65.83
C	134.66	14.01	11.11	16.52
sum		126.10	100.00	148.67

Table 3 Shapley method (average of first in, second in and last in)

	"First in"	Average "second in"	"Last in"	Average	Implied allocation (%)	Implied capital
A	67.64	46.49	56.25	56.79	38.20	56.79
B	67.54	46.24	55.84	56.54	38.03	56.54
C	66.96	25.03	14.01	35.33	23.76	35.33
sum				148.67	100.00	148.67

Table 4 Aumann–Shapley method (contribution to loss scenarios beyond 1 in 100)

	Class contribution	Implied allocation (%)	Implied capital
A	62.58	42.09	62.58
B	62.27	41.88	62.27
C	23.81	16.01	23.81
sum	148.67	100.00	148.67

Total capital required (expected value beyond 1 in 100) 148.67

The independent or "first in" method allocates capital pro–rata to the assessed stand-alone capital for each portfolio and gives each portfolio broadly the same capital requirement. The sum of the stand-alone capital amounts is greater then that of the company together due to basic portfolio theory. If A, B and C are not perfectly correlated, then the 1 in 100 year for portfolio A may be a good year for portfolio C, say. This method gives no reward to a portfolio that is uncorrelated with the rest of the group.

The "last in" or marginal capital method calculates how much additional capital requirement a portfolio would add if added to the existing company. For example, if portfolio C were added to a company comprising of portfolios A and B, it would require and extra US$14.01 million of capital. The total capital is then split pro-rata to these marginal capital amounts. This method over-rewards lack of correlation.

The Shapely method looks not just at the amount of capital required if "first in" or "last in", but also second in, third in etc. The resulting calculation is coherent, the method understandable (if not obvious why it should be valid), but calculation can involve thousands of possible ordering permutations and becomes practically impossible when allocating capital over many portfolios.

A possible compromise candidate is the Aumann–Shapley method, which is coherent and understandable. Here all simulations that cause a failure of capital are identified, and the contribution of each portfolio towards this failure calculated and summed. Thus we can see the degree that portfolios contribute towards events that cause the company strain and so can allocate capital proportionately.

Clearly reinsurance could affect the required capital at both the whole company and department level, allowing proper determination of the value of that reinsurance locally and at group level.

Whatever method is chosen, a DFA model can provide transparency about capital allocations, to satisfy both local management concerns about equity, and local regulator concerns about financial stability.

CONCLUSION

Dynamic financial analysis is here to stay. Every (re)insurer of any size around the world has either implemented a DFA, or more likely, is talking about implementing a DFA. Very often rationalisation of reinsurance purchase is the prime driver. However, the increasing focus upon capital by regulators and rating agencies, and the focus upon return on capital by investors and analysts, is driving a new, more structured way to look at reinsurance value and cost benefit. But a DFA model does not determine the optimal reinsurance structure; it is certainly no substitute for human judgement.

It is the role of management to determine the objectives of the company and to design and implement a strategy to deliver these objectives. A DFA model will help judge which strategy best meets the balance between required reward and unwanted risk. The optimal strategy will depend heavily upon the assumptions used in the model, which in themselves should reflect the assumptions currently being made in the business.

It is vital that management fully understand the assumptions being made in their business and their possible effects. This is not a responsibility that they can delegate to specialists or subordinates.

The mad cow crisis in the UK in the 1990s demonstrated the dangers of hiding behind expert opinion. Scientific opinion was that, based upon available evidence, mad cow disease was unlikely to spread to humans. Government policy was driven solely by scientific opinion (at least that was the public position of ministers). But how robust was this opinion? Clearly it was low given the uncertainly about the nature and spread of the disease and its long incubation period. But the consequences if the scientific opinion was found to be wrong could not be more profound, as was later proved. It was clearly wrong for ministers to shelter behind scientific opinion as it was the ministers' duty to assess the balance of risk, costs and consequences to the public, clearly a political decision not a scientific one.

Similarly in an insurance company, management not actuaries or modellers should decide. Yes they should use the best advice, but ultimately they must "own" the assumptions and accept the consequences. A well designed DFA model can help management in this process. It can clearly capture the assumptions used in a business and demonstrate the consequences of the failure of that assumption, an important aid to understanding of the dynamics of the business.

DFA models can bring clarity and transparency to decision making. For example, a model can assist a reinsurance manager to design a reinsurance strategy that best meets the board's objectives. The reinsurance manager can then use the model to convince his finance director. The finance director can use the model to convince his board. The board can then use it to convince investors and/or analysts and/or regulators and/or rating agencies about the validity of their decision making and, more broadly, to demonstrate that they are a well managed company.

The model, or a broker variant, can also be used to convince reinsurers to write the risk on the basis of mutual benefit by cedent and reinsurer.

In summary, DFAs will not be the salvation of bad management, rather a vital aid for good business management. They do not provide the answer to rational reinsurance purchase, rather they are, or will become, an increasingly indespensible tool to aid the process. But a DFA is no substitute for rational thought.

Part III

Integration of risk management with capital management

10

Economic and Financial Perspectives on the Demand for Reinsurance

James R. Garven and Joan Lamm-Tennant

Hankamer School of Business, Baylor University;
GeneralCologne Re

"The ideas of economists and political philosophers, both when they are right and when they are wrong, are more powerful than is commonly understood. Practical men, who believe themselves quite exempt from any intellectual influences, are usually the slaves of some defunct economist. Madmen in authority, who hear voices in the air, are distilling their frenzy from some academic scribblers of a few years back."

John Maynard Keynes
The General Theory of Employment, Interest and Money (1936)

INTRODUCTION

The first section of this book provides a glimpse into the minds of a number of experts involved in setting the reinsurance strategies for leading multinational insurance companies. These authors identify a number of important issues that affect effective reinsurance strategies. Robert Stevenson (Zurich Financial Services) focuses on the crux of the challenge; that is, setting the reinsurance policy. Policy must be determined prior to setting strategy; and only then can insurers transact as well as benchmark the effectiveness of their reinsurance decisions. Nick Golden (Royal and Sun Alliance) and Chris Milton (American Insurance Group Inc.) argue that reinsurance is a capital source intended to either back the risk in the existing book of business or alternatively, back the risk in new ventures. Therefore, the policy guiding reinsurance strategy is essentially a subset of the insurer's capital management policy.

Moving beyond the more philosophical issues addressed by Stevenson, Golden and Milton, Philippe Derieux (AXA), Herbert Sedlmair (Allianz) and Milton demonstrate two alternative business models for purchasing reinsurance; one very centralised and the other decentralised. These authors show, among other things, that the appropriate model for a given insurer depends upon various structural and cultural characteristics.

In this chapter, our preference is to frame the theory of the demand for reinsurance as a "special case" of the more general question concerning how one might design contracts, business organisations, and markets in order to allow for the efficient allocation, pricing and management of risk. Traditional approaches to risk management typically focus upon the analysis of a specific type of operating or financial risk without considering how such risks interact.[1] Here, we consider more of an integrated approach.[2] The framework for this approach is based in large part upon theoretical advances in finance and economics. In the spirit of the quote by noted economist John Maynard Keynes, by focusing on theory we hope to broaden the reader's perspective beyond the more practical and strategic perspectives that have already been offered in the earlier chapters of this book.

The primary question we wish to address in this chapter is whether risk is costly, and if so, how can reinsurance be used to reduce the cost of risk for insurance companies? The answer to this question is of obvious importance, because insurers who do not manage capital and risk effectively put themselves at a comparative disadvantage in the competition for scarce capital resources. We will address this question by analysing the economic and financial conditions that are necessary in order for reinsurance to add value to the insurance enterprise. In the first section, we consider the set of conditions under which reinsurance policy may not particularly matter. This model will discipline our analysis by providing a "null hypothesis" against which we can "test" alternative theories that are discussed in subsequent sections. The second section of the chapter will examine the impact that taxes have upon incentives for risk bearing. This will be followed by a section that addresses the effects of direct and indirect costs related to financial distress (eg, costs of bankruptcy and moral hazard). The fourth section will present a discussion of some implications of adverse selection in reinsurance and financial markets. The last section examines the impact that managerial compensation contract design has upon the risk appetite of the insurer. Finally, the chapter finishes with a summary conclusion, including some thoughts concerning how economic and financial insights into the demand for reinsurance help lead to consistency between policy, strategy, reinsurance buying behaviour and benchmarking.

WHAT IF REINSURANCE DIDN'T MATTER?

For reasons that will soon become apparent, in this chapter, we prefer to view the reinsurance decision as a risk and capital management decision. This perspective differs significantly from traditional theories of reinsurance markets that were developed in the economics and actuarial science literatures. These literatures typically view insurers as owner-managed underwriters who differ primarily with respect to their appetites for bearing risk. For example, the famous Norwegian actuary and economist Karl Borch models reinsurance as a market where risk-averse insurers participate in a reinsurance pool in which they optimally share insurance risk. What emerges from Borch's model is that reinsurance is demanded and supplied on a proportional, or quota share basis, where the share for any given insurer depends upon the degree to which that insurer is averse to or tolerant of risk. Subsequent authors – including Borch himself (Borch, 1985) – built upon the Borch model by introducing factors such as the risk of becoming insolvent.

While the Borch model is of substantial theoretical interest, the most apparent "deficiency" of his model is that most insurers are not owned and operated by individual entrepreneurs; rather, they comprise a complex set of (implicit and explicit) contracts among various stakeholders, including policyholders, shareholders, managers, regulators and tax authorities.[3] Consequently, this raises the question of whose welfare should such an insurer look after, and how one might manage conflicts (along with related costs) between these stakeholders.

Under the assumption (to be relaxed later) that the insurer can costlessly enforce its various stakeholder contracts, the optimal decision criterion is for the insurer to maximise the value of its shares.[4] Within this framework, Doherty and Tiniç (1981) show that as a method of reducing the riskiness of returns to the owners of the insurer, the reinsurance policy of the insurer should not matter. The logic behind this result is compelling. Insurers can alter their risk profile by ceding or assuming reinsurance. However, shareholders can also alter their risk profile by trading shares. Suppose the insurer seeks to reduce the risk of its shares by purchasing reinsurance. While some shareholders might approve of such a change, others might have an appetite for more insurance risk that can be satisfied by buying shares in riskier insurers. Thus, shareholder risk management is a close (if not perfect) substitute for insurer risk management. In such a world, reinsurance is a redundant feature of the insurance marketplace.[5]

CORPORATE INCOME TAX EFFECTS

Now that we have our null hypothesis in place; ie, that reinsurance is a redundant feature of the insurance marketplace, we are in a position to determine whether it is possible to reject this hypothesis in favour of various alternative hypotheses. The first alternative hypothesis that we consider is the effect of the corporate income tax. In many countries, corporate income tax rates vary as a function of the level of income and are typically progressive in nature; ie, the firm pays a higher marginal rate at higher levels of total income. It is also common for tax authorities to limit the ability of firms to write off the full value of corporate losses.[6] Mathematically, these features imply that firms face non-linear tax schedules in which varying marginal tax rates introduce a firm-specific source of risk that can be more effectively managed by the firm than by its shareholders.

In order to show how non-linear taxes create incentives for firms to insure risk, consider the following simple numerical example. Suppose a firm will earn US$1,000,000 if no loss occurs and US$500,000 if there is a loss. The probability of a loss is 50%, and the firm may purchase an (actuarially fair) insurance policy for US$250,000 that fully covers this loss. Also suppose that the firm must pay a 15% tax rate if income is US$500,000, 25% if income is US$750,000 and 35% if income is US$1,000,000. Should the firm purchase the insurance policy? In order to answer this question, we must compare the expected value of after tax income under the two alternatives (risk retention versus risk transfer). In Tables 1

Table 1 Retain risk

Loss outcome	Probability	Taxable income (US$)	Taxes (US$)	After-tax income (US$)
No Loss	50%	1,000,000	350,000	650,000
Loss	50%	500,000	75,000	425,000

Table 2 Transfer (insure) risk

Loss outcome	Probability	Taxable income (US$)	Taxes (US$)	After-tax income (US$)
No Loss	50%	750,000	187,500	562,500
Loss	50%	750,000	187,500	562,500

and 2, we compute the after-tax income distributions that occur under each possible loss outcome.

Comparing the two risk management strategies listed above, we find that the effect of insuring risk is to simultaneously reduce the volatility and increase the expected value of after-tax income:

Strategy 1 expected taxable income = 50% × US$1,000,000 + 50% × US$500,000 = US$750,000.
Strategy 1 expected taxes = 50% × US$350,000 + 50% × US$75,000 = US$212,500.
Strategy 1 expected after-tax income = 50% × US$650,000 + 50% × US$425,000 = US$537,500.

Strategy 2 expected taxable income = 50% × US$750,000 + 50% × US$750,000 = US$750,000.
Strategy 2 expected taxes = 50% × US$187,500 + 50% × US$187,500 = US$187,500.
Strategy 2 expected after-tax income = 50% × US$562,500 + 50% × US$562,500 = US$562,500.

The reason why insurance raises the expected value of after-tax income by US$25,000 is that the firm is able to lock in a certain level of income (US$750,000) at which it is favourably taxed relative to the risk retention strategy in which a low tax is paid in the event of a loss but a high tax is paid when there was no loss.[7] The effective tax rate when risk is retained is US$212,500/US$750,000 = 28.33%, compared with the 25% tax rate that applies when risk is insured. In the academic literature, the problem of non-linear taxation is commonly referred to as the tax convexity problem.[8]

Interestingly, insurance is irrelevant if the marginal tax rate is constant. Consequently, tax convexity constitutes a sufficient (although not necessary) condition for risk transfer to matter. To illustrate this point, suppose that we replace the progressive tax schedule from the previous numerical example with a tax rate of 25% that applies to all levels of income. Under this assumption, the firm's expected tax liability is unaffected by the volatility of its taxable income; specifically, it will be US$187,500 irrespective of whether risk is transferred or retained. Therefore insurance would be irrelevant from a tax perspective.

Now we shall consider the problem of tax convexity (and the associated incentive to hedge risk) in the real world in which insurers actually operate. Tax convexity in the real world is quite a bit more complicated than in our numerical example, and it can vary significantly from firm to firm. For any given firm, the degree of tax convexity depends not only upon the schedule of marginal tax rates published by the tax authorities, but also upon a number of firm-specific characteristics, including past, present and future expected profitability, whether the firm is subject to the alternative minimum tax, and whether the firm has any investment tax credits or net operating loss carrybacks and carryforwards. Graham and Smith (1999) provide empirical evidence of the effect of tax convexity on the incentive to hedge risk by using financial data for a large cross section of US industries over the period 1980–1994. While their study is based on firms drawn from many industries, we have no *a priori* reason to believe that a qualitatively different result would necessarily obtain for the insurance industry. In summary, Graham and Smith find that firms with the greatest tax-based incentives to hedge were small to medium-sized, with earnings that were expected to be near zero and frequently shifting between losses and profits. Conversely, firms with weaker tax-based hedging incentives tended to have higher market values, lower leverage, higher levels of income, less frequently reported losses, lower income volatility, more investment tax credits and fewer net operating loss carryforwards. Overall, Graham and Smith found that the average tax savings from a 5% reduction in the volatility of taxable income represented 5.4% of expected tax liabilities, and in extreme cases, these savings exceeded 40%.

Recognising that reinsurance is a hedging vehicle, the demand for reinsurance will be greater among firms facing convex tax functions.[9] Therefore, we may generalise Graham and Smith's findings to suggest firm characteristics among insurers who utilise reinsurance more extensively for risk-hedging purposes. Furthermore, reinsurance may be a rational choice even if the contract is priced in excess of the expected loss due to the associated tax savings. Garven and Loubergé (1996) present an analytical model of underwriting capacity and insurance market equilibrium under a convex corporate tax schedule which, among other things, shows this to be the case.[10] In the Garven–Loubergé model, reinsurance markets enable insurers to reallocate tax shields to those firms that have the greatest capacity for utilising them, in much the same manner as leasing companies share tax shield benefits with lessees in leasing markets. Garven and Loubergé view reinsurance as an efficient mechanism to yield the optimal allocation of tax shield benefits. In this framework, reinsurance markets provide the insurance industry with an important tax arbitrage mechanism. Specifically, reinsurance enables the insurance industry to minimise the aggregate value of tax claims on overall industry income.[11] Finally, Garven and Loubergé extend their model to a consideration of the international reinsurance market, where they note that their model predicts the emergence of "tax clientele" effects that arise when tax rates differ among countries. An empirical implication of the Garven–Loubergé tax clientele hypothesis is that average net retention ratios for insurers should be inversely related to corporate tax rates. Using data from 1988 and 1989, Outreville (1994) provides corroborating empirical evidence, in that he finds that a statistically significant negative relationship exists between retention ratios and corporate tax rates using data from 42 countries. Specifically, net-ceded reinsurance tends to be higher on average in countries that have high marginal corporate tax rates.

THE EFFECTS OF BANKRUPTCY AND MORAL HAZARD COSTS

Recall the assumption underlying the Borch model such that the insurer can "costlessly" enforce its various stakeholders' contracts. Let us now relax this assumption and recognise that the various stakeholders (owners, policyholders, bondholders, shareholders, managers) do, in fact, have contracts that cannot be enforced without the imposition of some costs. For example, firms expend real economic resources in upholding the promise to owners by establishing the board of directors. Likewise, bankruptcy costs and the costs associated with moral hazard are examples of real costs incurred when firms fail to protect the rights of policyholders and/or bondholders. It is exactly these costs and the recognition of these costs that explain why, in fact, reinsurance does matter. Other owner-creditor agency problems are underinvestment (passing up projects with positive net present value) and asset substitution (replacing safe with risky investments).

Jensen and Meckling (1976) set forth the definition of a firm as being a legal fiction, which serves as a nexus for a set of contracting relationships among individuals. These contracts define a set of agency relationships under which principals engage agents to perform some service on their behalf and subsequently the principals delegate the decision-making authority to the agent. The agent may not always act in the best interest of the principal because it might not be in the agent's self interest to do so. The ownership structure of the insurance company (stock, mutual, reciprocal, Lloyds) determines the relationship between the various stakeholders (also referred to as agents) in an insurance organisation. For example, stock insurers separate the functions of the manager, owner and policyholder; whereas the mutual merges the owner with the policyholder and Lloyds merge the owner with the manager. Incentive conflicts exist between these agents and costs (eg, negotiation, administration, information and litigation costs) are incurred controlling the incentive conflicts. Because these agency costs are real, ownership structure matters when we set out to maximise value for the firm. That is, we must attempt to minimise these agency costs in order to maximise firm value.

In the context of the insurer, we focus primarily upon the following principal–agent relationships: (1) stockholder (principal)–manager (agent), and (2) stockholder (owner)–policyholder (creditor). In accordance with the agency theory of Jensen and Meckling, conflicts occur between shareholders and managers if managers' interests have not been aligned with the value creation demands of the shareholders. One mechanism providing ballast to incentive differences between managers and owners is to compensate managers with options or restrictive stocks. Furthermore, owner/manager conflicts are monitored by establishing a board of directors and the costs associated with maintaining a board, both explicit and implicit, become agency costs.

Under the stock form of ownership structure, the owner (shareholder) function is separate from that of the creditor (policyholder). A conflict exists between stockholders (owners) and policyholders (creditors) in that stockholders would prefer profitability while policyholders would prefer low premium charges. Alternatively, creditors may prefer less risky investments resulting in guarantees that the debt obligations will be met; whereas, shareholders, who claim rights to residual wealth, may prefer more risky investments. Because the stock insurer separates the owner from the customer, the potential for "ripping off" policyholders by risk shifting does exist. Recognising that the potential exists such that the owners may abstract value from the policyholders, the policyholders will ask for something in return such as lower premiums, surplus cushion, the purchase of reinsurance or participating policies, etc. When the financial health of the insurer becomes stressed, the costs associated with monitoring the conflict between owners and creditors are worsened. In the case of a mutual organisation, these conflicts do not exist because the owners and the creditors are combined in one function – the policyholder.

In the insurance industry, both the mutual and stock forms of ownership co-exist. In the mutual organisation, owner–creditor conflicts are eliminated and the associated monitoring costs are not incurred. A naive extension of the theory might suggest that the mutual form of ownership is preferred over the stock form since the structure naturally eliminates one set of conflicts. Mayers and Smith (1981) established the managerial discretion hypothesis suggesting that differences exist in costs of controlling incentive conflicts between shareholders and managers vs policyholders and managers, and these differences influence the choice between stock and mutual form of organisation. Mayers and Smith point out those managers with the greatest decision authority have the greatest potential to operate in self-interest at the expense of the owners. Mutual managers tend to have greater decision authority than do stock managers because of less effective or less intense corporate governance. Mayers and Smith predict that the cost of controlling management is significantly higher for mutual insurers as compared to stock insurers; consequently mutuals should be more prevalent in lines of business where management exercises little discretion. Likewise stock insurers should be more dominant in lines where management discretion is more important.

Lamm-Tennant and Starks (1993) empirically investigate risk differences between the two types of ownership structure in the property-liability insurance industry to better understand why both co-exist. The managerial discretion hypothesis derived from agency theory would suggest that mutuals would be associated with activities that require less managerial discretion. Lamm-Tennant and Starks provide empirical evidence supporting the managerial discretion hypothesis suggesting that stock insurers have more risk than mutuals where the risk inherent in future cash flows is proxied by the variance of the loss ratio. Further evidence suggests that stock insurers write relatively more business than do mutuals in lines and states having higher risk. The risk differences between stocks and mutuals have interesting implications suggesting differences in reinsurance strategy due to ownership structure. If mutuals concentrate in less risky states and less risky lines of business, one might conclude their appetite for hedging may be muted. Likewise, to the extent that a mutual holds an exposure in a risky state or risk line of business, the mutual insurer may be more prone to reinsurer or hedge the risk resulting in a net position aligned with their limited risk appetite.

As previously mentioned, two interesting problems occur when owner–creditor conflicts are not controlled; under-investment and risk shifting (also known as asset substitution). Under-investment suggests that insurers in financial distress may fail to exploit positive net present value opportunities since the value creating will not accrue to the shareholders but, instead, will simply prop up the debt otherwise in default. That is, due to agency conflicts between owners (shareholders, in the case of a stock company) and creditors (policyholders, in the case of a stock company), insurers may pass up opportunities in the market that would otherwise provide economic value to the firm. To the extent risk management removes or relaxes the threat of insolvency, agency conflicts are muted. Likewise the absence of agency conflict results in decision-makers rendering the optimal economic investment decisions avoiding under-investment, see Garven and MacMinn (1993).

Risk shifting is the propensity of highly levered firms to favour more risky investment choices (post the debt offering) because these choices accrue to the benefit of the shareholders at the expense of the bondholders. Again we see the conflicts between bondholders and owners affecting the risk appetite of the insurer. One might suspect insurers with poor controls between bondholder and owner conflicts would prefer more risk than less and would likewise hold higher nets or avoid reinsurance altogether.

IMPLICATIONS OF ADVERSE SELECTION IN REINSURANCE AND FINANCIAL MARKETS

Groucho Marx's famous comment that he would prefer not to belong to any club that would have him as a member captures the essence of adverse selection. Adverse selection occurs whenever a buyer or seller of a good or service has an informational advantage over his/her counterparty and tries to profit from this asymmetry in information. If unchecked, adverse selection may lead to market failure. Akerlof (1970) demonstrates how market failure may occur when sellers have an informational advantage over buyers concerning product quality.[12] For example, the seller of a used car knows whether the car is a "lemon". Surely, if the car is in pristine condition, the seller would be more likely to transfer ownership to a friend or family member. Consequently, by placing the car on the used car market, the seller inadvertently signals to potential buyers that the product is in all likelihood a lemon. Knowing this, the buyer will offer a lower price for the car in anticipation of it being a lemon. Sellers come to realise that used car prices reflect asymmetric information penalties, so eventually good used cars are crowded out by the lemons in the market for used cars. Akerlof showed that in the absence of adequate mechanisms to assure, verify and enforce contract provisions regarding quality (eg, via credible third-party certification), markets may either fail or do an otherwise poor job of allocating resources. Akerlof's work has important implications for the organisation and regulation of any number of markets, including product markets, labour markets and insurance markets.

The adverse selection model that is of more direct relevance for the study of insurance is that offered by Rothschild and Stiglitz (1976). Rothschild and Stiglitz set up an insurance market in which potential insureds are identical in all respects other than their accident probabilities. Although the insurer knows these accident probabilities, for whatever reason it is not possible to determine who the bad risks vs good risks are. This creates an obvious dilemma for the insurer.[13] Specifically, how can the insurer offer insurance and avoid adverse selection? Rothschild and Stiglitz's solution to this problem is rather clever. They solve the problem by restricting the menu of available insurance policy choices. The goal of this strategy is to induce self selection, in that one makes it economically attractive for the good risks to purchase the good risk policy and the bad risks to purchase the bad risk policy. In the Rothschild–Stiglitz equilibrium, the good risks will not purchase the bad risk policy because this would lower their economic welfare, and similarly, the bad risks will not purchase the good risk policy for the same reason. The insurer offers a bad risk policy that provides full coverage at a premium that is actuarially fair for bad risks, and she offers a good risk policy that provides partial coverage at a premium that is actuarially fair for good risks. The theory has very practical implications for the demand for insurance. Specifically, if you are a good risk, then you should purchase insurance with a high deductible; to do otherwise would involve overpaying for coverage. This may be an important reason why rates on line in the reinsurance market are lower at higher attachment points; essentially, the reinsurer is anticipating that the worst risks will be those who want low attachment points on their excess of loss reinsurance treaties.

Not only is there adverse selection in insurance and reinsurance markets; adverse selection is also a problem in financial markets, and this also has implications for the insurer's reinsurance policy. The adverse selection problem in financial markets derives from the fact that corporate managers have better information about the firm's future prospects than do outside investors. Consequently, managers are more likely to issue new equity when the firm is overvalued. However, investors are aware of this incentive, so they infer the announcement of a secondary equity offering by a publicly traded firm as a signal that the firm's equity is overvalued. Therefore firms prefer to rely upon internal equity since funds can be raised without conveying adverse signals (and consequently bearing related costs) about the value of the firm. However, if external financing is necessary, then firms prefer to rely upon financing sources such as bank loans, commercial paper, notes, bonds, preferred stock and convertible securities, and issue external equity as a last resort. The logic for this "pecking order" strategy is straightforward; essentially, there is less room for differences in opinion concerning the values of securities whose terms are contractually fixed (eg, debt), compared with equity which resembles a residual claim on the firm that is paid only after all of the other fixed claims upon the firm are satisfied.[14] Consequently, just as a good risk will gravitate toward higher attachment points in the case of a reinsurance purchase, it is also the case that the "good" firm will manage its risks so that it can minimise the probability of incurring adverse selection costs when it obtains contingent financing. This creates a bias in favour of pre-loss financing strategies (eg, purchasing reinsurance) in place of post-loss strategies (eg, retaining risk and issuing equity after the fact). An important benefit of pre-loss vs post-loss financing is that pre-loss financing guarantees liquidity at a future date on favourable terms.[15] Following a loss, the unhedged firm might experience difficulty raising additional capital on favourable terms due to adverse selection costs and also because of the possibility of financial distress.

In the reinsurance markets, the insurer ceding the risk will likely have better information about the underlying risk than does the reinsurer. The asymmetry in information is exacerbated depending on the nature of the underlying risk. For example, we would expect less information asymmetry surrounding high-frequency, low-severity risk such as automobile physical damage than low frequency, high severity such as commercial liability. The greater the information asymmetry, the greater the imputed charge imposed by the reinsurer on to the insurer when transferring the risk through reinsurance. This imputed charge for information asymmetry may be mitigated though long-standing relationships, joint risk sharing or improved information flows. Therefore, we may expect differences in insurer risk policy and strategy depending on nature of the underlying risk written by the insurer. In a paper entitled "The Design of Private Reinsurance Contracts", Jean-Baptiste and Santomero (2000) demonstrate how information problems affect the efficiency of the allocation of risk between insurers and reinsurers, and how long-term implicit contracts between insurers and reinsurers allow the inclusion of new information in the pricing of both future and past reinsurance coverage. Because of these features (long-term relationships and the inclusion of new information in the pricing of future and past coverage), Jean-Baptiste and Santomero show that the ceding company purchases a more efficient quantity of reinsurance and at a more efficient price with long-term implicit contracts or relationships between the insurer and the reinsurer.[16] The authors (Garven and Lamm-Tennant, 2002)) are currently working on an empirical study that we expect will provide empirical support for the Jean-Baptiste and Santomero hypotheses.

MANAGERIAL COMPENSATION CONTRACT DESIGN

Until this point, the chapter has made the implicit assumption that shareholders and managers of insurers have perfectly aligned incentives, such that managers are primarily interested in maximising shareholder welfare. Next, we consider the implications of relaxing this assumption.

It is reasonable to expect that managers may have different objectives than shareholders. Corporate managers are often not as well diversified as shareholders since they may own disproportionately large firm-specific human capital investments as well as investments in their firm's shares. Consequently, managers have natural incentives to reduce their firm's exposure to risk, even when it may not necessarily be in shareholders' best interests to do so. An important aspect of corporate governance relates to the role of managerial compensation contract design in aligning shareholder and managerial incentives. A substantial literature has developed in the economics and finance literature concerning the relationship between managerial compensation contracts and decision making.[17] Generally, economists have found that compensation contract design is important in the sense that managers tend to respond quite predictably to the incentives that are conveyed by these contracts.

Here, we will consider the impact that very elementary aspects of contract design may have upon risk management decision making. Doherty (2000) develops a simple model based upon the framework provided by Aggarwal and Samwick (1999). In Doherty's model, the firm can select any of three different (mutually exclusive) compensation contracts:

1. flat salary;
2. direct share ownership; and
3. executive stock options.

All three of these compensation contracts are competitively priced relative to each other as well as to contracts related to alternative employment opportunities outside the firm. However, they convey different incentives in terms of what might constitute an optimal risk management decision. Specifically, Doherty's model produces the following set of predictions:

- Firms that offer compensation based upon direct share ownership are likely to hedge risk.
- Firms that offer flat salary may still hedge, but the incentives to do so are weaker (since the linkage between managerial welfare and firm risk is less direct).
- Firms that offer executive stock options to their managers are not likely to hedge.

Although these contract choices (share ownership, salary and options) are not mutually exclusive in the real world, it is nevertheless interesting to note that the predictions have strong empirical support in papers by Tufano (1996) and Geczy, Minton and Schrand (1997). In Tufano's study of the risk management practices of gold mining firms, he finds that when firms weight compensation more heavily in favour of direct share ownership, there is a greater propensity toward active management of gold price risk. On the other hand, firms that rely more on option executive stock options tend to be much less concerned about managing gold price risk. Geczy, Minton and Schrand study foreign exchange risk management by non financial firms, and they obtain results that are qualitatively similar to those of Tufano.

Insurance industry-specific studies of executive compensation have been published by Mayers and Smith (1992, 2001). Mayers and Smith document, among other things, that cross-sectional regularities exist in managerial compensation contract design across organisational forms. For example, stock company Chief Executive Officer (CEO) compensation tends to be more responsive to firm performance than mutual CEO compensation. This may reflect a number of factors, including the obvious fact that direct share ownership and options on shares are not feasible forms of compensation for a mutual insurer. Although there has yet to be a comprehensive study of the risk incentive effects of insurance industry compensation, we have no reason to believe that qualitatively different results from the findings of Tufano and Geczy, Minton and Schrand would necessarily obtain for the insurance industry. However, we are confident that real world reinsurance decision making is quite sensitive not only to the insurer's ownership structure, but also to the nature of its compensation contract designs for management.

SUMMARY AND CONCLUSION

Keynes (1936) wrote, "The ideas of economists and political philosophers, both when they are right and when they are wrong, are more powerful than is commonly understood". While the work of Karl Borch is eloquent, it clearly fails to explain the role of reinsurance. Nevertheless, by relaxing the underlying assumptions we begin to understand why firms reinsure (hedge). Furthermore, we gain insights into the differences in firm characteristics that explain or justify varying reinsurance policies and strategies. And last of all, we begin to appreciate that evaluating the effectiveness of reinsurance may require more financial rigour than merely striking a difference between premium and losses ceded since the very motive for purchasing reinsurance is entangled with both financial and cultural organisational characteristics.

By recognising taxes, the effects of bankruptcy and moral hazard costs, adverse selection and managerial contract compensation design, we begin to understand more clearly the role played by reinsurance when firms seek to maximise value. Furthermore differences among firms in terms of these characteristics explain why different reinsurance policy, strategy and buying behaviour are appropriate for different firms. The challenge is for firms to recognise how their organisation structure, both financial and culturally, effects taxes, bankruptcy and moral hazard costs, adverse selection and managerial compensation design, and then align reinsurance decisions accordingly.

While that chapter has evaluated each of these influences on reinsurance decision independently, in reality they interact and converge on an optimal choice. Beginning with taxes, we have presented evidence suggesting that the demand for reinsurance will be the greatest among firms facing convex tax functions and that reinsurance may be a rational, value-maximising choice even if the contract is priced in excess of the expected loss due to the associated tax savings. In the international reinsurance markets the emergence of tax clientele effects suggests that when tax rates differ among countries, the objective is to purchase reinsurance allowing insurers to reallocate tax shields to those entities that have the greatest capacity for utilising them. Hence we suggest that the average net retention ratio for insurers should be inversely related to corporate tax rates.

Organisations may not "costlessly" enforce their various stakeholders' contracts. Agency costs are incurred to monitor conflict between the various stakeholders. A conflict exists between the owner (shareholder) and creditor (policyholder) in a stock insurer which is eliminated though organisational structure amongst mutuals. Because of the owner–creditor friction, the chapter has suggested that the policyholders of stock insurers would ask for lower premiums, surplus cushion reinsurance and/or participating policy mechanisms to ballast any incentive by shareholders to expropriate wealth from policyholders. Furthermore, because the cost of controlling management is higher or less effective for mutuals than stock insurers, managers of mutuals may have more discretion. Since traditional managerial control mechanisms are less effective for mutuals, we would expect mutual insurers to concentrate in lines of business and states/countries having less risk. By concentrating in less risky lines, a mutual would have less of any need for reinsurance. To the extent that a mutual does have an exposure in a more risky line, albeit small, it would be more prone to reinsure resulting in a net positioned aligned with their limited risk appetite. To the extent that under investment and risk shifting occurs due to conflicts between owners and creditors, reinsurance would also provide real economic benefits.

Information asymmetries do exist such that the insurer is more informed than the reinsurer regarding the underlying risk. These information problems affect the efficiency of the allocation of risk between insurers and reinsurers. Also, long-term implicit contracts between insurers and reinsurers allow the inclusion of new information in the pricing of both future and past reinsurance coverage. The chapter suggests that long-term relationships between insurers and reinsurers that allow for the inclusion of new information in the pricing of future and past coverage, will result in the ceding company purchasing a more efficient quantity of reinsurance and at a more efficient price.

Differences in managerial compensation design leads to a set of predictions such that:

1. firms offering compensation based upon direct share ownership are likely to hedge risk;
2. firms offering flat salary may still hedge, but the incentives to do so are weaker (since the linkage between managerial welfare and firm risk is less direct); and
3. firms offering executive stock options to their managers are not likely to hedge.

Given that mutual insurers are restricted to compensating management with flat salary, the chapter suggests that mutuals are less incented to hedge with reinsurance.

We derive a set of predictions regarding reinsurance, some backed by convincing empirical evidence published in the academic literature, for the reader's consideration.

1 Operating risks include uninsurable business risks such as loss of competitive position, product substitution and obsolescence, as well as risks for which private insurance is often available, such as property-liability risks and workplace risks that can adversely affect employee life and health. Financial risks include credit risks as well as risks that result from market fluctuations in the prices of commodities, currencies and financial assets. Insurance and derivatives are commonly used to control the cost of "insurable" operating and financial risks, whereas alternative contract designs and organisational structures are commonly employed as risk control mechanisms for "uninsurable" business risks that are inherently more difficult to quantify and manage.

2 In recent years, integrated risk management has become increasingly popular in professional as well as academic circles. This change in approach and philosophy has been motivated significantly by the convergence of insurance and

financial markets, along with the ever-increasing frequency and severity of natural and man-made catastrophes. Indeed, as noted in a recent Economist article, "The business of financing companies is converging with the business of insuring them." See "The New Financiers," *The Economist*, September 2, 1999.

3 It is worthwhile noting that Borch's reinsurance model anticipated the development of the Sharpe (1964)-Lintner (1965)-Mossin (1966) Capital Asset Pricing Model (CAPM) for which Sharpe received the Nobel Prize in 1990. The parallels between Borch's model and the CAPM are striking, since the CAPM posits that investors should hold proportional shares in a "market portfolio" of risky assets. Given that some investors are more risk averse than others, they can satisfy their appetites for risk by varying the proportion invested in the market portfolio and a riskless asset. The development of the CAPM along with the "efficient market theory" helped to popularise indexed mutual fund strategies in which investors passively vary proportions invested in various indexed asset classes.

4 However, as Fama and Jensen (1983) note, everything changes if we relax the assumption of costless contracting. With costly contracting, the cost of doing business is determined by summing contracting costs along with other costs such as production and distribution costs and the costs related to compliance with external legal and regulatory constraints. Differences in the costs of managing incentive conflicts between stakeholders constitute an important reason why ownership structures in the insurance industry are so diverse, comprising the stock, mutual, reciprocal and Lloyds forms of organisation. Although a discussion of ownership structure in the insurance industry is well beyond the scope of our survey, we refer interested readers to Mayers and Smith (2000) for a succinct and lucid discussion of the theory and evidence underlying the industrial organisation of the insurance industry.

5 The reader should note that the above analysis implicitly assumes that there are no transaction costs associated with buying reinsurance (eg, in the form of premium loadings) and trading shares in capital markets (eg, in the form of trading costs). However, if the transactions costs are higher for insurers to cede and assume reinsurance than it is for investors to buy and sell shares, then investors would obviously be better off without a reinsurance market.

6 Although the US tax code mitigates this effect somewhat by allowing for loss carrybacks and carryforwards, the net effect is still one in which corporate gains are effectively taxed at higher rates than losses are rebated. See Doherty (2000, pp. 199–204) for a lucid discussion of these issues.

7 Depending upon the competitive structure of the insurance market, one might expect that the tax benefits associated with insuring risk are likely to be shared between the insurer and the insured, with the insured appropriating most (if not all) of the tax benefits in a competitive insurance market and the insurer benefiting if insurance markets are not competitively structured.

8 The definition of tax convexity follows directly from a mathematical theorem known as Jensen's inequality. According to Jensen's inequality, if a function $f(x)$ is convex, then $E(f(x)) > f(E(x))$. In our numerical example, we showed that the tax on insured income $f(E(x))$ is less than the tax on uninsured income $(E(f(x)))$; consequently, we have tax convexity.

9 A reinsurance contract is a type of hedging contract whereby the ceding company puts the losses on the reinsurer subject to some trigger event.

10 In Garven and Loubergé, convex taxes are sufficient to cause insurance prices to be actuarially unfair, and the expected return on capital invested in the insurance business reflects the probability of paying taxes. The notion that competitively determined insurance prices must incorporate a corporate tax loading is

also a well-known result from the more general insurance pricing literature; eg, see Fairley (1979), Hill (1979), Doherty and Garven (1986), Hill and Modigliani (1987), and Myers and Cohn (1987).

11 The parallels between the Garven-Loubergé model and Miller's (1977) capital market equilibrium model are striking, since the Miller model posits that a central role of corporate finance is to perform a similar tax arbitrage function for investors.

12 The 2001 Nobel Prize in Economic Sciences was awarded to George Akerlof (University of California-Berkeley), Michael Spence (Stanford University), and Joseph E. Stiglitz (Columbia University) "for their analyses of markets with asymmetric information". Akerlof (1970) analyses the role of third party certification in resolving adverse selection, whereas Spence (1973) focuses on the role of signalling. Rothschild and Stiglitz (1976) show that adverse selection in insurance markets can be largely mitigated through contract designs.

13 Although Rothschild and Stiglitz present an extreme case, in the real world there are obvious limits to risk classification that may be due to any number of factors, including technology or legal and regulatory factors.

14 The concept of a "pecking order" in terms of preferences for different forms of financing is due to Myers and Majluf (1984). Froot, Scharstein and Stein (1993) apply the pecking order theory as a way to explain corporate risk management decision making. There, risk management represents a device for ensuring the firm's liquidity so that cash is always available to make value-enhancing investments.

15 The notion that insurance provides liquidity was recently advanced by Peter Bernstein, see Bernstein (2000). Bernstein notes that insurance enables investors to reverse the consequences of unfavourable outcomes, and thus reduce the risk of investing in a particular asset that would otherwise be unbuyable and unsellable due to its lack of liquidity.

16 Garven and Lamm-Tennant (2002) have designed an empirical test of this hypothesis using Schedule F data for all insurers reporting to A.M. Best from 1980 to 2000. While Schedule F does impose numerous data limitations, preliminary results appear consistent with Jean-Baptiste and Santomero. That is, the longer the term of the relationship between the insurer and the reinsurer the greater the reinsurance purchases. Garven and Lamm-Tennant are not capable of testing the pricing implications directly.

17 For a comprehensive review of the executive compensation literature, see Murphy (1999).

BIBLIOGRAPHY

Aggarwal, R. K. and A. A. Samwick, 1999, "The Other Side of the Trade-off: The Impact of Risk on Executive Compensation", *Journal of Political Economy*, 107, pp. 65–105.

Akerlof, G. A., 1970, "The Market for Lemons: Quality Uncertainty and the Market Mechanism", *Quarterly Journal of Economics*, 84 (August), pp. 488–500.

Bernstein, P., 2000, "Risk Management, Financial Markets and Insurance", *Contingencies* (November/December), pp. 20–26.

Borch, K., 1985, "Do we need utility theory in insurance?", Paper presented at the Annual Seminar of the European Group of Risk and Insurance Economists, Brussels, September.

Doherty, N. A., 2000, *Integrated Risk Management: Techniques and Strategies for Managing Corporate Risk*, (New York: McGraw-Hill Professional Publishing).

Doherty, N. A, and J. R. Garven, 1986, "Price Regulation in Property-Liability Insurance: A Contingent Claims Approach", *Journal of Finance*, 41:5, pp. 1031–50.

Doherty N. A. and S. M. Tiniç, 1981, "Reinsurance under Conditions of Capital Market Equilibrium: A Note", *Journal of Finance*, 36 (September), pp. 949–53.

Fairley, W. B., 1979, "Investment Income and Profit Margins in Property Liability Insurance, *Bell Journal of Economics*, 10, pp. 192–210.

Fama, E. F., and M. C. Jensen, 1983, "Separation of Ownership and Control," *Journal of Law and Economics*, 26, pp. 301–25.

Froot, K. A., D. S. Scharfstein and J. C. Stein, 1993, "Risk Management: Coordinating Corporate Investment and Financing Policies", *Journal of Finance*, 48 (December), pp. 1629–58.

Garven, J. R., and J. Lamm-Tennant, 1999, "The Demand for Reinsurance: Theory and Empirical Tests", working paper, Louisiana State University and Villanova University.

Garven, J. R., and J. Lamm-Tennant, 2002, "Empirical Perspectives on the Demand for Reinsurance", working paper, Baylor University and GeneralCologne Re.

Garven, J. R., and H. Loubergé, 1996, "Reinsurance, Taxes and Efficiency: A Contingent-claims Model of Insurance Market Equilibrium", *Journal of Financial Intermediation*, 5 (January): pp. 74–93.

Garven, J. R. and R. D. MacMinn, 1993, "The Underinvestment Problem Bond Covenants and Insurance", *Journal of Risk*, 60 (December), pp. 635–46.

Geczy, C., B. A. Minton and C. Schrand, 1997, "Why Firms Use Currency Derivatives", *Journal of Finance*, 52 (September), pp. 1323–54.

Graham, J. R. and C. W. Smith, 1999, "Tax Incentives to Hedge", *Journal of Finance*, 44 (December), pp. 2241–62.

Jean-Baptiste, E. L. and A. M. Santomero, 2000, "The Design of Private Reinsurance Contracts", *Journal of Financial Intermediation*, 9, pp. 274–97.

Hill, R.D., 1979, "Profit regulation in property liability insurance", *Bell Journal of Economics*, 10, pp. 172–91.

Hill, R.D., and F. Modigliani, 1987, "The Massachusetts Model of Profit Regulation In Non-Life Insurance", in: *Fair Rate of Return in Property-Liability Insurance*, J. D. Cummins and S. E. Harrington (eds) (Boston: Kluwer-Nijhof Publishing Company)

Jensen, M. C., and W. H. Meckling, 1976, "Theory of the Firm: Managerial Behavior Agency Costs and Ownership Structure, *Journal of Financial Economics*, 3 (October), pp. 305–60.

Keynes, J. M., 1936, *The General Theory of Employment, Interest, and Money* (New York: Harcourt Brace Jovanovich).

Lamm-Tennant, J., and L. T. Starks, 1993, "Stock Versus Mutual Ownership Structures: The Risk Implications", *Journal of Business*, 66 (January), pp. 29–46.

Lintner, J., 1965, "The Valuation of Risk Assets and the Selection of Risk Investments in Stock Portfolios and Capital Budgets", *Review of Economics and Statistics*, 47, pp. 13–37.

Marx, L. M., D. Mayers and C. W. Smith, 2001, "Insurer Ownership Structure and Executive Compensation as Complements", *Journal of Risk and Insurance*, 68 (September), pp. 449–63.

Mayers D. and C. W. Smith, 1992, "Executive Compensation in the Life Insurance Industry", *Journal of Business*, 65 (January), pp. 51–74.

Mayers D. and C. W. Smith, 2000., "Organizational Forms Within the Insurance Industry: Theory and Evidence", Chapter 23 in *Handbook of Insurance*, Georges Dionne, editor (Norwell, MA: Kluwer Academic Publishers), December 2000, pp. 689–707.

Mayers D. and C. W. Smith, 1981, "Contractual Provisions Organizational Structure and Conflict Control in Insurance Markets", *Journal of Business*, 54 (July), pp. 407–434.

Miller, M.H., 1977, "Debt and taxes", *Journal of Finance*, 32 pp. 261–275.

Mossin, J., 1966, "Equilibrium in a Capital Asset Market," *Econometrica*, 34, pp. 768–783.

Murphy, K. J., 1999, "Executive Compensation", in O. Ashenfelter and D. Card, eds., *Handbook of Labor Economics*, Volume 3 (North-Holland).

Myers, S. C. and R. A. Cohn, 1987, "Insurance Rate Regulation and the Capital Asset Pricing Model" (chapter 3 in *Fair Rate of Return in Property-Liability Insurance*, J. D. Cummins and S. E. Harrington (eds.) (Kluwer-Nijhof Publishing Company, Boston).

Myers, S. C. and N. S. Majluf, 1984, "Corporate Financing and Investment Decisions when Firms have Information that Investors do not have", *Journal of Financial Economics*, 13, pp. 187–221.

Outreville J. F., 1994, "The demand for reinsurance in developing countries", UNCTAD working paper, United Nations Geneva.

Rothschild, M. and J. E. Stiglitz, "Equilibrium in Competitive Insurance Markets: An Essay on the Economics of Imperfect Information," *Quarterly Journal of Economics*, 90(4), November 1976, pp. 629–649.

Sharpe, W. F., 1964., "Capital Asset Prices: A Theory of Market Equilibrium Under Conditions of Risk", *Journal of Finance*, 19, 425–442.

Spence, A. M., 1973, "Job Market Signalling", *Quarterly Journal of Economics*, 87 (August), pp. 355–374.

The Economist, 1999, "The New Financiers", September 2.

Tufano, P., 1996, "Who Manages Risk? An Empirical Examination of Risk Management Practices in the Gold Mining Industry", *Journal of Finance*, 51, pp. 1097–1137.

11

Alternative Capital Sources

Morton Lane

Lane Financial LLC

> **Capital** ... 2. n. ~ city: ~ letter: stock with which company &c. starts, accumulated wealth used or usable for producing more, money lent at interest, **~ists** as a class (*hampered by lack of ~; fixed ~*, land, buildings, machinery, &c. *circulating* or *floating ~*, goods, money, &c.; *lost both ~ & interest*; *~ & labour*, employers & employed; *~ goods*; goods to be used in producing commodities, opp. *Consumer goods*; *~ levy*, confiscation of a proportion of all property; *make ~ out of*, turn to account in argument &c); head or cornice of pillar. **~ist** (or Kapit-) n., person who uses or possesses ~, rich man; **~ism** (or Kapit -) n., organization of production by **~ists** for their own profit (cf. *collectivism*); **~istic** a. (*ically*). **~ize** v.t. (*zable*), use as ~, compute or realize present value of (income, property), turn to account, use to ones advantage; ...
>
> *Pocket Oxford Dictionary* (1969)

The above definition of "capital" captures two things; first, the essential meaning of capital as the resource necessary for production of wealth and, second, the fact that capital can mean many things to many people. On the other hand, one thing that may be missing is any reference to the relation between risk and capital. The definition was written before the modern capital market theories were expounded, yet it does capture the essentials – present value of income, etc – before the significant contributions of

Black, Scholes, Merton and other modern finance theorists formalised the concepts. The theories contributed by these Nobel Laureates added to our general understanding of capital markets, and the insights allowed a proliferation of new, innovative instruments by which capital can be accessed and managed. Swaps, options, futures, collateralised debt obligations (CDOs), converts, caps, floors, collars, Remics, collateralised mortgage obligations (CMOs) and derivatives of all kinds are aids in the use of capital to produce wealth.

Inadvertently perhaps, this proliferation of instruments may also have clouded the essential perception of capital. Thirty years after the above definition was written, in talking to insurance market executives about alternative capital markets, a most persistent question is "What exactly are the 'capital markets'?" It is possible after all to visit the bookshop and pick up a book entitled *Capital Markets Revolution* which scarely mentions the words equity or capital (neither is even mentioned in the index).[1] What is going on? Instead of sounding like Tom Joad travelling from Oklahoma to California muttering "What is them Reds?" insurance executives would prefer to be well informed about why the new capital forms exist and of what relevance they are to insurance.[2] Conversely, exhibiting more confidence they may ask "Why is it that insurance capital markets have developed differently from other forms of corporate finance?". An exploration of the latter can be quite revealing about the nature of capital, and its alternatives.

INTRODUCTION

This chapter briefly reviews the history of capital formation in the insurance world. This necessarily involves a visit to Lloyds of London and the original form of capital – unlimited liability – together with Lloyds new embrace of corporate, ie, limited liability, capital. The chapter then reprises the reasons for holding capital, its modern forms and proceeds to describe the alternative forms of capital available today that may not have been accessible in the past. In covering this ground, however, there is perhaps one central thought to keep in mind: Capital is required to produce wealth. Wealth creation is risky. Capital is required because there are risks. Only a few things can be done with risk. It can be mitigated, transferred or retained. Capital is the agent that facilitates each of these processes.

PRE-HISTORY

The storied history of insurance, and of Lloyds, begins with the idea that wealthy merchants underwrote the value of ships and contents against loss from storms at sea. Their object was said to be that "...the losse lightethe rather easilie upon many, than heavily upon fewe."[3] The load was spread among many underwriters in exchange for "some consideracon of money". Clearly the concept of risk transfer and premiums were embedded in the insurance from the beginning. Merchants could "make any great adventure (speciallie into remote partes)" without fear of extreme loss. Without that insurance, the adventure would necessarily be more hazardous financially, necessitating fewer ventures at one time (mitigation) or more capital to be able to withstand extreme loss and stay in business (retention). Insurance (risk transfer) allowed them to conduct more adventures because the extreme risks (loss of cargo and ship) were transferred to others. Insurance and reinsurance is therefore at the heart of risk transfer and capital provisioning.

Over time, and through the tested process of abuse by scallywags and scoundrels, underwriting standards were set and improved. However, the promise to pay was generally only extended by, and accepted from, the very wealthy. They were the ones who could be relied upon to make good on their promise. They had what might today be called "political capital" or "credit", emanating from their good name. By transferring risk to them, merchants substituted their own capital needs for the underwriter's available political capital or credit worthiness. In some sense, that process has continued to the present day at Lloyds (or at least up until 5–10 years ago).

The promise of the wealthy was further embellished by making the promiser liable to the full extent of his wealth. This was the principal of unlimited liability. The underwriters of early ventures were liable "down to their cuff-links". Actually it was worse than that, they were jointly and severally liable, ie, down to their co-underwriters' cuff-links as well as their own. This was a powerful promise, especially when it involved some of the richest men of the realm. But, in 16th-century England, unlimited liability was not confined to insurance, it was the norm; most commercial ventures involved unlimited liability. Deadbeats ended up in debtor's prison. Only "incorporated" companies were able to limit their obligations. Incorporated companies were treated with the same status as individuals, ie, they were liable for their debts to the extent of the corporate net worth, but not beyond. Furthermore, incorporation was confined to state-granted monopolies such as the Hudson's Bay Company, East Indian Company, etc.

So powerful was the concept of unlimited liability that when new methods of raising capital – such as the joint stock company – ran into trouble through the South Sea Bubble fiasco, parliament passed a law (the notorious Bubble Act of 1720) limiting incorporations and forbidding the exchange of shares by any unincorporated joint stock company. Incorporation, of course, was an expensive parliamentary procedure and the lack of it arguably slowed the early deployment of capital to the industrial revolution.

In this environment unlimited liability in insurance did not seem out of place. In fact, the government sanctioned only two incorporated insurers (Royal Exchange Assurance and London Assurance Companies) and forbade the writing of marine insurance by any other corporation. What it did not do was outlaw underwriting of ventures on a private or individual (unlimited) basis and this private mechanism flourished. Indeed, insurances companies (as well as Lloyds syndicates) and private stock companies with unlimited liability were the principal way of raising capital for the next century. Despite their tenuous legal standing, private joint stock companies proliferated. Not until 1855 did parliament pass the Limited Liability Act. It actually formalised what had been a growing practice among unincorporated joint stock companies of indemnifying certain capital contributors and of creeping limited liability. Known as the "rogue's charter" the concerns of the day were evident in the Act's sobriquet. Even the redoubtable economist Adam Smith had earlier said "incorporation with limited liability could only be justified if the capital required was so great that private ventures would not otherwise provide it and the industry was of the greatest public utility." Reluctance due to moral hazard was overcome because of the capital needs of the nation.

A MORE RECENT ERA

Arguably, insurance and capital markets practices began to diverge at this point. The private limited company (the modern form of the incorporated joint stock company) has financed most of the industrial development for the past 150 years in both the US and UK. As a mechanism for raising capital it is surely one of the most successful ever devised. It provides capital for general corporate purposes as well as for insurance companies. However, Lloyds as the exemplar of insurance innovation, continued with unlimited liability as its signature promise for another 140 years. It has only recently given up the ghost. It is not alone. General Partnerships, the other part of the finance world where unlimited liability continued to exist, particularly for the accounting, legal and other professions, have also seen a decline.

Before conceding that Lloyds is bowing to a superior mechanism, it is worth spending a moment to examine what unlimited liability did achieve.

On the negative side of the ledger stand two things; first, unlimited coverage and, second, separation of capital and risk. To explain, there is a tendency to say that because capital is unlimited then coverage should also be unlimited. To be sure, modern policies have occurrence, aggregate and individual limits, but far too many casualty policies exist without limit. (Asbestos, mould or sideways marine and aviation exposure might serve as specific contemporary examples.[4]) In truth, an unlimited liability is always limited (at the cuff-link point) and it seems it would appear sensible to always have coverage limits as well. But, once started, such practices are competitively tough to move away from. (Again, by way of illustration from another market, why do US borrowers of fixed-rate mortgages continue to have the right to cancel at will without penalty? Try changing it.)

The other potentially negative point – separation of capital management and underwriting – is a double-edged sword. As originally conceived, the promise of the wealthy underwriter was backed by his capital – whether that capital was invested in Scottish land, US equities or raw commodities. In order to raise more "wealth capital", over the years Lloyds expanded its membership to included non-UK residents, women and (God forbid!) Americans and Canadians. The agents who raised the membership

Figure 1 Membership, capacity, losses and number of syndicates, Lloyds of London 1975–2002

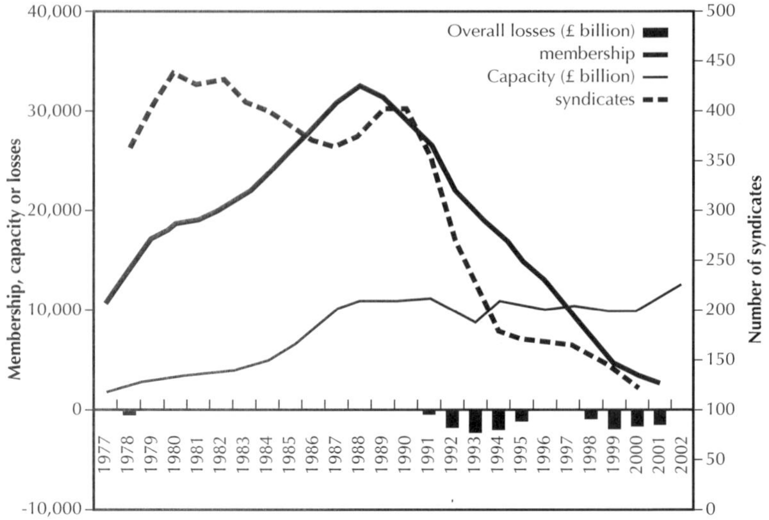

Source: Morgan Stanley, courtesy Doherty and Lamm-Tennant research paper.

rolls were paid according to membership numbers rather than syndicate results and there was inevitably a disconnection between agent and principal. This "flaw" was not exclusive to Lloyds. It is present in all corporate offerings by investment bankers, but somehow it was writ large in the case of Lloyds. Figure 1 shows both the recent growth and withdrawal of expanded membership of Lloyds.

Not unlike the Japanese stock market, membership peaked in 1989 at around 32,000 names (as shown in Figure 1). Today there are fewer than 3,000 names still operating on old unlimited liability principles. This low number was last seen in 1960. Under the 2002 renewal proposals, no new names will be admitted after January 2003. Quite a reversal of practice, but we are getting ahead of ourselves.

The separation of capital management and underwriting does have its beneficial effects. As long as adequate capital is maintained, with attendant liquidity, there is no reason why capital investment should be commingled with underwriting. Indeed, the recent stock market experience of European insurers has shown that investing in an insurer exposes the investor to both the insurer's underwriting and the insurer's asset management results. Both can be poorly done. If one is an asset manager oneself, acquiring a good underwriting result can be a great diversifier. Acquiring the insurer's underwriting result bundled with his asset management can be less attractive. It can compound one's own results rather than diversify them.

In this case, the evolved Lloyds practice – to invest in underwriting and self-manage the assets necessary to make good on the promise – seems to have got it right and is a preferred solution, provided good security can be established.

The underwriting–investment management separation can now be seen to explain why so many insurance executives have difficulty relating to capital markets: they never had to before. Names agents solicited the wealthy and the commitment of their wealth to underwriting. And as long as underwriting returns were positive, participation in Lloyds was an attractive add-on to the names self-wealth management. To join Lloyds was to join an elite club; discussing ones capital, its form, let alone its price, was not only unnecessary, it was considered bad form. Comparisons with alternative forms of capital were redundant as long as profits flowed.

As Figure 1 shows, however, the profit compact was breached with losses in 1978 and then hugely in the early and late 1990s. It is interesting to speculate whether Lloyds would still be in business the old fashioned way today if they had continued to deliver old fashioned profits.

Another aspect in which the unlimited liability crowd may have got it right is the discipline of an annual venture. Each year syndicates were required to close the account and let their investors know the projected result and solicit the names' intention to continue underwriting the following year. In modern finance this can be analogised to mark-to-market requirements, or to the ability to exit periodically from a hedge fund. It is a practice generally applauded. Not that it is easy to effect in the context of insurance. Long tail obligations must be represented by a single current value in order to close a year. This can be done by acquiring "reinsurance-to-close" from a competitor. The premium of such reinsurance represents the value of the book of outstanding obligations. Failure to obtain reinsurance-to-close means that value cannot be agreed upon, or is high. In either case, the investor's capital is not released for the next year's underwriting. It is judged to be lost completely or at least seriously impaired. Unfortunately, such reinsurance-to-close was often only obtained within the Lloyds market where it was subject to manipulative abuse. Again this "flaw" is not exclusive to Lloyds, as any number of rogue trader incidents of mismarking trading inventories can attest – see for example Barings.

Whether abused or not, whether well intentioned or not, the annual venture is unfortunately expensive. Imagine if stock companies had to return capital to investors each year and then bid for it back – oh the fees! Lloyds had to maintain a names agent structure to support their continued re-election. This is almost as undesirable, and costly, as the money raising activities of local politicians. Furthermore, Lloyds had to compete with stock insurance companies who encountered no such costs. Each year public insurance companies report their result to their investors and the public through their annual (or quarterly) statements. Investors or new entrants are then free to buy or sell their stock at the prevailing market price. The capital is permanent (in the sense that it does not have to be retired at any time) but the price of it and ownership of it may change at will. Of course, no system is without its abuses. Stock company insurers can be chronic under-reporters of loss, thus distorting the fair price at which their stock will trade. They may raise new capital as disingenuously as any derived from a contrived reinsurance-to-close. It could be that the losses that Lloyds discloses in a particular year are no more or no less than the stock company's market, but the annual venture forces earlier and more rigorous disclosure of loss than their competitors and they thereby garner worse publicity. (Actually Lloyds practice involves an annual venture, but a three year accounting of that annual period, so that the rigour of forcing annual results out into the open is delayed two years even at Lloyds.)

Notwithstanding the virtues of unlimited liability, the battle to maintain existing practice has been lost at Lloyds by dint of poor performance. Allowed for the first time in 1996, corporate (ie, limited liability) capital now is the predominant form of capital used at Lloyds. Within several years it may be the only form of capital. Figure 1 shows the decline of the number of private members. It shows the decline in the number of syndicates (indications of economies of scale at work) but it also shows that "capacity" has been stable or slowly rising for the last five years. Corporate members have more than made up for the private names in terms of their capacity to take risks. The fraction of names now on a limited liability basis has risen from 0% in 1995, to 60% in 1998, to 80% in 2001.

The current articulation of this switch at Lloyds is the 2002 renewal programme. It seeks to turn Lloyds into a franchise and to make it more investor friendly. To that end, Sax Riley, Lloyds chairman at the time of writing, says "Lloyds can no longer sustain financial performance which goes from profit to heart attack every five years. If we do not do this right, any debate about the provision of capital to the market will be academic. Capital providers will just stop putting up their money – it is as basic as that. ... The concept of unlimited liability is no longer viable in this era ... potential future investors in Lloyds are interested in profit, performance and return on capital."

So, if Sax Riley is to believed, Lloyds rejoins the capital markets that parted company from them a century and half ago. Those capital markets have not stood still, indeed the pace of their change has accelerated markedly in the past two decades. Lloyds, and those insurers built on similar practice, have a lot of catching up to do. First and foremost they must adjust to a world where their results are not an add-on but must be measured against other competing investment alternatives.

MODERN CAPITAL MARKETS

Christopher Culp identifies half a dozen reasons why the general corporation holds capital.[5] They include:

1. financing new investments;
2. maintenance of ownership and control;
3. risk mitigation;
4. financial shock absorber (financial slack);
5. signaling to both suppliers, clients and potential investors the strength of the corporation; and finally
6. regulatory requirements.

Collectively, these motivations determine the amount of capital that the firm will hold, although not its form.

Traditionally, limited liability is provided in the form of equity capital. The equity holders own the company. Theoretically, at

Figure 2 Type of issue by issuing entity, October 2001–January 2002

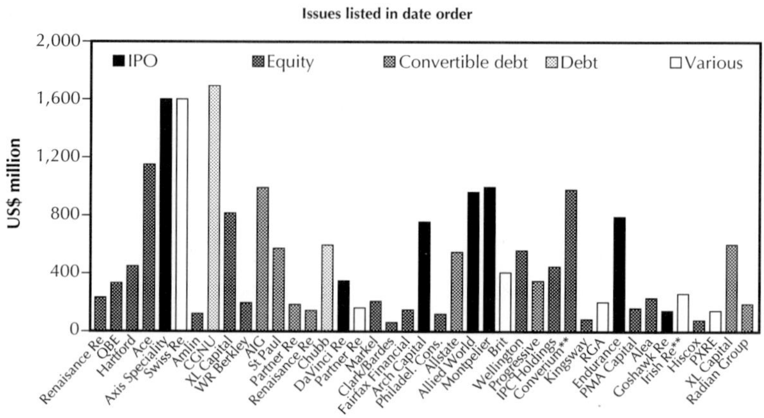

Source: Morgan Stanley, courtesy of Doherty and Lamm-Tennant research paper.

least, they appoint management and a board of directors to look after their interests. If the firm is successful they may reward themselves with a stream of dividends and reserve for themselves the decision about winding up or selling the company. Typically, firms try to leverage the return to themselves by borrowing funds for investment purposes. Debt usually, but not always, is cheaper than equity. It is, for instance, tax deductible. So, if investment can be funded by debt instead of new equity, the returns to existing equity will be higher. Of course there is a limit; too much debt and the vulnerability of capital to financial and or business shocks increases. In any case, this is the traditional form of capital provisioning; debt and equity. Different industries experience different volatility and so norms in the amount of debt or equity differ by industry. Cigna, the large US property casualty insurer, aims to have debt no higher than 20% of its surplus. Catastrophe insurers may have no debt or very little.

Without doubt the majority of capital for insurers and for corporations alike is raised in the traditional market for capital. Equity is raised privately by subscription or publicly via initial public offerings. The shares in the company are then traded in the secondary market – the New York Stock Exchange and its ilk. Debt is usually distributed in the same way and is traded privately via the over-the-counter bond markets. Any doubt that this is the mainstream practice will be put to rest by Figure 2.[6] It shows how capital was raised by new and existing insurers immediately following

September 11, 2001. Clearly, the insurance market is a dedicated user of traditional capital markets; but that now includes some Lloyds syndicates as well. One might also reflect on the efficiencies of the modern capital market. Some US$20 billion new capital was raised in the three months following September 11, compared with the eight years it has taken Lloyds to transition to a US$16 billion corporate capital.

Traditional markets have used these forms – debt and equity – or certain variants for 150 years. However, about 30 years ago perceptions of the nature of equity and debt changed and the new insights by the aforementioned Black, Scholes and Merton energised considerable financial product innovation.[7] Let's be clear, debt and equity did not change, rather the way we looked at them did. Think an earth-centric vs a Copernican view of the universe. The planets are no different, the perceptions are.

Essentially, the insight was that equity and debt are options on the assets of the firm and that the price of the equity or debt is exactly equivalent to the price of those options. Further, the options price formula can be articulated mathematically, calculated and even synthesised. This is important because once such a general formula exists other options can be valued and traded. And the world of finance is full of options both implicit and explicit. Put another way the world is full of choices, and now those choices can be valued financially. As one simple example, when lessors of equipment are given the option to return equipment to a manufacturer or lessee, that option is valuable, but without option pricing theory it is difficult to quantify precisely.

The famous Barnum & Bailey circus notice "this way to the 'Egress'" served to increase throughput in the menagerie; it may also serve to illuminate the character of viewing debts and equity as options. When a venture is terminated, consciously or involuntarily, the debts of the firm have to be paid off first. The remaining assets of the firm are "put" to the debt holders first. Debt holders are short a put on the assets.[8] However, creditors can never reclaim more than they have lent the firm, so strictly they are short a "put spread" on the assets. The rate of interest paid on the debt is actually equal to a) the risk-free price of money over time, plus b) the value of the "put spread". Only after the creditors have been satisfied can the equity holder claim the residual assets. Ergo, equity is a "call" on the firm's remaining assets.

The picture gets more complicated when there is more "capital structure", but the essential message is the same – each point in the structure can be represented as a simple or compound option and independently valued. If there is bank debt, senior debt, subordinated debt, convertibles, preferred stock and then common, each must be paid off in full in turn via the "waterfall" of claims before remaining assets can "egress" to the equity shareholder.

Each claim in the structure has a different cost (option premium) and the highest cost is the equity. Why? Because the firm's assets are assumed to be risky – their value is volatile. If the termination of the firm is at an inopportune time (which it usually is) then the remaining value of the assets may not be enough to pay off all preceding claimants. There may be a good chance that the equity holder will get nothing. Shareholders therefore need inducement, high expected return, to invest in equity. At the other end of the spectrum, people will compete to be at the head of the waterfall – the front of the queue – in the senior position. The cost of a senior option will be considerably lower than the cost of equity. (It is worth remarking that even senior debt costs will rise dramatically if perceptions about asset values or volatilities shift significantly – see, eg, fallen angels.)

Summarising, claims to assets can be characterised as options and options values are driven by volatility. It follows that the lower the volatility of asset values relative to expected earnings, the more valuable the option. The lower the volatility, the lower the cost of capital.

It also follows that any attempts to reduce asset volatility would lower the cost of capital. Insurance is a traditional way to reduce the volatility from events beyond the control of management. An oil driller may experience an extreme financial loss if his/her rig is wiped out in a hurricane and he/she has no insurance. Similarly, a shipper will suffer major, perhaps bankruptcy inducing, loss if hit by an environmental suit following an oil spill. Management, therefore, protects shareholders by buying insurance – transferring the risk to a third party.

Commercial insurance then is surrogate capital. It replaces downside loss and protects capital values from fortuitous

Figure 3 Capital solutions by broad categorisation

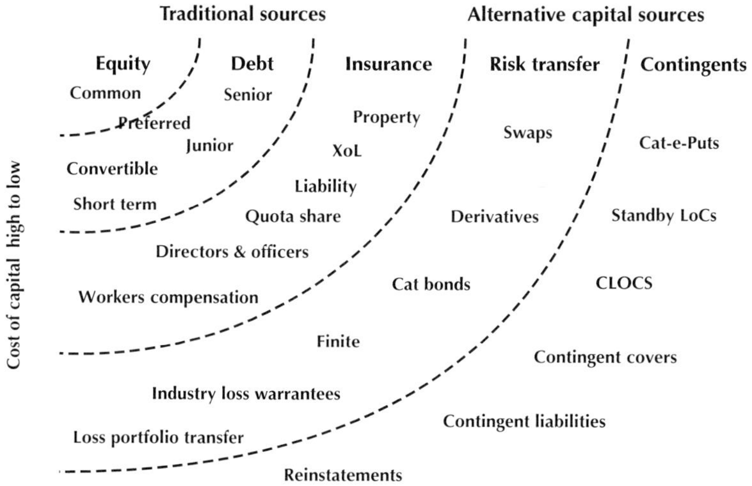

events. It is part of the traditional fabric of the corporate landscape. It is time to move to alternative sources of capital for insurers.

One last piece of the jigsaw is necessary to put it in to the modern finance context. Various capital forms can be characterised as options as heretofore described. Volatility drives options. But options can be synthesised. A long "call" plus a short "put" position is the financial and algebraic equivalent of a forward or future position in the underlying stock. This simple identity can be used to construct new instruments and to deconstruct existing ones. US fixed-rate mortgages are the equivalent of a bond plus a "put" option. A convertible bond is a bond plus a "call". Etc, etc.

Modern financial markets have instruments such as futures, swaps, options, structured notes, asset-backed securities, collateralised mortgage obligations, collateralised debt obligations and many more. This chapter is not the place to explore each of these. Suffice it to say that all are possible because of the ability to construct and deconstruct the options equivalents; each of them is a component part of the capital market; each is designed to shift risk or mitigate it and thereby reduce firm volatility. The instruments are not capital, but they shape the risk return profile of capital and therefore are surrogate capital in the same way as insurance is.

The alternative sources of capital that are the subject of this chapter are the insurance doppelganger of what has happened in modern corporate finance. The relative positioning of these alternative forms is illustrated in Figure 3.

ALTERNATIVE SOURCES OF CAPITAL IN THE INSURANCE MARKET

Alternative capital can now be broadly defined as monies and other devices beyond traditional equity, debt and insurance that serve to reduce volatility of results and thereby reduce the need for traditional capital. Figure 3 shows two broad swaths of alternative capital beyond the traditional sources. These are direct risk transfer instruments and standby or contingent instruments. The first category contains catastrophe (cat) bonds, derivatives, industry loss warrantees, swaps, finite and loss portfolio transfers. The second group contains contingent equity, debt and insurance – which are pre-arrangements of traditional capital sources. This chapter will comment on each in turn.

Risk transfer through cat bonds

By far and away the most talked about and widely heralded concept of alternative capital sources are cat bonds. More broadly defined as "insurance-linked securities" (ILS) so as to include non-cat insurance lines, the widespread appreciation of the concept has not yet lead directly to wholehearted embrace by either capital or insurance markets. The concept, in other words, has not been fully perfected. Nevertheless, there is a persistent drum beat of attempts to cross the acceptance threshold and the record is shown in Figure 4. Nearly 50 securitisations have been completed representing a total risk transfer of US$8–US$10 billion. This issuance has taken place since 1996, therefore equalling a rate of transfer of a little over a US$1 billion per year. There is a certain roughness in the numbers because the market is private and not all deals reach the public light of day. The lists in Figure 4 represent deals that have been publicised in the press, although even then not all details of the transaction are fully or consistently exposed (ie, while every attempt has been made to be accurate, the exact numbers are subject to error).

Figure 4 Catastrophe bond issues 1966 – date listed in reverse chronology

Issue Date	Issuer	Ceding Insurer	Amount
June-02	**Pioneer 2002 Ltd.**	Swiss Re	$2 billion authorized($255 million issued)
June-02	**Pioneer 2002 Ltd. Class A**	Swiss Re	$85 million
June-02	**Pioneer 2002 Ltd. Class B**	Swiss Re	$50 million
June-02	**Pioneer 2002 Ltd. Class C**	Swiss Re	$30 million
June-02	**Pioneer 2002 Ltd. Class D**	Swiss Re	$40 million
June-02	**Pioneer 2002 Ltd. Class E**	Swiss Re	$25 million
June-02	**Pioneer 2002 Ltd. Class F**	Swiss Re	$25 million
May-02	**Fujiyama Ltd.**	Nissay Dowa General Ins. Co., Ltd.	$70 million
May-02	**Residential Re 2002 Ltd.**	USAA	$100 million
April-02	**K3**	Hannover Re	$230 million
April-02	**St. Agatha Re**	Hiscox Syndicates Ltd.*	$33 million
March-02	**Redwood Capital II, Ltd.**	Swiss Re	$200 million
December-01	**Redwood Capital I, Ltd.**	Lehman Re	$165 million
December-01	**Atlas Reinsurance II p.l.c.**	SCOR	$150 million
June-01	**Trinom Ltd.**	Zurich Insurance Co.	$161.856 million
May-01	**SR Wind Ltd.**	Swiss Re	$120 million
May-01	**Residential Re 2001 Ltd.**	USAA	$150 million
March-01	**Halyard Re BV**	Sorema SA	$17 million
March-01	**Gold Eagle Capital 2001 Ltd.**	American Re	$120 million
February-01	**Western Capital**	Swiss Re	$100 million
November-00	**Mediterranean Re p.l.c.**	Assurances Generales de France I.A.R.T. ("AGF")	$129 million
November-00	**PRIME Capital Hurricane Ltd.**	Munich Re	$165 million
November-00	**PRIME Capital CalQuake & EuroWind**	Munich Re	$135 million
July-00	**NeHi**	NeHi Re, LP**	$50 million
May-00	**Alpha Wind 2000-A Ltd.**	Arrow Re***	$90 million
May-00	**Residential Re 2000 Ltd.**	USAA	$200 million
March-00	**Atlas Reinsurance p.l.c.**	SCOR	$200 million
November-99	**Namazu Re**	Gerling	$100 million*
September-99	**Kelvin Ltd.**	[Koch Energy Trading]	$44 million
Jun-99	**Residential Re III**	USAA	$200 million
June-99	**Juno Re**	Gerling	$80 million
May-99	**Concentric Ltd.**	Oriental Land	$100 million
May-99	**Circle Maihama**	Oriental Land	$100 million
May-99	**Halyard Re**	Sorema	$17 million
April-99	**SECTRS 1999-1**	Namur Re SA****	Euro455 million
March-99	**Domestic LLC**	Kemper Insurance Co. & affiliates	$80 million
February-99	**Reliance/SLF Re IV**	Reliance National and affiliates	$10 million
December-98	**Trinity Re 1999**	Centre Solutions	$55.6 million
December-98	**Gemini Re**	Allainz	$150 million
July-98	**Gramercy Place Insurance Ltd.**	[Toyota Motor Credit]	$566 milliom
July-98	**Pacific Re**	Yasuda Fire & Marine Ins. Co. Ltd.	$80 million
July-98	**X.L. Mid Ocean**	Mid Ocean Re and XL Global Re	$200 million
June 15, 1998	**Residential Re II**	USAA	$450 million
June 1, 1998	**Mosaic Re**	USF&G	$50 million
April 1, 1998	**Reliance/SLF Re III**	Reliance National and affiliates	$20 million optionable note (assume note issuance)*
February 1, 1998	**Trinity Re I**	Centre Solutions	$83.6 million
January-98	**Reliance/SLF Re II**	Reliance National and affiliates	$10 million
November-97	**Parametric Re**	Swiss Re*****	$100 million
July-97	**SR Earthquake Fund**	Swiss Re	$137 million
June-97	**Residential Re I**	USAA	$477 million
March-97	**Reliance/SLF Re I**	Reliance National and affiliates	$10 million
November-96	**Winterthur**	Winterthur	Sfr 399.5 million ($280 million)
October-96	**George Town Re**	St Paul Re	$68.5 million
July-96	**[Unknown/Guernsey?]**	AIG Combined Risks******	[$10 million]

Note: On occasion the insured is different the ultimate reinsured

* Lloyds Syndicate 33
** Vesta Fire Insurance Corp
*** 3State Farm Companies
**** Gerling Global and Gerling Credit Insurance Group
***** Tokio Marine
****** PXRE

Some important names are shown to be cedents to the market, testifying to its experimental importance. In fact, only a few reinsurers of note do not appear to have issued cat bonds. Since most of the cedents are reinsurers rather than insurers, ILS have been seen mostly as retrocessional substitutes, but they should work for insurers or even insureds equally well. Going against the tide, the most prolific – a six-time – issuer is the insurer United Services Automobile Association (USAA).

The process works like this: A ceding (re)insurer buys insurance coverage from a special purpose reinsurer (SPR). The SPR has been set up exclusively to write that specific coverage to the cedent. The SPR then issues bonds to capitalise its obligation under the written coverage. Those bonds are sold directly into the bond markets by the investment bankers representing the SPR. The proceeds of the bond sale are then placed in trust by the SPR, thereby collateralising the exposure, and are released to the cedent if and only if a legitimate claim is made under the cover.

At the end of the transaction, if no claim has been made, the funds are returned to the bondholder as repayment of principal and the SPR is liquidated. The bondholder will have received interest, (premium plus a (near) risk–free return, usually LIBOR) on his principal or deposited funds. The insurance premium from the cedent and passed through the SPR to the bondholder corresponds to the "spread over LIBOR" that the bondholder would expect to receive from corresponding corporate bonds that compete for attention. The premium paid by the cedent is comparable to what would be paid to a traditional reinsurer for similar coverage received.

The advantage to the cedent is two-fold. First, the ILS represents a diversifying source of capital – the bond market – and second, since the insurer's obligation is pre-funded, the coverage has near zero credit risk. In current times when insurers are looking for new sources of capital and casting a wary eye on reinsurance recoverables these are not inconsiderable advantages. For the bondholder there are also two benefits to purchasing cat bonds. First, acquisition of a diversifying risk to the bondholder's normal corporate exposure (stock markets and earthquakes are not highly correlated) and second, a good expected excess return compared to corporate alternatives. The appeal to bondholders ought to be similar to the appeal that Lloyds had for wealthy individuals of the past, namely an expected excess return over and above non-correlated alternatives.

Evidently, however, there are disadvantages to both sides, which offset the advantages. If this were not the case more cat bonds would be forthcoming. Start with the obvious. Cat bond premiums paid by the cedent must be competitive with the conventional reinsurance alternatives and equally the "spread" received by the bondholder must be competitive with bond spreads. In a deep liquid market such a fortuitous alignment of prices would be brought about by arbitrage. In a nascent illiquid market the alignment is more difficult to achieve. It is much more hit or miss.

Among the other perceived disadvantages is the consequence of an asymmetry of information; bondholders do not know as much about the underlying risks as the insurers. They are understandably afraid of being taken advantage of. When the risk transferred is based on the outcome of the insurer's book of business (on the indemnity principal) the asymmetries are at their greatest. Indemnity was necessary to comfort cedents in early deals, but later it became necessary to comfort bondholders. As a consequence, the fraction of bonds issued on an indemnity basis has dropped from 99% in 1999 to only 17.5% in 2002.[9] The alternative to an indemnity issue is an issue with a more objective measure of loss – an index – that serves the cedent while putting the bondholder and cedent on a more equal informational footing. Three approaches have been tried.

The first index approach is to use an industry measure of loss, rather than the loss experienced directly by the cedent. This solution, already used by the traditional industry in certain contexts, necessarily introduces a "basis risk" for the cedent. A basis risk is the exposure that the insurer encounters because the recovery under an index deal may not exactly equal actual loss. Under conventional insurance coverage using a principal of indemnity, such basis risk is minimised. (It is not eliminated as some would have you believe.) Clearly, any substantial basis risk assumed by the cedent detracts from the benefits from improved security, cost and diversification.

The other approaches to the problems of asymmetry are paying losses based on "modelled loss" or based upon a "parametric" measure. The modelled loss approach takes a computer model of the cedent's book and puts the model in escrow to be used to calculate the loss later on. The model is either made available to bondholders or to independent verifiers on the bondholder's behalf. Typically, the verifiers are one of the modelling agencies, RMS, EQECAT or AIR. These modelling agencies are also used in the parametric process. Parametric measures link the loss payment to some physical measure of disaster such as wind speed, or earthquake severity in particular locations.

Cochran Caronia estimates that 25% of deals have been indemnity-based, 19% are industry loss-based, 21% are modelled loss and 25% are parametric.[10] Among Figure 1's listings, Namazu and Trinom deals are modelled loss, Parametric and Atlas II are parametric, SR Earthquake and Redwood Capital I are index-based and Residential Re is the most consistent indemnity issuer.

Several other features define cat bonds, such as the term to maturity, perils covered, whether single or multiple perils and any embedded optionality. In the context of alternative capital, however, the important point is that all these features can be tailor-made to the cedent's capital needs. Cat bonds can protect against volatility in the same way that insurance can, and may even be superior.

Insurance derivatives

Before cat bonds hit the street in 1993, various exchanges in the US and Bermuda experimented with derivatives that paid losses based on indices. The Chicago Board of Trade initially used an "Insurance Services Office" index and later improved it with a "Property Claims Service" index. The experiment lasted for about five years and several hundreds of millions of risk was so transferred. However, the soft markets of the mid-1990s reduced interest, and eventually put paid to the experiment. Yet one is left with the impression that those ideas may someday be revived. The exchanges' current experiment is with weather derivatives. Even so, the early exchange attempts are behind us and do not currently represent viable public sources of alternate capital. However the concept is still available to private parties and certain transactions can be done on a derivative basis. For example, derivatives could be drawn up on an outstanding security, say PRIME Cal Quake and Euro-wind. The derivative would then mimic PRIME and if Munich Re were a counterparty to an independent investor, it would provide additional capacity to Munich Re without the expense of issuing a whole new security.

Industry loss warrantees

An industry loss warrantee (ILW) is analogous to a cat bond written on an industry loss index basis, with two important differences. Typically, the ILWs are written by and between insurers and are not pre-funded. Secondly, ILWs have a second trigger based on indemnity losses. The indemnity loss is set low so that it will almost always trigger when the industry loss triggers, thereby releasing payment. The reason this is important is that the presence of the indemnity trigger ensures that the coverage provided by an ILW can be accounted for as insurance cover. Cat bonds with non-indemnity indices may not be given insurance accounting treatment, and may have to be recorded as investment transactions. The bottom line effect to the income statement will be the same for a purchased ILW as a similarly designed cat bond, but the composition of the income statement will be different. The ILW will show a lower net written premium (since its cost is a deductible premium expense), the similarly designed cat bond may not. This underscores the point that while all surrogate capital is equally good from a strictly cashflow point of view, not all will be good from other, perhaps cosmetic, points of view. If analysts view net premium as a measure of exposure for the company, the lower net written premium company appears less risky.

The ILW market is perhaps the natural successor to the exchange-traded insurance derivative market. The market supplies derivative-like instruments with accounting benefits and there is a quite healthy trading market which has also allowed non-insurance participants to get "alternative capital" to insurers. Some other subtle differences involve payout. ILWs are usually binary. There is either a full payout of the cover, or none. In comparison, cat bond covers pay out proportionate to the size of underlying loss. There are often also reinstatement provisions (more of which is described in the "Contingent liabilities" section).

Insurance swaps

Paralleling the exchange-traded interest derivative market in the financial markets is the enormous over-the-counter interest rate swaps market. Literally trillions of dollars worth of notional value is swap-traded between fixed vs variable interest rates. It seems quite natural that as insurance markets experiment with doppelganger instruments for insurance, they would also experiment with swaps. Tokio Marine and State Farm have led the charge in this direction. Swaps do not provide capital in the sense that they reduce volatility directly by funding losses, they instead accommodate or achieve less volatility in the income stream by reducing exposure from one line of business and assuming another diversifying line and thereby improve the existing capital position.

Tokio Marine swapped Japanese earthquake risk for State Farm's US wind risk.[11] Neither wrote those risks directly. Usually the swap is done on a zero premium basis, provided the differences in riskiness can be agreed upon. (Finding equivalence of different tail risks is a non-trivial task in itself.) Thus, both parties get reduced tail risk and improved diversification at no cost. Is this capital? Maybe not, but it reduces capital need or at least makes the existing capital more efficient. It is likely that the practice will grow (Tokio Marine has since done several others including with Swiss Re) and may even mutate into the various forms that cat bonds have taken. Swaps on an index, modelled loss or parametric basis and with zero premium effect would take away the adverse accounting effect of cat bonds and would also allow direct access to the non-insurance market.

Finite reinsurance

So-called finite insurance is probably the hardest to define precisely among all the types of alternative instruments, but it is the oldest. Essentially, finite reinsurance recognises that catastrophic risk is lumpy and that it would be better if the cost of loss could be spread over several years. US insurance regulation requires that cat losses only be expensed after a loss; no reserve or bank can be built up prior to the potential loss. Clearly a "bank" would smooth the impact of a catastrophic loss. Not all jurisdictions have the same conservatism and finite reinsurance can be seen as a regulatory arbitrage allowing smoothing for domestic insurers via purchase of reinsurance in other jurisdictions. Not all finite is of this form and all must now contain a significant amount of risk transfer. But once again, finite is not alternative capital in the sense of a financial shock absorber, primarily because such covers are designed so that the cedent eventually pays the loss. It is an accounting shock absorber. The non-risk transfer component of finite reinsurance may be considered faux capital in the sense that it can reduce the appearance of volatility year to year without necessarily reducing ultimate long-term volatility.

Loss portfolio transfers

The sister of finite coverage is the transfer of whole portfolios of risk. Typically, a premium is paid to the new carrier of the risk which is calibrated to defease the portfolio obligations over time. Usually the carriers of such portfolios gain because they have to hold reserves on a non-discounted basis and usually pay the assumer on a discounted basis in those jurisdictions where discounting is permitted. There is an income statement gain and there may be an improved capital position, although items are removed from both sides of the balance sheet.

All the risk transfer solutions described above involve a beneficial effect of volatility reduction and efficient use of capital. Those solutions will be all the more utilised if they are cheaper than traditional sources. For example, if investors begin to pay up aggressively for the diversification implicit in cat bonds or ILWs, then this form of alternative capital may become much more attractive. It is also worth noting that risk may be transferred but it does not get extinguished, it simply gets moved. Holders of cat bonds or finite reinsurance assume volatility from others. Presumably, those assumers are better able to absorb the volatility and market efficiency is achieved.

CONTINGENT EQUITY, CONTINGENT DEBT AND CONTINGENT COVERAGE

If the Army, Navy and Air Force of a country are the capital counterparty of equity, debt and insurance, namely the first line of defence against volatility, then the Marines and Special Forces are the equivalent of alternative capital that can be used in a variety of volatility-reducing theatres. Continuing the thought then, the Army, Naval and Air National Guards are the equivalent of contingent capital. The National Guard (or the Territorial Army) is committed to serve in the event if they are called. It costs something to keep the guard on call, but not as much as the standing army. If the standing force is engaged in a conflict, the presence of a reserve that is partially, perhaps fully, trained to take their place adds to a country's strength.

In the case of insurance, contingent forms of capital exist for equity, debt and coverage. The most visible equity standby was coined by Aon as a "cat-e-put". The insurer acquiring the cat-e-put gained the right to put preferred stock to the option writer. In order to reduce cost and to tailor the circumstances to those occasions when extra capital was required, the option could only be exercised after the occurrence of a pre-specified catastrophe. Since the put writer in those circumstances would only want to buy stock if the firm was still a viable franchise, there was often a restriction that the loss should not be too large. Prudent as it was, this last restriction probably slowed the development of a promising structure. Nevertheless, several deals have been consummated that are quite useful as back up capital.

The debt equivalent of the cat-e-put has the eponymous name CLOCS (for committed long-term capital solutions). Invented and named by Swiss Re, they been used in significant transactions for Royal Bank of Canada (for regulatory capital purposes), Michelin (standby credit) and MBIA (credit wraps for ratings maintenance). Although none of these examples are insurers there is no reason that they could not be. Similarly, the CLOCS can be used for debt and equity combinations.

Another example of a contingent debt securitisation was Circle Maihama, which gave the Oriental Land Company the right to put a note to the standby investor if and only if there was an earthquake of a prescribed size around their Tokyo Disney Land holdings. This deal was partnered with a cat bond (Concentric Ltd) so the "insured" first received a loss payment then the contingent loan. Notice that "insured" was placed in quotations because no insurer was involved. Investors took the role of the insurer. Circle Maihama represent a case where the insured went directly to the capital markets for coverage rather than via the insurance markets – a development to perhaps cause insurers a certain wariness.

Completing the National Guard line up is contingent coverage. In these cases the option buyer buys the right to acquire reinsurance coverage if and when the option is exercised. Unlike contingent debt or equity, which will affect ownership structure and seniority claims, contingent coverage is capital structure neutral. Three cedents have publicly utilised contingent cover through securitisation; Reliance National (with SLFIII), Allianz (with Gemini) and Converium (with Trinom) all listed in Figure 4. Like other contingents the trigger is usually exercisable only after a major event. Obviously, contingent coverage provides a back up capital to absorb financial shocks after the first such shock.

When contingent covers are written they usually pre-specify the price at which the debt, equity or coverage is put in place, if and when exercised. Usually this is close to the current market – "at-the-money". Replacement coverage is the main objective. If however, the price is set "out-of-the-money" relative to current prices, these options a) are cheaper and b) take on the character of a cap on the price of future replacement coverage. When exercisable, coverage may or may not be cheaper in the underlying market. If it is less than the "out-of-the-money" price the option will not be exercised, and vice versa. There is a significant reason to use contingents simply as price caps rather than capital sources.

REINSTATEMENTS

Both ILWs and conventional reinsurances often have reinstatement provisions attached to them. Strictly, these reinstatements are contingent options (that reinstate the coverage after a first loss) with mandatory exercise provisions. Since reinstatements force new coverage for the buyers from the sellers they once again provide a "belt and suspenders" financial shock absorber. Note, however, ILW reinstatement terms often fix the reinstatement premium at the original level (so-called "one at 100%"). Since the reinstatement may be invoked at any time during the year the effect is one of de facto rising reinstatement premiums as the year unfolds.

CONTINGENT LIABILITIES

If the addition of contingent capital is an asset for the firm, then it follows that the reduction in contingent liabilities is also an asset. Both increased contingent capital and reduced contingent liability are reducers of shareholder volatility. Several deals by airline manufacturers British Aerospace and Saab have securitised their contingent liabilities by putting them into the capital market. Another line where contingent liabilities have been reduced is in auto leasing, eg, by Toyota Motor Credit Corporation (TMCC). In the Gramercy transaction TMCC obtained protection from low residual values of autos coming off lease contracts. Generally there is a growing appreciation of residual value as a separate asset class. Most of the deals ended back on insurers' balance sheets as they were quicker to recognise the diversifying virtues of the risk to their portfolios. In that sense insurers were alternative capital sources to corporates. Provided the residual value contract is profitably underwritten it can be as valuable as a swap for capital efficiency purposes.

CONCLUDING REMARKS

Much general market underwriting practice in insurance is in step with, and originates from, the early practices of Lloyds of London. On the other hand, capital acquisition practice by Lloyds has been quite out of step with conventional markets for a century or more. Lloyds has begun to move toward conventional financial markets and are encountering a bewildering variety of capital instruments. There is in Lloyds, and, reflexively, in other insurance markets, an ever increasing appreciation of the demands of capital and the innovativeness of those capital markets. Over the past 5–8 years we have seen experiments in insurance with what we have called doppelgangers of a myriad of finance market instruments – derivatives, swaps, etc. Collectively, all these instruments – traditional and alternative – are the capital markets. The current alternative capital markets for insurance are still in their infancy. They are likely to grow to be much more significant in future.

This chapter has laid the context for these significant changes ahead. It also sought to identify the principal instruments that will shape those changes. The rationale for executing any such changes is the improvement and efficiency of capital. In conclusion it should be noted that while such experiments are likely to be positive in direction, they are not likely to happen without some stress. In the most conventional of capital markets there is a natural tension between the desires of debt and equity holders; debt holders are naturally conservative, whereas equity holders are more aggressive. Similarly, in insurance markets, tensions can grow between shareholders and policyholders as well as debtholders. These issues have presented themselves in the US in the controversies surrounding de-mutualisation initiatives, and in the UK it has been asserted, eg, that payments to Royal and Sun Alliance shareholders in 1999 may have had a deleterious effect on policy holders in 2002. Whatever the merits of either argument, the discussions expose the fact that capital must serve many masters. Innovative solutions that address each constituent's concern can only evolve with intelligent use of new capital market alternatives. The future of capital market alternatives for insurance has only just begun. It is a future that appears both exciting and challenging.

1 Young and Theys (1999). To be fair this interesting book addresses new electronic forums for trading capital rather than capital itself, but it neatly illustrates how easy it is to be misled.
2 Steinbeck (2000).
3 From the preamble to the Insurance Act of 1601. Recorded in Raphael (1994).
4 The practice of insuring "each and every loss" or "each and every event" is a manifestation of unlimited cover.
5 See Lane (2002), Chapter 6.
6 Source: Morgan Stanley and chapters by Joan Lamm-Tennant and Neil Doherty in Lane (2002).
7 See *Capital Ideas*, The Free Press, 1992, by Peter Bernstein for an excellent exposition of these changes.
8 Sometimes the respective options roles of debt and equity are described differently. However, these other descriptions may not be incorrect. Often they are equivalent statements that can be reconciled by reference to "put–call parity" theorem. This says that an asset may be expressed as equivalent to a long call and a short put position. Hence, by algebraically rearranging, equity (a call) is the financial equivalent of being long the assets of a firm and long a put (the debt). The debtholder is short the put.
9 See Lane Financial LLC (2002).
10 See Lane (2002), Chapter 3.
11 See Lane (2002), Chapter 5.

BIBLIOGRAPHY

Bernstein, P., 1992, *Capital Ideas: The Improbable Origins of Modern Wall Street* (The Free Press).

Lane, M., 2002, *Alternative Risk Strategies* (London: Risk Books).

Lane Financial LLC, 2002, "Review of Trends in Insurance Securitization", August.

Raphael, A., 1994, *Ultimate Risk* (London: Bantam Press).

Steinbeck, J., 2000, *Grapes of Wrath* (London: Penguin).

Young, P. and T. Theys, 1999, *Capital Market Revolution* (New York: *Financial Times*–Prentice Hall).

Part IV

Alternative perspectives

12

The Future of Electronic Trading

Kathrine Huelster

inreon

For years the reinsurance industry has been criticised for its apparent reluctance to embrace new technology; while other financial sectors were quick to incorporate electronic transactions into their everyday procedures, reinsurers lagged behind. Previous e-commerce initiatives failed to live up to their billing or establish widespread support. Indeed, those considering the future of electronic trading for the industry must surely have identified with the words of Argentine author Jorge Luis Borges who famously wrote: "The future is inevitable and precise, but it may not occur."[1]

The picture is not all doom and gloom. It might be argued that a more cautious approach has in some ways benefited reinsurers, saving them from costly false starts made by other so-called "early mover" industries. In the United States, for example, Potomac Electric Power launched an online exchange for companies in the Washington and Baltimore areas to buy a range of different business products services. The initiative promised to save time, reduce errors and trim costs, but after just four months it closed down after discovering that "the current demand for business-to-business marketplaces was not as robust as anticipated", according to a company press release. Dell Computer also shut its Dell Marketplace, an online exchange for buying products from Dell or select third parties after only four months of operation.

Opting out of the race altogether, however, is neither a realistic nor sensible option. And there are a now a number of signs that reinsurers are beginning to sit up and take notice of online trading possibilities.

Few would now argue that there are not enormous benefits to be gained from the market implementing a successful e-commerce strategy. A Goldman Sachs study in the US has suggested that technology could reduce the insurance industry's operating costs by an incredible US$45 billion over the next few years (see Goldman Sachs, 1999b). That figure is equal to 5.8% of operating costs and is cautioned to be a conservative benchmark for world-wide estimates. Clearly there is a great deal at stake. Industry technology budgets over the next five years will total US$25 billion, believes Goldman Sachs, with 30% spent on e-commerce activities.

INDUSTRY PROGRESS TO DATE

Already a degree of maturity in the e-commerce offerings available to the industry can be detected. Just 18 months to a year ago there were a wide range of different solutions available to the market. As the market has developed, however, a number have fallen by the wayside or been absorbed by stronger propositions. inreon, for example, acquired Risk Transfer Exchange (RTX) in June 2001 taking on its rivals' facultative expertise and marketing presence in the US. In December 2001 further consolidation took place with the acquisition of reway, a market-wide e-trading platform established by the German reinsurer, Gothaer Re. Additional unions are likely as the reinsurance e-commerce landscape continues to evolve.

Other platforms that have made a mark include e-Reinsure, a platform that has begun significant volumes of business from its sponsor Chubb. RI3K meanwhile has made progress with its business model to speed up the information flow and cash handling involved with reinsurance transactions. Lloyds of London has signalled its intention to push electronic trading with the implementation of "Project Blue Mountain".

inreon itself has seen acceptance of its virtual marketplace rise steadily with a 100%+ increase in membership over the first six months of 2001. There are now around 100 members of the platform, including a panel of 17 blue chip reinsurers. More than 50% of capacity available from the world's top 25 reinsurers is represented by inreon and original premiums in excess of €270m have been submitted.

Figure 1 Cumulative productivity improvement in banking, reinsurance and insurance

BUSINESS TO BUSINESS (B2B) E-COMMERCE MARKETS

Elsewhere, other industries are already realising such benefits. According to an analysis of revenue per employee data from Bloomberg and AM Best by consultants Accenture, productivity in the banking sector increased by 4% in the six years between 1995 and 2001 (as shown in Figure 1).[2] During the same period, productivity among reinsurers decreased by 5% while insurers suffered a dramatic 14% decline. The gaping chasm between the two financial sectors was largely put down to different levels of advancement in process reengineering and automation. Banking had successfully tackled the problem of handling standard cases without manual intervention while insurance had not.

A private Accenture study done specifically for inreon predicts that global e-commerce revenues across all industries will climb steadily over the next few years. By 2004, overall worldwide revenues are predicted to have reached in excess of US$3,200 billion. This forecast is made in spite of the dot com crash which saw electronic marketplaces fall from grace in the late 1990s. At one point, analysts were predicting that there would be as many as 10,000 e-marketplaces flourishing by 2004. But very quickly reports of B2B e-markets in financial trouble and issuing profit warnings

Figure 2 Global e-commerce revenues (US$ billion) B2B

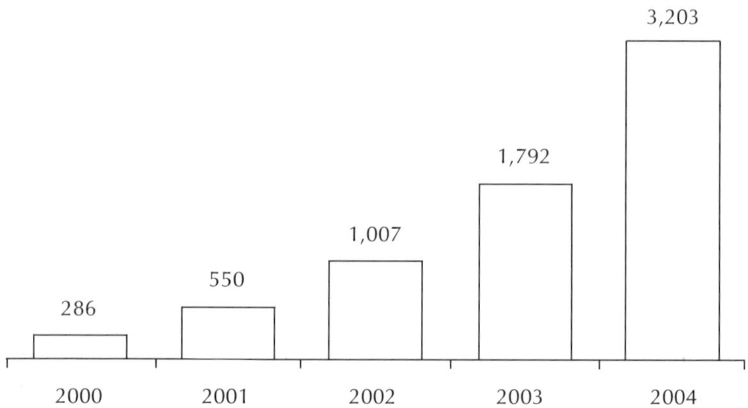

Source: Accenture 2001

were almost as much a regular feature of daily news bulletins as the weather forecast.

There are still, however, around 500 e-marketplaces in Europe, observes Accenture. Most of these are reported to have experienced their first transactions in the first year of their foundation. In the chemicals industry an online marketplace, ChemConnect, was established in 1995 and claims case studies showing individual sellers have achieved US$3 million in new business while buyers have cut costs by 12% through access to new suppliers. Omnexus was founded by leading companies in the plastics industry in 2000 and provides members with access to more than 20 global suppliers, online order placement and tracking and a simplified ordering process. The aerospace and defence industry meanwhile has supported Exostar, a standardised online platform for transactions and business development. Further examples can be found in securities and automobiles.

E-TRADING FOR THE REINSURANCE SECTOR

The key question for the reinsurance industry now is what type of e-trading capability does it want? In arriving at a credible answer to this debate it is useful to look at the experiences of other sectors. What lessons have already been learned? Are there any common features of successful e-markets and if so what are they?

Perhaps the first argument to be had concerns the merits of a single market e-trading platform vs many different proprietary systems. A completely independent market platform, not tied to any existing industry participants may struggle to obtain acceptance and generate the necessary support to survive and prosper. Developing proprietary platforms meanwhile allows individual companies to maintain greater control over development.

But ultimately such a myriad of different solutions can only mean greater cost for the industry as a whole. While proprietary systems may suit clients who maintain a close relationship with one reinsurer, any cedents looking to access several different companies will face a potentially frustrating process. In order to access all the business partners they wish, they may have to re-key data into, or build interfaces with, a number of different systems.

A single market-wide solution however, minimises the need for such re-entry and maximises opportunities for expanded distribution and cost savings. Users only have to access one platform and can receive data from a variety of different business partners in a single standardised format.

As previously mentioned, however, independently establishing a successful e-marketplace is no easy task. Initially, perceived low barriers to entry enabled a large number of participants to establish e-trading solutions in a number of industries. According to Accenture's research, uncertainty created by such large numbers prevented many potential users from taking business online. Thus, "a main reason for recent failures of B2B marketplaces was their inability to gain critical mass."

Any successful e-trading solution for the reinsurance industry as a whole therefore must be able to command widespread support from the industry on a global basis. Typically only two or three significant e-trading solutions can possibly survive in each industry, predicts Accenture: "This is based on the assumption that buyers will move their transactions to the marketplace with the highest liquidity. Thereby demand will concentrate on few marketplaces. Moreover, in order to defray high investments and ongoing costs a high number of transactions are needed by the marketplaces."

The conditions necessary to achieve such a critical mass create something of a paradox; without influential industry support in the initial start-up phase, any trading platform will find it difficult, if not impossible to get off the ground. Yet being too closely tied to any single particular market player invites accusations of bias and lack of genuine independence.

It was this dilemma that prompted Munich Re and Swiss Re to co-operate in forming the Internet-based trading platform inreon. Despite a fierce rivalry, the world's two largest reinsurers appreciated that neither company on its own could realistically expect to promote an "independent" solution. Together they hoped to use their market-leading position to launch an e-solution that could credibly be seen to maintain an important position of independence and stand a reasonable chance of achieving critical mass. In order to become truly independent, however, the platform will need to further expand its shareholding to properly reflect all interests within the industry.

LINES OF BUSINESS FOR E-TRADING

Another vital component for the success of future B2B e-marketplaces will be an ability to expand their service offering, claims Accenture. An important reason why some ventures failed in the past "lay in the fact that their business models misjudged how much, and for which services, customers were willing to pay".

A concentrated and targeted product offering is vital. In reinsurance the early development of products was relatively straightforward with facultative contracts an obvious area for improvement. Already fairly commoditised facultative business was seen as ideally suited to Internet trading because of the relative uniformity of many contracts and absence of more protracted contract negotiations. Various lines of business were identified for the process change with property a pioneer followed by among others liability, engineering, marine and aviation.

If, however, trading efficiencies could be identified and proven in one area, it was inevitable that other areas of business would soon also come under consideration for e-trading.

By definition treaty reinsurance is more complex than facultative. And its greater financial value to both buyer and seller means that much more time and discussion is spent on making sure the right deal is struck at the right price.

But the increased amount of detail and negotiation required can be overcome by introducing enhanced levels of dialogue before a risk is quoted. In particular treaty catastrophe covers, already widely syndicated, are thought to lend themselves well to an electronic platform. The need for a more efficient method of placing this line of business is paramount. Shortages of capacity are far from uncommon. Cedents and brokers are often forced to canvas a wider group of reinsurers in order to satisfy their placement needs while new reinsurers entering the market have needed to establish simple and efficient distribution networks to attract trading partners.

These features do not, of course, apply to all treaty covers and there are some that are unlikely to obtain major advantages from being transferred online. More complex programmes with specialised requirements will continue to require bespoke solutions structured after detailed face-to-face negotiations. Yet certainly some treaty covers do benefit and 2001's renewal season saw a number successfully bound in this manner. Catastrophe excess of loss cover, for example, is already widely syndicated and its structured risk data transfers relatively simply to an Internet-based trading process.

Another area where the future may see electronic trading playing a significant part in the reinsurance market is indexed catastrophe covers – contracts where the reinsured's ability to collect loss recoveries depends as much on the size of any overall market loss as his own individual liabilities.

A US-based industry (or original) loss warranty (ILW) product of this type is already being submitted and quoted online. Claims payments are triggered according to an index of market loss events supplied by Property Claim Services, part of industry statistics provider Insurance Services Office (ISO).

In recent years there has been growing interest among both primary insurers and reinsurers in using this type of product for covering exposures to so-called mega-cats like 1992's Hurricane Andrew. They are also now being increasingly considered for their ability to limit the impact of smaller events on a company's financial wellbeing.

ILW covers are thought to be ideally suited to Internet-based trading because of their structured data and process. Certainly, the use of an independent agency to determine the value of industry indexes upon which any claim will depend greatly simplifies

Figure 3 Traditional process

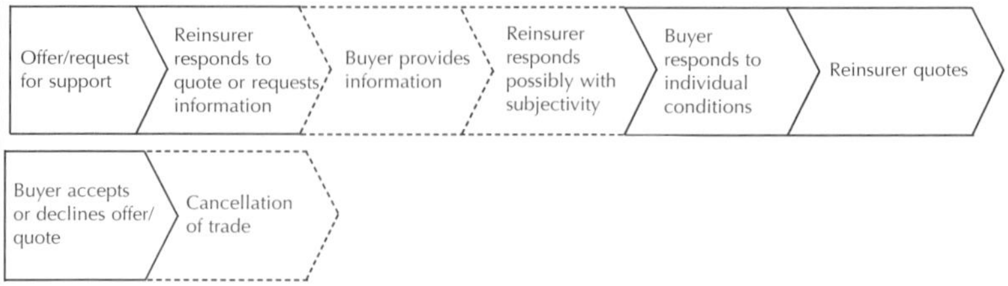

both the underwriting and claims process of more traditional contracts.

Only time will tell the true extent of reinsurance business suitable for electronic trading, but it seems clear already that the scope might be wider than many analysts previously thought. E-trading will never completely replace the traditional face-to-face methods of many reinsurance deals. In time, however, it is likely to play at least a part in a very significant proportion of the market's activities.

THE E-TRADING PROCESS AND ONLINE ADMINISTRATION

The methods and processes widely used to place reinsurance business today are really little changed from those employed a century ago. Risk is transferred through a multitude of complex individual operations and the result is highly customised structures and documents that are costly to administer.

Each risk placement progresses through a lengthy series of different stages where data is re-entered into a number of different systems. Every transaction, even the most simple and straightforward, requires time-consuming, labour-intensive assessments. The potential scope for errors is vast and inefficiency rife.

Electronic trading enables these traditional processes to be much simplified. Data is captured once in a single standard format and then made available to those who require it at different points along the placement chain. Re-keying of information is minimised and thus the scope for error greatly reduced.

Thus e-trading standardises the process of placing reinsurance. It is important to note here that it is the process that is standardised, not the products themselves. Much debate surrounding the

Figure 4 inreon process

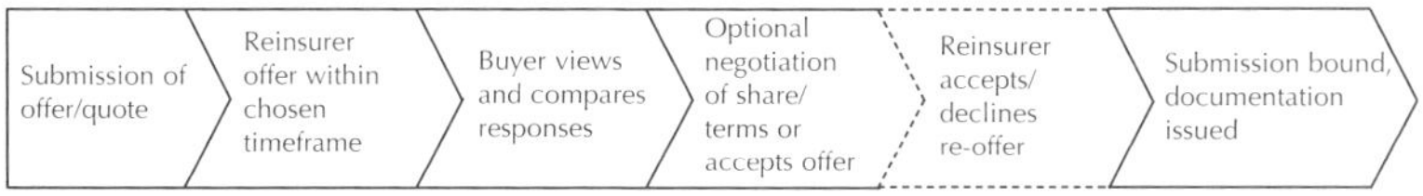

migration of business online has focussed on the resultant standardising of reinsurance contracts, but this can be misleading. A good analogy is the case of Microsoft whose computer software is used in offices around the world. Would it be true to say that Microsoft has standardised the way in which all offices function? Of course the answer is no and the reason for that is because there is enough flexibility within the Microsoft product offering for different offices to operate as they wish. The same may be said of e-trading in reinsurance. Each risk may be submitted and placed in the same standard manner, but within that process there should be enough flexibility to cope with the different features and characteristics of each individual submission.

All trades operating online may progress through four basic prescribed steps or trading phases instead of the many found in a traditional placement process (as can be compared in Figures 3 and 4).

1. The reinsurance buyer – whether broker or primary insurer – begins an initiation phase where a submission for cover is entered.
2. Key parameters for the risk coverage are defined within specific fields.
3. A reinsurer, after being alerted to a new submission, analyses these key parameters together with any other information provided and responds.
4. The buyer may then enter an order online and then contractual documents can be prepared and despatched to involved parties.

In many countries electronic signatures are legally accepted and enable quotes to be offered and bound online. There are still some exceptions, such as Germany, where the picture is less clear-cut, but this problem can be comfortably overcome through the use of a

Membership Agreement which must be signed before reinsurance market participants begin trading on an industry platform. This is a legally enforceable contract that states that members of the platform agree to be bound by its rules, including that all quotes offered online are binding.

But it has never just been through the online placement of reinsurance business that the industry has hoped e-trading will cut costs and improve efficiency. In order to obtain maximum benefits any future solution must contain back office administration advancements as part of the package. Indeed, it is in this area that many analysts have always felt the potential gains could be greatest.

The US property/casualty industry, for example, could save US$30 billion annually by transforming the way it processes claims, according to a recent report by management consulting firm AT Kearney.[3] An analysis conducted in an effort to assess the impact of the September 11, 2001 terrorist attacks showed the introduction of effective new technologies could have a dramatic influence on profitability.

Cost savings were estimated at anything between 12 and 25%. Extrapolating savings of 12% to the overall industry claims cost would shave 10 points off the US Property and Casualty sector's projected combined ratio of 120 in 2001, stated the consultancy. AT Kearney's report found that costs associated with reviewing and settling claims typically account for around 65% of an insurance company's total revenue.

Premium processing, claims processing and endorsements, all with technical accounting capabilities are likely to be conducted online as a matter of course in future.

It is likely that there are a number of potential opportunities still yet to be fully recognised in the considerable progress being made in e-banking. It is quite conceivable that in the near future once a trade has been completed, the client merely enters a code accessing an on-line account creating the premium payment and the onwards movement of funds to reinsurers, all without further intervention.

All insurers, of course, have a view of how a claims system should function and the information it should provide. Such opinions are shaped by the markets in which they operate and the classes of business they write. It is clearly impossible to replicate all these different visions, but a market platform should aim to provide as comprehensive a functionality as possible.

THE BENEFITS OF E-TRADING

In recent years there has been any number of e-commerce initiatives aimed at the reinsurance market and the subject remains a hot topic for debate, continually discussed at conferences and in the trade press. Such interest obviously indicates there is a great deal at stake for the industry in developing an effective e-strategy, but pinning down the real benefits is not always as straightforward as might be expected. Generally, the advantages of electronic trading can be grouped into four main categories:

Expanded distribution

Submitting a risk to a dozen or more reinsurers can be completed online just as simply as submitting a risk to one reinsurer. Once data has been captured by a genuine market-wide electronic trading platform it can be submitted at the click of a mouse. There is no need for separate, different submissions to be prepared for different business partners. This can be a particularly important advantage during hard markets when capacity is scarce. Under such market conditions reinsurance buyers are often forced to seek new trading partners in order to fulfil their coverage requirements. Even in a soft market accessing new reinsurers and obtaining a greater variety of quotes with minimal extra effort can help reduce the cost of cover. From a reinsurer's point of view the ease of making an online submission may enable them to win new clients they were perhaps unaware of, or had previously simply found too uneconomic to service.

Cost reduction

Cost reductions are difficult to quantify and will of course vary from company to company according to the nature of existing processes. E-trading will, however, allow cedents and brokers to enter and view consistent information for every transaction and easily compare terms across a range of responses. Reinsurers too are able to receive and analyse risks from a range of different clients in a single standard format. All transaction information can be accessed in a single location and contracts can easily be retrieved from documentation management systems. Automated binding, meanwhile, eliminates significant manual processes and paperwork and a much-simplified trading process minimises errors. According to an analysis conducted by one leading European insurer with inreon, use of the platform for all property facultative placements would save between 4% and 7% of reinsurance premium expenditure.

Streamlined processing

Ultimately the goal for e-trading will be to provide the reinsurance industry with "straight-through processing" whereby data is captured once and then made available throughout the value chain to whichever parties require it. A single market platform capable of handling both the placement process and back office administration will greatly help this ambition of course, but there will still be a need for some integration with the internal systems of individual companies. Interfaces based on XML and ebXML technology will enable market participants to link their existing data pools and legacy systems with an online exchange.[4] Such a seamless flow of data between different applications eliminates any need for rekeying and will be a vital component of any e-trading solution for the industry.

Improved management reporting

The introduction of a standardised process for risk placement provides an unprecedented opportunity for better management reporting. Trading transparency is a major difficulty for many of today's cedents, particularly large multinational operations who may be purchasing reinsurance cover from a range of local offices around the globe.

Through the use of structured submission templates with predefined data entry fields, high quality data is automatically captured. This can then be used to compile comprehensive, bespoke management and accounting reports as well as tools for portfolio analysis. These reports are available online and can be instantly updated to include the latest information. They will be of benefit both to individual underwriters seeking to record their day-to-day activities and to managers aiming to monitor all aspects of the placement process.

Each trading member can have access to reports detailing their own activities. This information must of course remain strictly confidential. But anonymous, aggregate market reports may also be complied once trading volumes reach a sufficient level on a single market platform. Such statistics are likely to prove invaluable to other market entities including ratings companies and other analysts.

MARKET PARTICIPATION

If the reinsurance industry is to have a prosperous e-trading future it is essential that the benefits outlined above are apparent to and felt by both buyers and sellers of capacity. Consultation and collaboration with representatives of all participants in reinsurance market – reinsurers, insurers and brokers – will be vital in building a successful electronic trading solution. No platform can prosper by representing only the narrow interests of one single group. A genuinely effective reinsurance solution must work for and, ideally, be capable of representing the industry as a whole.

Such diverse participation will be a vital component in the successful future development of e-trading; the more market players prepared to offer their input into this development, the better any solution will be and the greater its chance of success. Of course it is here that the so-called "early mover" advantage comes into play. While those who wait to follow the lead of others may indeed minimise the risk of adopting such a position, they also exclude themselves from the potential benefit. Early movers will be able to provide the greatest input at the crucial early stages of development and therefore have the greatest influence over what a future reinsurance e-trading model looks like.

The comprehensive involvement of all market participants in the future of electronic trading should in no way exclude the broking community. There has been much debate in recent years over the prospect of disintermediation with some analysts predicting that brokers will find themselves gradually squeezed out of the reinsurance value chain. E-trading has been suspected of accelerating this process by providing easier access to reinsurers and reducing the need to go through a broker.

In order to sustain this prediction, however, it is necessary to ignore some important facts. The efficiencies offered by online trading and back office administration are just as relevant to many broking houses as to any other market participants. Indeed, inefficient processing has long been cited as an area for urgent attention by brokers. Improvements introduced by e-trading will allow brokers to more profitably concentrate on providing the services that they are best at – essential advice and instruction rather than paperwork and administration. All brokers worth their salt know there is no hope of survival in acting merely as an inefficient middleman. Market leaders benefit their clients by operating in almost a consultancy role. This is a function that no e-trading operation fulfils; no advice is offered and therefore no platform can ever completely replicate the role of a broker.

OBSTACLES TO A SUCCESSFUL ELECTRONIC FUTURE

Many of the benefits of e-trading are really quite obvious and those who are utterly against the idea in principle are rather thin on the ground in today's industry. The debate generally has moved on from "should e-trading be adopted?" to "how should it be adopted and where can it be most effective?"

Given the clearly apparent nature of these advantages, the immediate question that springs to mind is why has there not been wide-scale adoption already? Old habits die hard of course, but there are also a number of real obstacles that must be overcome. Clearing these hurdles will not happen overnight.

A degree of inertia when faced with new technology is perhaps inevitable, especially in an industry built on analysing the past as much as looking ahead to the future. Insurers can be cautious people – if they were not it is unlikely they would be any good at their job of analysing risk. Thus, any revolutionary change in working practices will naturally be very carefully scrutinised and deliberated before being implemented. The introduction of electronic trading is without doubt a revolutionary change for the reinsurance industry. And it has also drawn a certain amount of rather unjust suspicion from groups and individuals fearful of being replaced by technology and seeing their roles become obsolete.

There are, however, also a lot of visionary people within the industry who do appreciate and are enthused by the enormous possibilities. The major obstacle to their ambitions is the problem of integrating existing systems within the market into a bright new electronic future. The industry is littered with a myriad of different legacy systems. Individual companies all have their own individual methods of working and have tailored their IT requirements accordingly. Interfaces can and must be built in order to ensure these differing systems are all able to connect in future with the industry's electronic trading platform. But, with the nature and quality of data provided from different companies varying greatly, building such interfaces will take time and effort.

In order to overcome this obstacle, the role of industry data standards as promoted by the ACORD organisation will be paramount. The non-profit association's mission is to facilitate the development and use of standards for the insurance and related financial services industries. It was established in 1970 to counter the proliferation of proprietary paper forms used in the insurance industry. Its work is just as relevant today, as without effective standards many of the benefits of e-trading will be diluted or even eliminated altogether. The expansion of client relationships will be inhibited, the sharing of data with trading partners will be inconsistent and inaccurate and investments in legacy systems will be written off.

A great deal of progress has already been made in establishing XML data standards for the reinsurance industry. ACORD's XML standards are based on development begun in 1992 under the direction of a joint venture comprised of European, UK and US standards bodies. ACORD assumed sole responsibility for management of these standards in 2001. The organisation has developed standards for all parts of the reinsurance business cycle, from placement through to accounting, claims and settlement – but there is still more work to be done.

An "eMerge" working group was established last year to meet the challenges of globalisation and deregulation of insurance and financial services, the expansion of new distribution channels and providing consistent data access across divisions and lines of business. Part of the work of this group is to establish new standards for the industry in previously untouched areas of data interfacing to a market e-trading platform.

Many leading industry players are already actively involved in the effort to establish effective data standards – ACORD members represent 70% of the top 10 reinsurers and the top five reinsurance brokers.[5] The full support of the industry in this standards programme will greatly advance the progress towards a successful e-trading future.

THE FUTURE OF REINSURANCE E-TRADING

The reinsurance industry is still some way from making the most of its electronic trading possibilities. Online trading volumes remain limited, but are now growing all the time. Significant progress is being made and it is likely there will be an exponential rise in the number of contracts conducted via the Internet in coming months.

The 2002/3 renewal season represents the first time there has been significant numbers of market players ready to trade electronically. Previous years have seen a number of individual companies experimenting with a limited number of trial risks. Now, however, there is evidence of several companies moving on from this early testing stage to committing whole books of business online. For the 2001/2 renewal season there were around 35 companies that had signed membership agreements in order to trade on the inreon trading platform. Going into the following year's renewals, that figure had jumped to around 100 – an increase of almost 200%. Certain markets are also now demonstrating a critical mass of e-traders. In Spain, for example, 17 cedents and brokers together with local reinsurers Mapfre Re and Nacional are all now prepared to do business online.

As the acceptance of new technology increases, the success of such developments is also more apparent. Continuing the above example, the commitment of the Spanish market has resulted in a much higher than average proportion of trades bound online. In another instance where one subsidiary of a major European insurer committed to placing a whole book of facultative risks online, the rate of bound submissions was as high as 85%.

Early trials of electronic trading were often conducted using distressed business that had not been successfully placed elsewhere. But as confidence in the technology grows the quality of business online has risen in addition to the quantity.

CONCLUSION

The 2002/3 renewal season is likely to see more risks effectively bound online than ever before. Slowly but surely, electronic trading is making its presence felt within the reinsurance industry. This progress comes after a number of false starts that failed to deliver the genuinely market-wide solution that the industry will require to trade successfully online. In order to achieve this necessarily comprehensive strategy, three key areas must be addressed.

First, any electronic marketplace must operate on a global basis. It cannot be limited to one geographical area; business should flow from across the major reinsurance centres in Western Europe, North America and Asia. Multi-lingual client support should be provided from local offices on each continent.

Second, a market-wide solution for e-trading must be able to rely on substantial and widespread support from within the industry. Such backing should be reflected in the ownership of any initiative to prove a level of independence from any single existing market entity. Ownership is also a key factor because of the substantial financial support necessary to launch and sustain a project through its early stages of development. Building a true market platform that is capable of serving all industry participants is not a simple or inexpensive task. If it were it would have already been completed long before now. Achieving this goal will require full commitment and not insignificant expenditure from strong, dedicated partners. Several reinsurance e-commerce initiatives in the past have floundered through lack of funds and no doubt they will not be the last.

The third vital area in which electronic trading must deliver for the industry is in the range of services offered. For the sector to get the most out of technological development it must have access to a full reach of online capabilities. This means the entire process chain must be available; it is of little benefit to offer just a placement facility or just an administration facility. On their own, such offerings may enable some savings and improvements to be made, but the real advancements will be made when both functions are reliably combined together. A full range of products is also necessary. Reinsurers and their clients do not want to sign up with several different e-trading systems in order to trade several different products; a market solution should offer both treaty and facultative capabilities in a variety of different business lines.

Developing these facilities should also be completed on a market-wide basis. Providing a bespoke e-trading service for individual clients may enable a more tailored solution for the industry participant in question, but does little to move the market forward as a whole. Indeed, such an approach actively inhibits the market since it raises new difficulties of integration and acceptance with business partners. Thus, when a new product or line of business is developed for electronic trading it should be available for everyone in the market to use if they wish, not just one favoured client.

All of the above requirements may be compromised or conceded to different degrees in order to provide a "quick fix" e-commerce strategy. But a diluted e-trading solution will have limited long-term appeal and must surely be destined ultimately for failure. If, however, all of these criteria are fulfilled then the industry can expect real benefits long overdue.

1 Borges (1952).
2 Principe and Meyer (2001).
3 AT Kearney(2002).
4 XML/ebXML stands for (electronic business) eXtensible Markup Language, which is a system for defining specialised markup languages that are used to transmit formatted data. Using these tools provides companies with a standard method to exchange business messages, conduct trading relationships, communicate data in common terms and define and register business processes.
5 These statistics are available from ACORD's website: http://www.acord.org.

BIBLIOGRAPHY

AT Kearney, 1952, "Insurance Companies Could Save $30 Billion Anually Through Aggressive Focus on Claims Costs", Press Release, February.

Borges, J. L., 1952, "Creation and P.H. Gosse/La creacin y P.H. Gosse" in: *Other Inquisitions/Otras inquisiciones* (University of Texas).

Goldman Sachs, 1999a, "E-Insurance If you build it, will they come?"

Goldman Sachs, 1999b, "E-Finance Internet Financial Services: A Meeting of the Minds".

Goldman Sachs, 2000, "Insurance United States".

Principe S., and T Meyer, 2001, "Business-to-Business Marketplaces in Europe", Accenture.

13

*Principles on Minimum Requirements for Supervision of Reinsurers**

Reinsurance Subcommittee

International Association of Insurance Supervisors (IAIS)

This chapter sets out principles on minimum requirements for supervision of pure reinsurers.[1] It identifies elements of the supervisory framework that should be common for primary insurers and reinsurers and those elements that need to be adapted to reflect the unique risks faced by reinsurers.

Captive insurers often operate as reinsurers. As a result, they are included in the scope of this paper. However, where captives only insure the risks of their owners and are part of the same organisation they may not pose the same risk to the financial system and separate regulations may be established recognising this reduced risk.

INTRODUCTION

Reinsurers contribute to the stability of insurance markets. They can improve the risk profile and the financial soundness of primary insurers by diversifying and limiting territorial accumulations of exposure, and consequently creating underwriting capacity. However, to have this stabilising effect these entities must be able and willing to meet their obligations as they fall due. Reinsurance cover is available either in a traditional format with full risk transfer to reinsurers or through certain alternative risk

*This article was originally published in October 2002 by the IAIS on their website (www.iaisweb.org) and has been adapted and reprinted here with their kind permission.

transfer (ART) products which usually have more limited risk transfer. Reinsurers provide services across borders either directly or by establishing subsidiaries or branches. While they operate on a global basis, their business has to take account of the location of the risks, types of business or differences in regulation among jurisdictions.

Currently, reinsurers in some jurisdictions are fully or partly directly supervised; other jurisdictions rely on rating agencies in assessing the security of a reinsurer. Some supervisors maintain a register of those reinsurers authorised to underwrite reinsurance in their jurisdiction, while others evaluate reinsurers writing business in their jurisdiction. Some jurisdictions require reinsurers to post collateral, covering the likely liabilities (or liabilities plus a margin). In most jurisdictions, a reinsurer who also acts as a primary insurer is subject to direct supervision. Internationally recognised principles for the supervision of reinsurers are needed because of the global nature of the business and the expectation that the business will continue to expand, into new regions, for example. They are also needed to ensure that new entrants in the reinsurance markets or existing entities that expand their business rapidly offer acceptable security.

There is an ongoing need for insurers to assess the security of the reinsurers with whom they deal.[2] Supervisors of primary insurers also need access to information on the reinsurers of their authorised insurers, including information on whether these reinsurers are subject to effective supervision elsewhere.[3]

Recognising that there will always be some differences in the supervisory regimes, the IAIS have identified minimum requirements for supervision of reinsurers. These requirements should be supplemented by effective systems for exchanging information. It is assumed that the move towards global principles will be an evolutionary process especially because, in a number of jurisdictions, the supervisor presently lacks the powers or the resources to supervise pure reinsurers.

The minimum requirements anticipate a global approach to the regulation of reinsurers. In such a system, the onus is placed on the home supervisor of the reinsurer. The home supervisor is responsible for effective supervision of the business and is responsible and expected to communicate effectively with supervisors in other jurisdictions where the reinsurer writes business. In the interest of policyholders and by improving comparability, minimum requirements could help define a minimum level of acceptable security of reinsurers.[4] Within the framework of the global approach some form of accreditation of home supervisors will be necessary. In addition, the minimum requirements and standards for accreditation should be at such a sufficient level that host supervisors can reasonably be expected to see no need for additional requirements. The development of an efficient global approach to regulation of reinsurers may present advantages to reinsurers, primary insurers and, therefore, to policyholders. These would include greater risk diversification, more effective use of available capital, minimisation of duplicative regulation, and the reduction of alternative methods for assessing the recoverability of reinsurance claims.

The minimum requirements for the supervision of reinsurers naturally differ from those for primary insurers. Conduct-of-business rules do not apply, since the policyholders of reinsurers are not consumers and do not require the same protection. Jurisdictions supervising reinsurers should apply principles reflecting the characteristics of the reinsurance business and the types of risks entailed (particularly in relation to their financial strength). Regulation should take account of and reflect best practices in the industry. It should not stifle innovation that would improve the efficiency and stability of the reinsurance market.

The principles recommended by the IAIS are set out below. Principle 1 describes where supervisory requirements and practices for reinsurers differ from those applied to primary insurers because of the characteristics of the business undertaken. Principle 2 identifies where the same methods can be applied.

PRINCIPLE 1:

Regulation and supervision of reinsurers' technical provisions, investments and liquidity, capital requirements and policies and procedures to ensure effective corporate governance should reflect the characteristics of reinsurance business and be supplemented by systems for exchanging information among supervisors.

Technical provisions

1. Supervisors should have the ability to assess the adequacy of procedures used by reinsurers to establish their liabilities.
2. Supervisors should take into consideration the limitations that reinsurers face. For example, they largely depend on information from primary insurers in establishing technical provisions.

As a result there may be significant delays in receiving claims information. Thus, it is particularly important that the reinsurers have adequate systems for establishing provisions for claims incurred but not reported (IBNR) or incurred but not enough reported (IBNER).[5] Generally, reinsurers and primary insurers use similar actuarial methods to establish and review their IBNR and IBNER provisions. However, the exercise can be more complicated for reinsurers because of non-homogenous portfolios, long tail classes, or information delays. Often, it is necessary to review individual treaties.

Investments and liquidity

Reinsurers, as well as primary insurers, must invest in assets that in terms of security, return, diversification and marketability are sufficient to cover their obligations as they fall due.

Reinsurers' investment strategies are further complicated because often they need to manage and match assets and liabilities in a number of currencies and different markets. In addition, they may have to reimburse the large-scale losses of primary insurers on demand. Reinsurers need to have effective tools in place to manage their investments and liquidity risks and monitor their cashflows.

Capital requirements

In setting capital requirements, supervisors should take into account risk profiles, including the volume of business and degree of diversification. The higher a company's sensitivity to risk, the greater the need for it to have strong risk management practices and capital to shore up its financial strength. Significant risks faced by reinsurers include underwriting (including accumulations and geographical diversification), retrocession, investments (liquidity and currency matching), taxation and, for reinsurers in a group, group risk. In addition, like primary insurers, reinsurers are exposed to a variety of operational risks, the sources of which could be:

- ❑ employees (eg, human error and internal fraud);
- ❑ technology (eg, technological failure and deteriorating systems);
- ❑ customer relationship (eg, contractual disputes); and
- ❑ external (eg, external fraud).

Also since reinsurers' operating results are potentially more volatile than those of primary insurers, they must hold capital that reflects the risks inherent in this type of business and that is sufficient to be able to withstand extreme but plausible loss scenarios. Reinsurers may use dynamic financial analysis tools or other risk models to determine the required economic capital.[6] Supervisors should be knowledgeable about these tools and have access to expertise as necessary. Provided the models in the future are sufficiently reliable, and provided they meet supervisory standards and are properly controlled, they may be used to facilitate mutual recognition of capital requirements of reinsurers.

Corporate governance

Standards should be present to ensure effective corporate governance of reinsurers. For example, there should be standards with respect to the roles and responsibilities of the board of directors. In many respects, reinsurers and primary insurers face the same problems. However, in the case of reinsurers, some of the problems may be different, and sometimes more acute and of greater magnitude. With this in mind, reinsurers should be required to have appropriate policies and procedures covering:[7]

- ❑ underwriting (including counterparties, integrity, management and business policy);
- ❑ provisioning;
- ❑ identification, handling and control of aggregates;
- ❑ accumulations (storm, quake, flood and hail);
- ❑ business line and geographical diversification;
- ❑ retrocession (cover and security);
- ❑ investments (including asset/liability matching and asset diversification);

- ❑ liquidity and cashflow; and
- ❑ currency matching.

Exchange of information on supervision of reinsurers

By exchanging information, supervisors can learn from each other's experiences. This is especially true given the international and the dynamic nature of reinsurance and ART business. In particular, supervisors should exchange information on supervisory methods and experience, including information and experience on catastrophes. Such exchanges will be subject to normal confidentiality provisions.

PRINCIPLE 2

Except as stated in Principle 1, regulation and supervision of the legal forms, licensing and the possibility of withdrawing the licence, fit and proper testing, changes in control, group relations, supervision of the entire business, on-site inspections, sanctions, internal controls and audit and accounting rules applicable to reinsurers should be the same as that of primary insurers.[8]

Legal forms

The law of the home jurisdiction should define the legal forms of reinsurance entities.

Licensing and the possibility of withdrawing the licence

Reinsurers must be licensed or authorised in their home jurisdiction before undertaking reinsurance activities. The supervisor has the right to revoke the licence if the company no longer fulfils the conditions for obtaining a licence, or is able, but not willing to fulfil its obligations. If the licence is revoked, the reinsurance company must stop writing new business.[9]

Fit and proper testing

Supervised reinsurers should be run by persons of good repute, with appropriate professional qualifications and experience. Thus, substantial owners, the board of directors and management should be subject to fit and proper tests. These tests should be made in accordance with the "IAIS Guidance Paper for Fit and Proper Principles and their Application", October 2000.

Changes in control

The home jurisdiction supervisor should have the authority to approve or object to shareholders with material interests in reinsurers.

Group relations

Reinsurers in a group should be supervised on a consolidated or solo-plus basis, incorporating all activities that could have an impact on the financial position of the individual licensed entities.[10] In particular, supervisors should assess capital adequacy, underwriting and other risk concentrations, and intra-group transactions including intra-group exposures on a group-wide basis.[11]

Supervision of the entire business

The home jurisdiction supervisor must make sure that all parts of the business of a reinsurer are subject to effective supervision. The supervisor should be able and willing to share relevant information with other insurance and reinsurance supervisors, subject to confidentiality rules.

On-site inspections

The supervisor should have the authority to carry out on-site inspections to review the business and affairs of the reinsurer, including the inspection of books, records and other documents.[12]

Sanctions

Supervisors must have the authority to take remedial action where problems involving licensed reinsurers are identified. The supervisor must have a range of actions available in order to apply appropriate sanctions to problems encountered, recognising that reinsurers and primary insurers may face different problems. The powers available to the supervisor should be set out in legislation and/or statute. Where there are serious doubts about the ability of a company to continue operations, the supervisor would be expected to notify other relevant insurance and reinsurance supervisors, on the condition that these other supervisors would maintain the confidentiality of the information according to the rules of the home jurisdiction.

Internal controls and audit

The supervisor should be able to review the internal controls that the board of directors and management approve and apply, and request strengthening of the controls where necessary. The supervisor should require accounts to be audited by external auditors. In addition, the supervisor may require auditors to certify compliance with certain requirements.

Accounting rules

Accounting rules should be in line with those applicable to primary insurers and should include valuation principles. Since reinsurance is a global business and most entities operate in several jurisdictions, all reinsurers should use similar accounting principles.

Access to non-public information

It is important that reinsurance supervisors have access to and receive information necessary to form a proper opinion on the risk profile of each reinsurance company domiciled in their jurisdiction. The information needed to carry out this review and analysis should be obtained from the financial and statistical reports, including accounts that are filed on a regular basis and supported by information obtained through special information requests, on-site inspections and communication with actuaries and external auditors. All reinsurance supervisors should be subject to confidentiality constraints in respect of information obtained in the course of their activities, including the conduct of on-site inspections.[13]

1 While this paper addresses the minimum requirements for supervision of pure reinsurers, the IAIS database of reinsurers includes insurers who provide a significant amount of reinsurance business. The principles described in this paper will, with the necessary adaptations, also be applicable to insurers whose main activity includes the issuance of reinsurance coverage.

2 The "OECD Recommendation of the Council on Assessment of Reinsurance Companies", C(98)40/FINAL.

3 "IAIS Standard on the Evaluation of the Reinsurance Cover of Primary Insurers and the Security of their Reinsurers", January 2002.

4 "IAIS Standard on the Evaluation of the Reinsurance Cover of Primary Insurers and the Security of their Reinsurers", January 2002.

5 Some jurisdictions refer to these provisions collectively as IBNR; in other jurisdictions they are referred to separately IBNR and IBNER.

6 This term is normally used to describe the capital needed to support a given risk profile of the company.

7 Additionally, the following IAIS Standards should be referred to: "Supervisory Standard on Asset Management", December 1999; "Supervisory Standard on Derivatives", October 1998; and "Standard on the Evaluation of the Reinsurance Cover of Primary Insurers and the Security of their Reinsurers", January 2002.

8 Some entities are given permission to underwrite reinsurance through authorisation; in this paper the term licensing will include authorisation.

9 Licensing should follow similar principles to those described in the "IAIS Supervisory Standard on Licensing", October 1998. This standard, however, refers to licensing of primary insurers only.

10 The concept of solo-plus supervision implies that in addition to the solo or stand-alone supervision of regulated entities supplementary supervision should also be applied on a group-wide basis. The supplementary supervision would normally include a review of the group's capital (ensuring that there is no double gearing or double leveraging), intra-group transactions or risk transfers (ensuring that they are conducted as if they were on an arm's length basis), risk concentrations, and co-operation among supervisors.

11 The following IAIS Standard may be referred to: "Supervisory Standard on Group Co-ordination", October 2000. Reference is also made to the Joint Forum papers: "Capital Adequacy Principles", February 1999; "Risk Concentration Principles", December 1999; "Intra-Group Transactions and Exposures Principles", December 1999; and "Framework for Supervisory Information Sharing", February 1999.

12 The following IAIS Standard may be referred to: "Supervisory Standard on On-Site Inspections", October 1998.

13 "IAIS Supervisory Standard on the Exchange of Information", January 2002.

14

*Supervisory Standard on the Evaluation of the Reinsurance Cover of Primary Insurers and the Security of their Reinsurers**

Reinsurance Subcommittee

International Association of Insurance Supervisors (IAIS)

This chapter provides guidance to supervisors in assessing how insurers manage their reinsurance arrangements. It discusses the policies and procedures that companies should have in place and supervisory approaches for evaluating the adequacy of each company's reinsurance cover.

The IAIS recognises that currently there are significant differences in supervisory approaches taken by member jurisdictions with respect to reinsurance. For example, reinsurers in some jurisdictions are directly supervised; other jurisdictions rely on rating agencies in assessing the security of a reinsurer. Some supervisors maintain a register of those reinsurers authorised to underwrite reinsurance in their jurisdiction, while others evaluate reinsurers actually writing business in their jurisdiction. Some jurisdictions require reinsurers to post collateral, covering the likely liabilities (or liabilities plus a margin) of the reinsurer, with the ceding companies. This chapter acknowledges the differing practices but does not purport to favour one regime over another.

*This article was originally published in January 2002 by the IAIS on their website (www.iaisweb.org) and has been adapted and reprinted here with their kind permission.

Additionally, in recent years, reinsurance has evolved with the introduction of many new products, commonly known as alternative risk transfer (ART) products. Much of the guidance provided in this chapter will also apply in the case of ART products.

INTRODUCTION

Insurance companies assume risk on behalf of policyholders. They mitigate these risks by acquiring insurance with reinsurers. Through the use of reinsurance, an insurer can reduce risk, stabilise its solvency, use available capital more efficiently and expand underwriting capacity. Reinsurance helps an insurer obtain a desired, prudent risk profile.[1] However, irrespective of the reinsurance obtained, the primary insurer normally remains contractually responsible for paying the full claim amounts to policyholders.

Reinsurance may be provided by pure (or professional) reinsurers or by primary insurers also authorised to write reinsurance.

TYPES OF REINSURANCE ARRANGEMENTS

Traditional

Most risk assumed by reinsurers is based on traditional contracts, which are normally either "treaty" or "facultative". Under treaty contracts, the reinsurer automatically participates in certain sections or portfolios of the insurer's business.[2] Facultative contracts allow the reinsurer to participate on an individual, risk-by-risk basis.

Contracts may be proportional or non-proportional. Proportional reinsurance is a form of reinsurance in which the premiums and claims of the insurer are shared proportionally by the insurer and the reinsurer. In non-proportional reinsurance an insurer pays a risk premium to a reinsurer and the reinsurer assumes a share of the insurer's obligations in excess of a certain amount which could be limited by another, larger, amount. Thus the reinsurance cover can be built up in layers. Typically, for non-life insurance, reinsurance contracts last one year and cover specified lines of business. Life reinsurance contracts are usually indefinite and contain a termination provision for new business only.

Alternative risk transfer

Insurance risk may be transferred to reinsurers and other counterparties by using ART techniques, such as financial reinsurance and securitisation. Securitisations commonly utilise either a "protected cell" or a "special purpose vehicle" to effectuate the transfer of insurance risk from the ceding company. To date, most securitisations have been fully funded, which means that the proceeds of the securitisation fully cover the risk securitised.

Similar cover can also be provided by other types of ART contracts some of which are provided by reinsurers. ART cover may be obtained on a multi-line, multi-year, and holistic basis, and can be retrospective or prospective. Contracts can provide protection against different operational and financial risks. For example, some ART contracts, like traditional reinsurance contracts, protect a primary insurer's solvency.

In some ART contracts the transfer of insurance risk is secondary to the transfer of financial risks, such as credit, liquidity or market risk. While called financial "reinsurance", most jurisdictions regard that such contracts provide valid reinsurance cover only to the extent they imply a real transfer of insurance risk. However, such contracts do play a part in the company's risk management; but they should not be considered to mitigate insurance risk unless there is a genuine transfer of this risk. In some cases the only intention of the cedent is to obtain a favourable impact for financial reporting, but ART contracts should not be used in order to distort true and fair reporting.

REINSURANCE STRATEGY AND MANAGEMENT PROCEDURES

Board of directors

Every insurer should have a reinsurance strategy, approved by the company's board of directors, that is appropriate to the company's overall risk profile. The reinsurance strategy will be part of the company's overall underwriting strategy. The board should review the reinsurance strategy annually (in the case of life insurers, possibly less frequently). In addition, the reinsurance strategy should be reviewed when there have been changes in the company's circumstances, its underwriting strategy, or the status of its reinsurers.

The reinsurance strategy should define and document the insurer's strategy for reinsurance management, identifying the procedures for:

- the reinsurance to be purchased;
- how reinsurers will be selected, including how to assess their security;
- what collateral, if any, is required at any given time; and
- how the reinsurance programme will be monitored (ie, the reporting and internal control systems).

The board should ensure that all legal and regulatory requirements are met. It should set limits on:

- the net risk to be retained; and
- the maximum foreseeable amount of reinsurance protection to be obtained from the approved reinsurers.

Senior management

Senior management should document clear policies and procedures for implementing the reinsurance strategy set by the board of directors. This includes:

- setting underwriting guidelines that specify the types of insurance to be underwritten, policy terms and conditions, and aggregate exposure by type of business;
- establishing limits on the amount and type of insurance that will be automatically covered by reinsurance (eg, treaty reinsurance); and
- establishing criteria for acquiring facultative reinsurance cover.

In order to avoid uncovered risks, the terms and conditions of the reinsurance cover should be compatible with those of the underlying business.

Limits on the net risk to be retained should be set either per line of business or for the whole account. The insurer may also set limits per risk or per event (or a combination thereof).

The limits must be based upon an evaluation of its risk profile and the cost of the reinsurance.

In particular, the insurer should have adequate capital to support the risk retained. Some insurers may use the results of dynamic financial analysis techniques (using the reinsurance cover as one of the variables) as input into these operating decisions.[3]

The insurer should maintain an up-to-date list of reinsurers that it has approved.[4] For each approved reinsurer, the appropriate level of exposure should be specified. To do this, the insurer should evaluate the ability and willingness of the reinsurer to fulfil its contractual obligations as they fall due (ie, its security). Such assessment is required whether collateral is posted or not. The assessment should take into account the effects of any collateral the reinsurer has posted in favour of other insurers. The insurer's credit guidelines should describe the system for controlling exposures to each reinsurer.

To improve the security of the overall reinsurance cover, insurers may choose to use a number of different reinsurers. Diversification may also be achieved by using certain ART techniques.

Generally speaking, if no requirements are placed on the choice of reinsurer or on the posting of collateral, the fewer the number of reinsurers used, the more an insurer should pay importance to the security of its reinsurers. If a company takes advice on the strength and security of a reinsurer, then it should satisfy itself that the advice given is sound. Similarly, if reinsurance cover is acquired through an intermediary, the company should evaluate the operational risk associated with the transaction.

Senior management should ensure that the management information system in place meets all the requirements of the board with respect to reporting frequency and level of detail. In addition, there should be adequate systems of internal control to ensure that all underwriting is carried out in accordance with company policy and that the planned reinsurance cover is in place. The underwriting control systems should be able to identify and report on a timely basis where underwriters infringe authorised limits, breach company guidelines or otherwise assume risks exceeding the ability of the company's capital base and reinsurance cover to service.

Internal control

There should be internal control systems in place to ensure that claims are reported to the appropriate reinsurer and that reinsurance claims payments are being promptly collected.

The underwriting control may include an actuarial assessment of the risk and whether it has been transferred as presumed. This assessment may also include a review of the reinsurance contracts. The board of directors should receive regular and comprehensive reports on the effectiveness and performance of the claims system and the reinsurance protection. Companies' internal control systems should be subject to regular audit examination.

SUPERVISORY REGIME FOR INSURANCE BUSINESS (REINSURANCE COVER AND SECURITY)

The supervisor should verify that the board of directors has established an overall strategy framework – addressing, among other things, underwriting and reinsurance. To evaluate reinsurance cover, reinsurer security and collateral that may be posted, the supervisor should have, or have access to, sufficient expertise. Usually the supervisor takes a risk-based approach – ensuring that the company has appropriate policies, systems and procedures in place and focusing more detailed examination work on areas posing specific and significant concern.

Before granting a license, the supervisor must be satisfied with the company's planned risk management and reinsurance strategies, and accompanying policies. When examining the business plan of an insurance company, the supervisor must evaluate if the proposed reinsurance covers maximum foreseeable loss. In the business plan the company must describe how, and to what extent, future policies will be reinsured. The supervisor should evaluate whether reinsurers offer sufficient security. In most cases, this evaluation could be enhanced or improved by the exchange of information between supervisors.

Companies should maintain adequate reinsurance cover at all times. Supervisors should regularly evaluate the reinsurance cover and risk profile of the insurers. While many reinsurance treaties operate on an annual basis, some treaties, especially for life business and some ART contracts, can operate for many years. In such cases, supervisors will wish to be assured that the reinsurer offers sufficient security to act as a long-term counterparty.

Supervisors must receive sufficient and relevant information on the reinsurers used and the reinsurance cover arranged. Relevant information may include:

- reports describing the reinsurance cover, reinsurance programmes or treaties; and

- financial statements, including the result of reinsurance, any amounts outstanding from reinsurers and the effect of ART techniques, including financial reinsurance.

Supervisors should be able to review the quality and validity of information submitted.

The information may be submitted in the form of:

- copies of contracts and amendments;
- copies of slips and cover notes;
- supervisory returns; or
- written contract descriptions and summaries.

Information obtained by supervisors in the process of assessing a company's reinsurance cover should be kept confidential. Using this information and other relevant information received during on-site inspection, the supervisor should evaluate:

- the prudence of the company risk profile including an evaluation of any risk concentration, ie, an aggregate exposure with the potential to produce losses large enough to threaten the insurer's financial health or its ability to maintain core operations;
- compliance with the company's reinsurance strategy;
- the sufficiency of the reinsurance cover and the insurance company's financial strength, in particular under extreme, but plausible loss scenarios;
- the sufficiency of the reinsurance security, taking into consideration a wide range of factors including financial strength, whether reinsurers are properly supervised and whether or not collateral is posted; and
- the appropriateness of any ART techniques, such as securitisation, used.

In making these evaluations the supervisor should consider the overall risk profile of the insurer. The supervisor should be aware of the security and adequacy of the reinsurance or ART coverage for long-tail business (where claims development is slow) and the top layers of catastrophe programmes (where amounts involved can be large).

The choice of reinsurance cover is a business decision made by management within the overall reinsurance strategy of the insurer. However, where insufficient or inappropriate reinsurance cover affects the company's ability to pay policyholders' claims, the supervisor must enter into discussions with the management of the company. The supervisor should have the legal and administrative power necessary to take remedial action in (among other things) cases of insufficient reinsurance cover, insufficient reinsurer security, non-compliance with company reinsurance strategy, insufficient collateral (where applicable) or use of non-admitted (ie, non-authorised) reinsurers.

Remedial action should include the power to disallow credit in whole or in part for reinsurance when calculating solvency requirements or technical provisions on a net basis or when determining the coverage of gross technical provisions by reinsurance recoverables. Additionally, the supervisor should be able to require the insurer to:

- obtain additional reinsurance cover;
- provide additional capital;
- establish additional technical provisions; and
- have additional collateral posted, if applicable.

Such action should be taken according to transparent principles and be based on objective criteria.

The supervisor may choose to provide insurers with comparative risk information, for example in the form of benchmarking data or comparisons. This information allows management to evaluate the quality of the reinsurance cover in comparison with market standards and to decide if its risk profile is acceptable and prudent.

1 The risk profile of a financial undertaking reflects the relation between the risks run by the financial undertaking and its financial strength.

2 Treaty contracts are also referred to as automatic reinsurance or automatic capacity.

3 Dynamic financial analysis evaluates an expanded universe of possible scenarios through computer modelling, as opposed to the traditional approach that involves interpreting historical trends and ratios (ie, static). With the power of a computer, a user can simulate multiple scenarios based on specified set of constants and probabilistic estimates for key variables, such as reinsurance pricing and coverages, premium volume, pricing adequacy, underwriting profit/loss, investment returns, reserve adequacy, catastrophes and cost of capital. The resulting distribution of these variables can then be used to influence management's operating decisions.

4 The OECD Recommendation of the Council on Assessment of Reinsurance Companies, C(98)40/FINAL.

15

Risk Measurement and Reinsurance

Jonathan Barber, Paul Koronka and Adam Rose

SERM Rating Agency Ltd; Charles Taylor Consulting plc; Falcon Asset Management Ltd

For many reinsurers, September 11, 2001 was the last straw. Results had been bad in 2000. 2001 was not looking much better. The reinsurance market learnt a number of lessons very quickly:

- the past is a poor guide to the future;
- risks that were thought to be uncorrelated may be highly correlated in a catastrophic loss (fire, explosion, PA WCA and motor); and
- the level of information on risk exposures provided by cedents may be poor.

The reinsurance market is undergoing significant change. For some companies, there is upheaval and uncertainty, Gerling Re, GE Frankona, while others have left the market altogether (Copenhagen Re, Fortress Re, for example). Of those companies that remain, many have changed their strategies and all are looking for ways to improve margins and recoup past losses.

One of the key components of profitability is dependant on decision-making, and making the best decisions is dependant on having the right background information, methods and models.

Bock and Seitz (2002) express the opinion that

> "....the insurance industry performs the functions of risk assessment, risk management and risk-carrying in a very efficient manner, by applying and continually refining

methods and models founded on risk theory and actuarial mathematics."

The phrase "continually refining methods and models" is key. To be competitive, insurers must constantly review their methods and models to check that they are up to date, and they must examine new factors. An area that is being increasingly considered by decision-makers in the insurance industry is that of risk measurement. Two important questions to be considered are:

1. How good is an organisation at measuring and subsequently reducing operational risk (including environmental and health and safety risks)?
2. What consideration does it give to less tangible risks (social/ethical)? If a company manages its less tangible risks well, it will also tend to have good control over the entire business.

When evaluating individual companies (or a portfolio), insurers have typically assessed risk on the basis of historical information and claims records. Some look for other methods to determine management quality (the predominate loss driver) and use credit rating as a proxy. This chapter will argue that they could enhance their assessment further if they also considered the manner in which a company manages the totality of its risk. An organisation that has effective risk-reduction programmes in place will be a better risk than a company that does not.

Furthermore, risk measurement criteria will have differing significance according to industry sector and geographical location. For example, a risk in the manufacturing industry may be of less consequence in the finance sector.

INTRODUCTION

This chapter looks at a model developed by the Safety and Environmental Risk Management (SERM) Rating Agency, which awards ratings to individual companies, based on their track record and risk-reduction programmes. Initially, this model was developed to enable fund managers to measure the operational risks of companies within their portfolio, but insurers and reinsurers are also beginning to realise that it has much to offer.

The rating process provides a quantified, systematic assessment that reinsurers can apply to their decision-making. The results are presented in an easily interpreted form, and may be incorporated into their decision support systems. Of course, it cannot offer any copper-bottomed guarantees, but it brings another new perspective to assessing risk.

Corporate customers could also benefit from adopting a similar approach. If systematically applied, they should be able to distinguish themselves from their competitors and secure wider amd more favourable coverage terms from their insurers. Alternatively, they could use such a system to band together with others and take a layer of risk out of the market altogther, thus raising considerably the attachment point for their insurance or reinsurance programme.

RISK MEASUREMENT

The term "operational risk" covers a wide range of types and sources of risk: "The risk of loss resulting from inadequate or failed internal processes, people and systems or from external events".[1] Examples include, Kings Cross underground fire, Bhopal, Chernobyl and Potters Bar rail crash.

The growth in the use of internal tools for testing and validation of operational risk has resulted in a revolution in its modelling. Organisations now have better definitions of risk and these are more quantifiable in statistical terms.

Within the financial community, attempts to formalise a market response to operational risk have largely been fragmented. (The banking community were the first to recognise the potential for operational risk disasters and the resultant Basel revisions to capital adequacy requirements on account of operational risk assessment.) However, the issue is now being discussed and implemented as part of mainstream business practice. Indeed, in 1998 the London Stock Exchange formalised operational risk by introducing its Combined Code (LSE September 27, 1998) for corporations listed on its exchange, which included a requirement that directors review and report on the effectiveness of all three types of controls, not just financial controls. It specified that:

1. companies must consider what are the key risks and assess how they have been identified, evaluated and managed;

2. companies must assess the effectiveness of the related system of internal control having particular regard to the impact of weaknesses that have been reported;
3. companies must consider whether necessary actions are being taken promptly to remedy weaknesses;
4. companies must consider whether the findings indicate a need for more extensive monitoring of the system of internal control;
5. companies must be informed about how the reviews giving rise to the reports have been undertaken; and ensure that, in accordance with an appropriate cycle, the reports, taken together, cover all aspects of internal control.

The type of costs that insurers are bearing are severe, examples are:

- *Environmental costs.* Hazardous waste "superfund" sites in the US. Where various estimates range from US$100 billion[2] for just the superfund sites to US$750 billion for all 33,000 hazardous waste sites in the US.[3]
- *Environmental costs.* Extreme weather events cause an ever-increasing amount of suffering and damage worldwide. The amount of economic losses has increased 8.6-fold if we compare the amount of losses from all great natural catastrophes in the 1990s with the amount in the 1960s. During the same period, the number of catastrophes only increased by a factor of 3.3 (Munich Re 2002a).
- *Environmental costs.* Notably, the number of hydro-meteorological events, such as floods, landslides and droughts, has increased more rapidly over the past decades than the number of other disasters. It has been suggested that if current loss trends continue, annual losses will reach US$150 billion in the next decade (UNEP-FI, 2002). The Intergovernmental Panel on Climate Change concludes in its Third Assessment Report that the frequency of extreme precipitation events has increased over the past 100 years (IPCC 2001a). Additionally, the Panel states that "Part of the observed upward trend in disaster losses over the past 50 years is linked to socio-economic factors, such as population growth, increased wealth, and urbanisation in vulnerable areas, and part is linked to climatic factors such as the observed changes in precipitation and flooding events." (Vellinga *et al.*, 2001).

- *Health costs*. Asbestos claims have spiralled into the hundreds of billions of dollars in the US with the Rand Institute for Civil Justice estimating that of the 82 corporate sectors 75 are now facing claims. Initial estimates of European exposure are also spiralling as companies state their exposure to claims.

The SERM risk rating system captures exposure to these types of historic and emerging liabilities. The risk to capital rating is also an indicator of the quality of management of the risks faced by companies. Robert Monks, the pioneering corporate governance specialist stated at the AGM of the UK Social Investment Forum that:

> "Over the next decade, I predict that sensitivity to societal and environmental concerns will be explicitly recognised as adding value to companies…we need to ingrain into the public consciousness the reality that only attention to sustainable values will allow corporations to achieve optimum value."

This statement is supported by a report "Sustainability Pays" by Forum for the Future, which reviews the academic research on sustainability issues (environmental, social and economic performance) and demonstrates that the majority of the research shows a positive correlation between environmental performance and share performance.

SERM's risk ratings of companies' non-financial performance also demonstrate a positive correlation with improved financial performance (share value). A thesis from the Copenhagen Institute for Investments (Christensen and Kyhl, 2002) back-tested the performance of several models.

"SERM is the model in the analysed period that best managed to identify the companies that outperformed the market. We isolated the risks due to ethics, environment and economy by splitting up SERM's model. Each of the dimensions contributed to the financial gain in the analysed period."

Their findings indicate a 900-point (9%) out performance of the market over an 13-month period. The reports that are produced from the model clearly have a benefit for assessing portfolios and selecting best in class stocks. Insurers can also use the reports that are produced by major organisations to supplement their risk assessment and pricing models. At a portfolio level reinsurers can use the assessment to measure the quality of risks that are being passed to them.

The SERM model can help inform the debate on companies' non-financial performance and the following sections demonstrate its philosophy and methodology.

A CRITICAL APPROACH TO OPERATIONAL RISK

Key to improving business performance is for companies to identify, effectively engage with and proactively manage the environmental, health and safety and social/ethical operational risks of their business. These direct risks cannot be disentangled from those intangible risks such as the reputational damage associated with a company's health, safety, environmental and social risks. These tangible and intangible risks are associated within a feedback structure. Such feedback connections can be observed as concern over direct risks within institutions has been reflected in the steady, albeit slow, growth in ethical and Socially Responsible Investment (SRI) over recent years. The term SRI refers to non-financial performance measures being included in the stock selection process resulting in their, positive inclusion (renewable energy companies); negative screening (omission of contentious companies, ie, nuclear and defence industries, etc) or a best in class selection process.

Recently there has been a rapid escalation of interest from the financial community as recent research work indicates (see Table 1).

Table 1 UK SRI Growth[4]

	1997	1999	2001
Church Investors	12.5	14.0	13.0
SRI Unit Trusts	2.2	3.1	3.5
Charities	8.0	10.0	25.0
Pension Funds	0.0	25.0	80.0
Insurance	0.0	0.0	103.0
Total	22.7	52.2	224.5

Source: Sparkes, R., UK Social Investment Forum Debate, November 21, 2002.

The US is an even more developed market and provides an indicator for UK market potential. The US SRI market continues to experience strong growth in a bear market with a 36% increase of the assets under management by socially screened investment portfolios between 1999 and 2001. This now amounts to over US$2.34 trillion influenced by SRI considerations and represents more than US$1 out of every US$8 under management in the US. This is a major increase from US$639 billion in 1995.

It is surely only a matter of time before the insurance industry follows these exponential growth rates.

Furthermore, SERM's ratings provide additional indicators of overall management competency; a company that manages its risks well is likely to have good control over most aspects of its business. Companies underestimate the influence of environmental, health and safety, and social and ethical operational risk at their peril. After all, the larger the company and its profile, the greater the potential risk associated with their operations.

The ethical/social, environmental, health and safety risks are implicit considerations when considering operational risk. Neglecting concerns over direct risks resulting from the environment is a failure to understand the devastating impact that intangible risks such as reputation – which is the most important asset of any organisation – can have on an institution's operation and even its financial performance. Management should be proactive in building and maintaining its reputation, not just be responsive to adverse events.

By implementing risk-reduction programmes, rather than just being responsive to past events, companies will not only build and maintain their reputation, but their efforts should be reflected in the cost and availability of appropriate insurance premiums. Those companies that have a lower risk level (a higher rating such as AA+ as opposed to B+) will be able to demonstrate a historically lower level of prosecutions, etc, than their peer group. They may also be able to demonstrate that their operations lie within sub sectors with lower risks.

THE SERM RATING METHODOLOGY

The mathematical model analyses 39 risks areas that cover environmental, health and safety, social and ethical (including corporate governance issues) and other intangble/indirect risks as outlined in Appendix A.

Figure 1 SERM risk profile

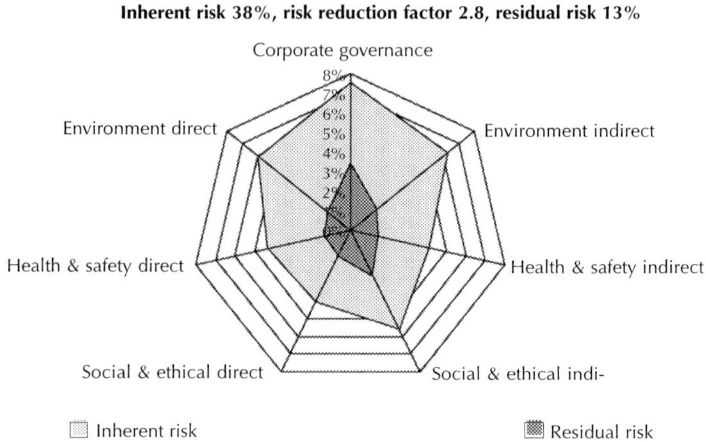

Source: SERM Rating Agency, January 2001.

These operational risks are individually weighted and the method effectively demonstrates how intangible risks can be seen along side tangible risks; the SERM method provides a good example. The assessment process starts with determining a company's safety, environmental and social "inherent risk" profile, covering its spread of sub-sector activities. Inherent risks are then divided by what are called "risk-reduction factors", reflecting the effectiveness of associated risk management systems and implementation, generating the company's "residual risk" profile.

Figure 1 shows the inherent and residual and tangible and intangible risk profiles for a major mining company. By presenting it in a common radar format, it provides stakeholders (especially the financial and insurance communities) with a powerful and visible corporate risk/liability "health check". It also identifies risk 'hot spots' and management underperformance.

HOW SERM CREATE THE RATING

Detailed research

Extensive research is carried out for industry sectors and individual companies.

- *Sector risks*: Over 100 industry sub-sectors are assessed, quantified and reviewed by the SERM advisory panel. This data is

Figure 2 Outline of the SERM algorithm inputs

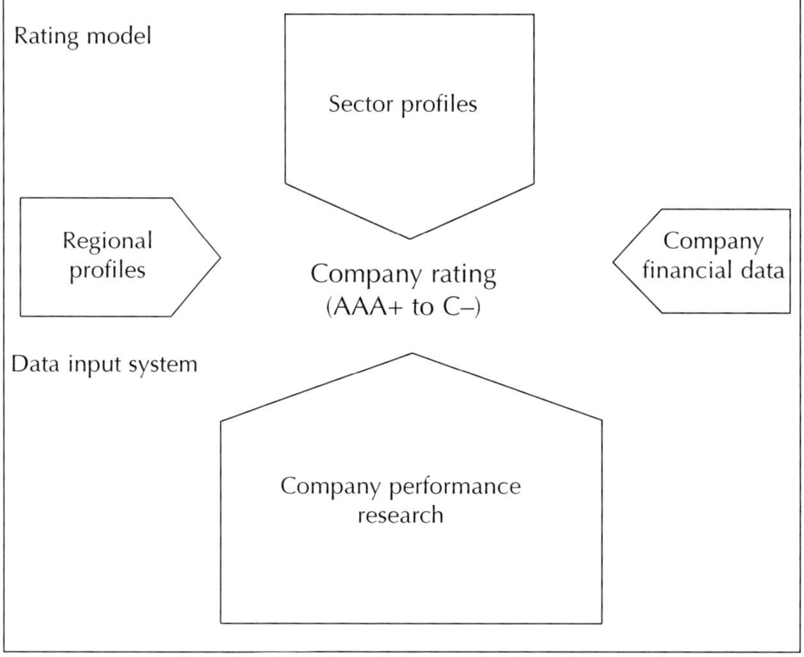

used to quantify the inherent risk that a firm faces by being present in different industries. Companies' emerging risks are also included, ie, climate change impacts, carbon tax increase costs to companies and product liabilities.

- *Company risk management*: SERM's business analyst research team collect performance data on individual companies. This is a detailed analysis of the steps taken by a company to reduce its inherent risk, synthesised into an overall grade.

There are two strands to the company research:

1. *Internal data*: A dedicated SERM analyst team enters factual data from company annual reports, interims and press releases into an on-line database.
2. *External data*: Another dedicated team enters data gathered from over 35,000 Internet and newspaper sources. These sources include global prosecution databases (like the UK's Health and Safety Executive), sector-based journals, regulatory sites and several proprietary data feeds.

Figure 3 Comparison of companies' performance within and between sectors

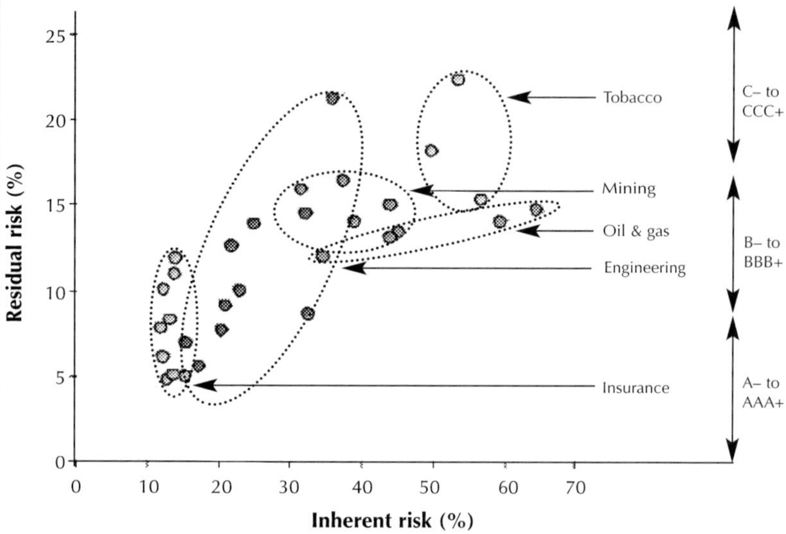

A rigorous algorithm

The collected data enables the SERM senior analysts to score a company's performance on each of the risk criteria.

These scores, along with their sectoral profiles (the proportioned risks due to their industrial sub-sector activities), feed into SERM's proprietary rating algorithm. They take into consideration the total cost (both tangible and intangible) of any potential incident and the likely effectiveness of risk management in avoiding or mitigating any such incident.

The key rating output is a point on a 27-point scale from AAA+ down to C- which is analogous to credit ratings with which the financial and insurance communities are familiar.

This rating can be interrogated to the lowest level of research detail.

The reports and graphs generated by the rating system can be used to analyse individual companies, industry sectors and customised portfolios. For example, Figure 3 shows a comparison of companies within specific industry sectors.

Additionally, as with the more conventional financial ratings from agencies such as Standard & Poor's and Moodys, SERM

Figure 4 Outliers within a portfolio

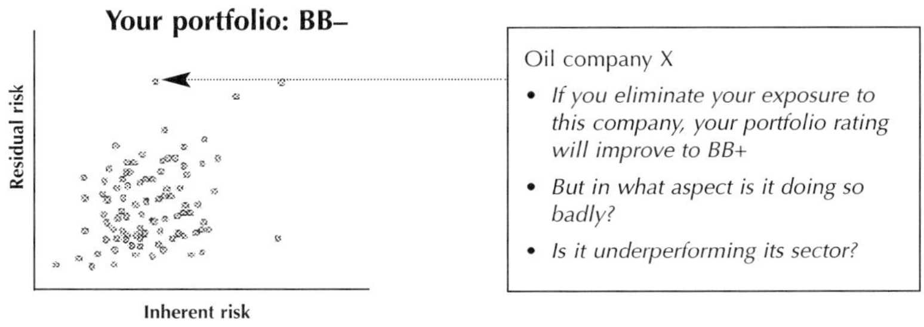

rating data can easily be factored in to decision support systems.

PORTFOLIO MANAGEMENT

Where insurers are looking to reinsure a book comprising multiple organisations, it is useful to be able to analyse the overall risk management performance of the entire group. The SERM model has a facility to define a customised portfolio of companies and to then calculate a composite rating, as shown in Figure 4.

By displaying the ratings in graphical form, it is possible to easily identify outliers in a portfolio. These are individual companies that are not managing risk as well as others. This prompts further investigation, such as:

- ❑ How does the risk change if the outlying company is removed from the portfolio?
- ❑ Why does the company have a poorer rating? Are there problems in particular areas and, if so, what relevance do they have? Can the company take any immediate actions to improve its rating?
- ❑ Shareholder engagement and activism to safeguard value and ensure that highlighted risks are included within companies' internal control systems.

Further analysis is possible by breaking down the rating of an individual company into different categories of risk, and comparing it with other companies in the same sector. Figure 5 shows that a specific oil company performs poorly with regard to social and

Figure 5 Comparisons within industry sector

Oil sector risk reduction potential

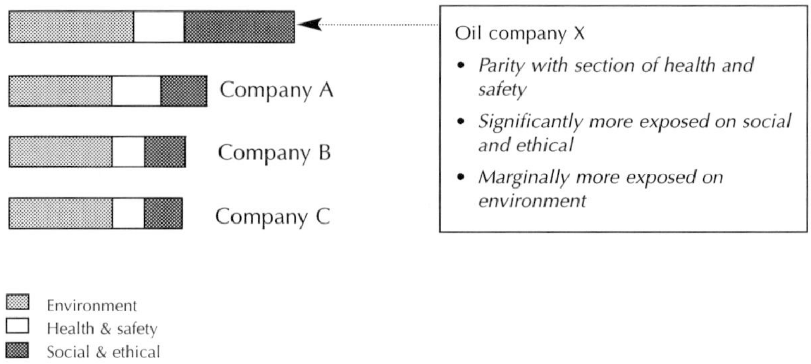

ethical risks compared to other oil companies, and is marginally worse for environmental risks.

If further investigations are required, it is possible to drill down in increasing levels of detail, right down to the detailed research on which the ratings were based. The written reports may be used to provide backup documentation during proposal preparation.

SRI funds are now being seen as an opportunity for superior performance for funds. The Good Money Industrial Average beat the Dow Jones by about 100% in the period 1977–2000.[5] The analysis of the SERM model by the Copenhagen Business School shows a 9% out performance of the FTSE All Share index over a period of 18 months.[6]

CONCLUSION

The insurance and financial communities are working more closely together, as business evolves and regulations change. In both industries, it is important to stay up to date with the latest modelling tools in order to remain competitive and profitable.

The fund management community is already making increasing use of the opportunity SERM provides to assess risk from a new standpoint, and the insurance market is poised to follow suit.

By providing an added dimension to risk evaluation, both parties within reinsurance negotiations are better placed to:

- make decisions on what risk to pass on and what to retain; and
- calculate/negotiate premiums.

Furthermore, SERM data could be used by a collaborative group of insurers/reinsurers and, as the number of users rises, the relevance increases.

Finally, it is important not to neglect the relevance to the original client – the company at the bottom of the chain, to whom a favourable rating is also beneficial. If they can demonstrate a high standard of risk management, in the form of measurement and reduction, they should find it easier to obtain insurance and at a lower cost.

One of the ways that organisations can use the methodology to their advantage is to demonstrate that they are superior risks compared to others in the market and are thus subsidising poorer risks. One way of avoiding this is through the establishment of selective mutuals or risk-retention groups. The theory is that this should enable such a group to achieve a structure that is closer to the optimum than could be achieved individually. The ability to persuade not only senior management but also the insurance industry of the value of such an approach depends almost entirely on the application of such techniques and how well they can be documented and quickly assimilated. Indeed, such an approach could be the only way forward if a group has a poor loss history. Another major advantage comes from the pooling of knowledge, and learning not only from your own mistakes, but also from the experience of others. Mutuals and other similar groups are natural organisms to achieve this end.

APPENDIX – CATEGORIES OF RISK

In order to provide some insight into some principal direct environmental, social/ethical and health and safety risks – which could have serious implications for an institution's indirect risks – the following paragraphs will describe those that are considered by SERM Rating Agency.

Environmental risk

Environmental risk looks at the extent to which the following risk factors are perceived as being principal environmental "aspects" of a company, in terms of significance of their impact.

1. *Environmental incidents*. Risk of emissions to air/land/water that cause a pollution incident and meets with severe regulatory/public reaction.
2. *Energy use*. Energy consumption profile throughout a company's operations, both in-process and support services (eg, office, business travel).
3. *Greenhouse gas (GHG) (production)*. Degree of GHG (eg, CO2, SO2, N2O) emissions generated throughout the company's operations as a result of production output.
4. *GHG (transport)*. Degree of GHG emissions generated during distribution (whether internal or outsourced) of production output.
5. *Water use*. Water consumption profile throughout the production operations, both in-process and support services (eg, office, truck cleaning, etc).
6. *Wastewater generation*. Volume/severity of wastewater generated as a result of the company's operations – industrial, wash water, municipal sewage, etc.
7. *Raw materials*. Extent (volume/type) of natural resources materials (excluding water) constituting inputs into the company's production operations.
8. *Waste generation*. Solid waste profile generated throughout the production process – both off-spec product output and waste by-products of the production process.
9. *Historical liabilities*. Magnitude of historical legacies of contamination/pollution, usually site-specific, eg, contaminated land, redundant/derelict structures, spoil heaps, etc.

10. *Amenity issues*. Extent of nuisance caused by any aspect of the company's operations, both internal (to workforce) and external (to public off-site).
11. *Other*. eg, other controlled/uncontrolled emissions/releases (volatile organic compounds, radiation, dioxins, etc).

Health and safety risk

1. *Health internal*. Current adverse health issues, both acute (short-term) and chronic (long-term), as they affect the workforce.
2. *Health external*. Current adverse health issues, both acute and chronic, as they affect users of the company's products/services and the public.
3. *Safety internal*. As measured by the extent of major/cumulative incidents causing injury/death to the workforce/contractors as a result of equipment malfunction/human error.
4. *Safety external*. Exposure to major/cumulative incidents causing injury/death to customers/suppliers and the public as a result of equipment malfunction/human error.
5. *Health and safety liabilities*. Magnitude of historical chronic ill-health issues that can be attributed to the company's operations (asbestosis, "black lung", repetitive strain injury, etc), including those continuing beyond cessation of operations.

New health issues are coming to the fore with potential large class actions, for instance against the long haul airlines in relation to deep vein thrombosis.

Social/ethical risk

1. *Poor corporate governance*. Extent to which a company's overall management is perceived not to reflect the perception of acceptable individual and business behaviour.
2. *Unrestrained corporate power*. Perception of excessive unrestrained power held by corporate management manifesting itself by: eg, the ability to dominate an industry by imposing standards that competitors must match, gaining concessions on major investment conditions, being the major employer in a location – related to size and international reach.
3. *Lack of corporate community involvement*. Extent to which an organisation neglects taking a participative community role and shows little concern with its general problems/needs.

4. *Adverse marketing practices*. Extent to which marketing/advertising of products/services is misleading/morally dubious, eg, marketing to children, cartels, price fixing, incorrect labelling, potential environmental damage, offensiveness to particular social groups.
5. *Adverse business practices*. Extent to which company's business practices are exposed in terms of, eg, not paying suppliers, exerting heavy pressure on franchisees, pressuring agents to sell, stealing intellectual property and other "sharp practice".
6. *Engagement in bribery and corruption*. Extent to which dubious practices are used to gain business advantage, eg, paying bribes, excessive corporate entertainment/gifts, money laundering, complicity in smuggling.
7. *Poor human resources management*. Extent to which the company's HR policies and practices are found wanting in terms of reducing/eliminating stress, discrimination, harassment, and protecting employee privacy.
8. *Abuse of human rights*. Extent to which an organisation's business practices are found wanting on issues such as working conditions, pay and hours, child labour, right of trade union recognition and dealing with oppressive regimes, use of local security forces.
9. *Natural resources degradation*. Attitudes to the extent to which the company's licensed operations disturb and/or degrade both environmental (land, air, water) and ecological resources.
10. *Negative impacts of technology*. Extent of perception that adoption of new technologies leads to effects on business practices and/or society (eg, teleworking), or carry unknown degrees of risk for present and future generations (eg, genetically modified organisms).
11. *Other*. eg, animal rights, high social dependence, cultural clash of different value systems, etc.

Intangible risks

The extent to which a range of intangible risk factors influence share price is vital information. These include: corporate reputation and individual brand values; regulatory regime and government reaction to public pressure; media and NGO interest; employee morale; and investor, lender and insurer confidence. Again, intangible risks are combined with tangible risks to provide the "missing link" between tangible risks and tarnished reputation.

The following are intangible factors that are considered by SERM:

1. *Corporate reputation.* Reflects key stakeholders' perception of the company's strength and corporate governance. This is a function of size and visibility.
2. *Individual brand values.* Reflects the relevant customer's perception of brand name and resultant loss of sales/increases in returned goods/inventory costs. Related to visibility.
3. *Alliance partners.* Reflects the effect on voluntary or imposed partnering due to operational structure.
4. *Regulatory regime.* Reflects changes to a company's operating environment beyond its control (eg, leading to imposed restrictions, loss of licence, likelihood of government intervention, etc).
5. *Government reaction to public pressure.* Reflects the extent to which perceived unethical business practices are becoming untenable (eg, Rip-Off Britain, Mergers & Monopolies Commission).
6. *Media interest.* Reflects the extent to which intrusive and maintained media coverage could adversely influence stakeholder perception.
7. *NGO interest.* Reflects the likelihood of NGO campaigns against some aspect of the company's operations (eg, Internet-based campaigns).
8. *Militant action groups.* Reflects the adverse pressure (unlawful direct action) against company over perceived malpractice (eg, Huntingdon Life, e-commerce crime/disruption).
9. *Employee morale.* Reflects the damage that could occur resulting in resignations/recruitment costs, loss of productivity, concerted trade union pressure.
10. *Investor confidence.*
11. *Lender confidence.*
12. *Insurer confidence.*

1 "Sensing Change in Operational Risk Exposure – SCORE Launch Event DTI HQ 23 November 2001", Martin Neil, RADAR group, Queeen Mary, University of London & Agena Ltd.
2 American Academy of Actuaries, Costs Under Superfund, Washington, D.C., American Academy of Actuaries, August 1995.
3 Waste Management Research and Education Institute, Hazardous Waste Remediation Project, The Superfund Process: Site-Level Experience, Knoxville, TN: The University of Tennessee, Knoxville, December 1991.
4 US Social Investment Forum survey – Trends report November 2001.
5 *Financial Times* fm 24/06/02.
6 The Copenhagen Business School (BCS) students won Denmark's annual prize for the best Master's thesis in finance and accounting 2002 for their work on this subject for SERM.

BIBLIOGRAPHY

Bock, K. J., and M. W. Seitz, 2002, "Reinsurance Vs Other Risk-Transfer Instruments – The Reinsurer's Perspective", in: M. Lane, *Alternative Risk Strategies* (London: Risk Books).

Forum for the Future and Co-operative Insurance Society (CIS), 2002, "Sustainability Pays", July.

Christensen, K., and B. Kyhl, 2002, "*Sustainable Investments – An analysis of the correlation between companies focus on 'the softer aspects' & and their financial development*", The Institut for Investments, Handelshøjskolen, Copenhagen, 1 June.

IPCC, 2001a, *Climate Change 2001: The Scientific Basis*, J. T. Houghton, *et al.* (eds).
http://www.grida.no/climate/ipcc_tar/wg1/index.htm.

IPCC, 2001b, *Climate Change 2001: Impacts, Adaptation and Vulnerability*, J. J. McCarthy, *et al.* (eds).
http://www.grida.no/climate/ipcc_tar/wg2/index.htm.

Monks R., UK Social Investment Forum Annual Lecture 2002.

Mueller B., 2002, *Equity in Climate Change: the Great Divide*, Oxford Institute for Energy Studies, EV 31.
http://www.oxfordenergy.org/pdfs/great_divide_executive_summary.pdf.

Munich Re, 2002a, *Topics Annual Review: Natural Catastrophes 2001*, Munich Reinsurance Company.

Red Cross, 2002, *World Disasters Report 2002: Focus on Reducing Risk,* International Federation of Red Cross and Red Crescent Societies, Geneva, Switzerland.

Repetto, R., and D. Austin, 2000, "Pure Profit: The Financial Implications of Environmental Performance", World Resources Institute.

Sparkes, R., 2002, *Socially Responsible Investment – A Global Revolution 2002* (London: John Wiley & Sons Ltd).

UNEP-FI, 2002, *Climate Change & The Financial Services Industry: A study by the UNEP FI Climate Change Working Group.* http://www.unepfi.net.

Vellinga, P., E. Mills, G. Berz, L.M. Bouwer, S. Huq, L.A. Kozak, J. Palutikof, B. Schanzenbächer, C. Benson, J. Bruce, G. Frerks, P. Huyck, P. Kovacs, X. Olsthoorn, A. Peara, S. Shida, and A. Dlugolecki, 2001, Insurance and Other Financial Services. In: *Climate Change 2001: Impacts, Adaptation, and Vulnerability,* J. J. McCarthy, O. F. Canziani, N. A. Leary, D.J . Dokken, and K. S. White (eds) (Cambridge University Press). http://www.grida.no/climate/ipcc_tar/wg2/321.htm.

16

Academia and Insurance: Bridging the Gap

Dougal Goodman

The Foundation for Science and Technology

INTRODUCTION

Although this is a book about the process of buying reinsurance, the various authors often return to the subject of risk. How can it be measured? Do we have faith in the measurement? Can it be transferred? Indeed it is evident from Chapter 8's discussion of emerging risk that much cannot be measured and priced; there is simply not enough knowledge out there.

There are two key questions to be considered:

1. There is much knowledge and many skills in the global academic community which could be of huge help to the insurance and reinsurance industry.
2. There is a major communication gap between the two; academics do not understand what insurance needs and insurers usually do not understand what academics are saying. How can this gap be bridged?

TSUNAMI

In 1997, seven companies – two insurance composites (Royal & Sun Alliance, Commercial Union – now Aviva), three Lloyds managing agents (Catlin, Faraday and BRIT Insurance) and two insurance brokers (Marsh and the Benfield Group) formed a consortium to undertake the TSUNAMI initiative to improve insurance industry competitiveness through the better application of research and development to industry problems. This initiative was managed by the Natural Environment Research Council (NERC) by the then deputy director of the British Antarctic Survey (BAS – a NERC research institute), a position the author held at the time. The initiative was successful in securing a grant of £480,000 from the DTI Sector Challenge and this sum was matched by the seven companies. The initiative ended in November, 2002.

TSUNAMI established an office at BAS in Cambridge with one, and then, two insurance industry secondees. A grant round, contract research, conferences, workshops, senior management presentations and other events were organised and funded. The Appendix summarises these activities.

All researchers participating in TSUNAMI projects were encouraged to publish their results in peer reviewed journals or in books. The tropical cyclone forecasting project resulted in the formation of a spin-out company offering long-range forecasts to the insurance market.

The selection of projects and quality of the science undertaken was overseen by a Science Committee chaired by Lord Hunt of Chesterton, CB FRS, former director of The Met Office.

In July/August, 2001 a three-week short programme was held at the Isaac Newton Institute for Mathematical Sciences in Cambridge on the theme of "managing uncertainty" partly funded by the insurance industry, BP, McKinsey & Co., the Engineering and Physical Sciences Research Council and the Leverhulme Trust. During this programme five one-day workshops were held on financial risk, insurance, economic risk, environmental risk and corporate governance at which industry and researchers came together to discuss how new mathematical methods could be applied to industry and governmental problems. Many ideas emerged from this meeting as to where research could be applied to industry and government problems.

TSUNAMI was a success. If one were to pose the question "is closer cooperation between insurance and academia worthwhile?" in the author's view the answer is a resounding yes. The Appendix, a table of projects achieved, reveals some really interesting and valuable work.

THE RISK GROUP

The question is how do we instutionalise this relationship for the future and lead the work from a UK Government-sponsored initiative to a self sufficient entity with a future? The remaining founder members of TSUNAMI continued and have established a successor organisation called The RISK (Risk, Insurance Science Knowledge) Group.

The concept of The RISK Group is centred on "industry pull" – what are the questions that companies are seeking to answer and where is the best place to find researchers who can answer these questions? The DTI-led "Foresight process" generated broad guidelines as to what the financial services and insurance sectors (FSIS) want in the long-term but there are immediate needs to which companies want answers. For example, the tragic events of September 11, 2001 have raised awareness among insurance companies of the need to undertake much more sophisticated analysis of possible single event catastrophes to estimate loss distributions and frequencies. Alternatively, after the problems of Equitable Life, the FSIS want to understand better how to model the non-stationary behaviour of morbidity data. How should a life company evaluate its reserving policy?

The RISK Group are aware that there are a number of existing and valuable partnerships with the insurance communities in various parts of the world: the Risk Prediction Initiative in Bermuda, the Benfield Greig Hazard Research Centre in London, Risk Frontiers in Sydney, the Geneva Association in Zurich. However, there is no single body taking an overall view of the needs of the market and able to identify and relate the advances in research to the changing global context.

The RISK Group is a new global, not-for-profit initiative that will establish and maintain a network of excellence in insurance risk research. Its aim is to deliver value by enabling cooperation between industry and the scientific community world-wide.

Discussions with leading insurers and reinsurers have elicited much interest in the concept of a global research facility, working first to identify the key subjects that are the primary source of concern and then accessing the global research and academic community. The current subjects under consideration include:

European flood risk assessment

Flood poses a major threat to Europe, both in terms of loss of life and destruction of property, and there is evidence that global warming might increase the magnitude of this threat. Flood risk assessment is currently an imperfect science. Flood mitigation – both physical and financial – is handled differently in each country.

The greatest difficulty is that at present there is no coherent approach to modelling damage at various return periods between institutions, such as the national water agencies, and commercial organisations, such as insurers and reinsurers. There remains a high level of uncertainty in all the models, which frequently leads to unnecessary risk aversion or inflated insurance pricing.

The project would tackle the current fragmented approach to the problem in Europe by commissioning the first pan-European assessment of the current modelling techniques with the objective of radically improving the level of skill available to the whole insurance community and the first study of financial approaches country by country.

The project will for the first time address the challenge of flood risk management on a multidisciplinary approach (both financial and technical). It will also be the first occasion when techniques and practices of individual countries are shared and developed to aid the European insurance community.

The project team would:

- ❑ Research the modelling changes required, develop conclusions, disseminate the knowledge, and assess the impact.
- ❑ Assess the financial implications of flood for each European country, compare and contrast the methods employed by each to transfer risk from the individual and identify the final risk holder.
- ❑ Establish, evaluate, compare and contrast the various methods of flood risk assessment, especially catastrophic risk and identify the research that needs to be undertaken to enhance the modelling capability.

Extreme value statistics

Recent advances in Bayesian Markov Chain Monte Carlo (MCMC) and mathematical modelling of extreme value statistics (EVS) make it possible to assess the chance of large losses in a statistically meaningful way.

In an unusual alliance of the signal processing research group at the Department of Engineering of Cambridge University and the insurance industry, a research project was commissioned in 1999 to assess the feasibility of analysing Y2K daily claims. Although the threat of Y2K receded, the results of this first research project were sufficiently promising to encourage a follow-up project to develop a computer program to apply the Baynesian methods using MCMC techniques to insurance problems. This second research project developed the software to a stage where some sample results could be calculated.

In pricing a risk the underwriter has information on the underlying exposures (eg, location in relation to a fault line or the distance from local fire services) as well as some historical facts (loss statistics on the particular risk and the class of business as a whole). Coupling these pillars of rational assessment with an intuition of chance of loss and the markets pricing structures enables an underwriter to set a premium for an insurance risk.

Three characteristics of risks placed in the London insurance market make them particularly suitable as candidates for analysis by EVS. First they are often high loss risks shunned by other markets, second – and related – there are usually few historical statistics available to assist pricing, and third, the risks are often underwritten "excess of loss" (known in EVS as "Points Over Threshold" for which a Generalised Pareto Distribution of loss exceedance generally holds true in the limiting case).

The basic idea is to apply the Bayesian paradigm of using evidence (loss statistics) to construct a more informative posterior distribution (technical rate) from a prior assessment of risk (underwriters' initial view of the rate) within the parameterised family of probability distributions given by EVS (which hold as limiting cases in a similar way to the central limit theorem).

The project would involve completion of the initial work and develop an Excel-based tool that would apply Bayesian MCMC methods to risk assessment and pricing. This will provide the insurance market with a valuable tool to test loss statistics and calculate technical rates.

CURRENT AND FUTURE PROJECTS

Other projects include a natural perils risk assessment for group and individual life accounts and an examination of the difficulties of supplying and pricing employers cover.

The next stage will be to invite interested parties to join and make a real difference to the way we all measure, price and transfer risk.

APPENDIX – TSUNAMI ACTIVITIES

The table below summarises the major activities of the TSUNAMI Initiative.

Project or Activity	Participating Organisation(s)	Objective
Tro pical cyclone forecasting	The Met Office, Benfield Hazard Research Centre, UCL and Reading University	Improved statistical estimation of tropical cyclone coastal arrival on the east coast of US and over Japan.
Extreme value and non-stationary time series analysis methods	Cambridge University (Engineering Department and the Newton Institute), University of North Carolina and ETH, Zurich (and many others who participated in the Newton Institute Programme on Managing Uncertainty)	Application of new methods for estimating the parameters to describe the tails of distributions and Bayesian non-stationary time-series analysis to insurance problems.
Extreme weather in NW Europe	University of East Anglia, UCL, Imperial College	Analysis of spatial extreme wind statistics across Europe to determine characteristic patterns.
UK flood	Universities of Southampton and Middlesex, Association of British Insurers	Evaluation of the social and regulatory framework for the risk to property from flood in the UK.
Uninsured losses	University of Surrey and IIASA	An evaluation of what was and was not insured in major loss events such as the Mississippi floods to understand the interplay between social and public response to major catastrophes.

Project or Activity	Participating Organisation(s)	Objective
Satellite risk	Mullard Space Science Laboratory and British Antarctic Survey	Analysis of historical data of the vulnerability of satellites in orbit to space weather events and the design of a detector for future measurements of energetic impacts.
Tsunami risks	UCL, University of Coventry, Health and Safety Executive	Development of a risk map and guidance notes for insurers on tsunami risk.
Earthquake risk map	British Geological Survey	Global risk map to show earthquake hazard.
El Niño study	The Met Office	Evaluation of the 1997–1998 El Niño event and the consequences for the insurance industry.
Conference at the Royal Society	Attended by 150 representatives of both the financial, insurance and science communities	Two-day conference with papers presented by TSUNAMI-funded researchers and break-out sessions led by insurers. Keynote speech by the Deputy Chairman of the Financial Services Authority.
Workshops on earthquakes, mathematical methods, flood forecasting, tsunamis, social science and others	Attended by 20–40 insurance representatives with 3–5 academics	Raising awareness of the strength and diversity of the UK science base and what science has to offer the industry.
Web site	Accessed by insurance company staff and academics	Archive of the reports of all the projects and information to help industry find science contacts in the UK.

BIBLIOGRAPHY

Coles, S., 2001, *An Introduction to Statistical Modeling of Extreme Values* (London: Springer-Verlag).

Embrechts, P., 2000, *Extremes and Integrated Risk Management* (London: Risk Books).

Embrechts, P., C. Klüppelberg and T. Mikosch, 1997, *Modelling Extremal Events* (Berlin: Springer-Verlag).

Fitzgerald W. J., R. L. Smith, A. T. Walden and P. C. Young, 2001, *Non-linear and Non-stationary Signal Processing* (Cambridge University Press).

Ruanaidh, J. J. K. Ó., and W. J. Fitzgerald, 1996, *Numerical Bayesian Methods Applied to Signal Processing* (London: Springer).

www.foundation.org.uk.

www.math.ethz.ch/~embrechts/.

www.newton.cam.ac.uk.

www-sigproc.eng.cam.ac.uk.

www.unc.edu/depts/statistics/faculty/rsmith.html.

Index

S